DEVELOPMENT OF
EDUCATION IN INDIA

AKANSHA PUBLISHING HOUSE
4649-B/21, Ansari Road
Darya Ganj, New Delhi - 110 002
Ph.: 23263193 / 9811582579 / 09435116718
Fax: 011-23263193
Email: ektabooks@yahoo.com
www.akanshapublishinghouse.com

Development of Education in India

First Published 2005
First Reprint 2006
Second Reprint 2010
Third Reprint 2012
Fourth Reprint 2021
ISBN 81-8370-000-4

PRINTED IN INDIA

Published by Akansha Publishing House, New Delhi and Printed at Harmain Offset, Delhi.

DEVELOPMENT OF EDUCATION IN INDIA

Dr. Vachan Singh
M.Sc. (Botany), B.Ed., Ph.D.

AKANSHA PUBLISHING HOUSE
NEW DELHI • GUWAHATI • VISAKHAPATNAM

Dedicated

to

All Educationists & Social Scientists
who have rendered yeoman service in the field
of Indian Education.

Contents

Preface

"Donot save your loving speeches
For your friends till they are dead;
Donot write them on their tombstone,
Speak them rather nor instead."

—Anna Cummins

Socrates says, "Education means bringing out of universal validity which are latest in the mind of every man." While Plato states "education (is) training which is given by suitable habits to first instincts of virtue in children... which leads you always to hate what you ought to hate, and love what you ought to love from the beginning of life to the end... in my view, will be rightly called education."

In fact, Education contributes to economic growth, poverty reduction, development of mental faculties, and growth of general awareness in all human societies all over. The education in India has had a chequered history. The education systems in India have seen many changes i.e. from Gurukul, Madarsa and Convent/Public School education to the era of distance education and e-education.

The indigenous system of education prevalent in India before the advent of the British rule was well developed. To quote Prof. A.N. Basu, "The elementary system was intended for the masses. It was a widespread system of education consisting of numerous primary schools scattered all over the countryside. Practically every village had its primary school." It is said that in Bengal alone, there were around the year 1835, hundred thousand such schools. The most significant feature of indigenous education in India was that schools were not meant for a particular caste or class of society. They were open to everyone who wanted to study. Higher education was also easily available.

Education in India during the British Government, was first ignored, then violently and successively opposed, then conducted on a system now universally admitted to be enormous and finally placed in its present footing. Lord Macaulay came to India as Law Member of the Council of Governor-General of India in June 1834. He was a learned scholar of English Literature. He was appointed as the Chairman of the Society of Public Instruction, Bengal. The modern system of education is said to be based on Macaulay pattern.

The basic goals and aspirations of the people of free and independent India as enshrined in the Indian Constitution have guided the development of education in the country during the last 60 years. In order to give concrete shape to these goals and aspirations several Commissions and Committees have examined the progress of education in its various dimensions from time to time. A comprehensive review of the whole gamut of education in the country was carried out by the Education Commission (1964-66) (i.e. the Kothari Commission). Based on the recommendations of the Education Commission a resolution on National Policy on Education was formally adopted by the Parliament in 1968. The principles enunciated in the National Policy on Education 1968 aimed to promote national progress, a sense of common citizenship and culture, and to strengthen national integration. Since the adoption of 1968 Policy, the country has witnessed considerable expansion of educational facilities all over the country at all levels. Particular attention has been paid to creation of basic educational facilities in rural habitation. Attempts have also been made to adopt a common structure of education throughout the country and laying down a common scheme of studies particularly at the school level all over the country.

Adoption of New Policy on Education (1986) is another landmark in the development history of education in India. Despite concerted efforts augmented by the government the slogan 'Education for All' remained utopia. Under WTO regime, currently education is gradually going to private hands and thus millions of poor are going to be deprived of quality higher education. Unfortunately there is no exaggeration to admit that 'Education' has become a marketable commodity turning educational institutions in industry with the prime motive of earning profits.

Amidst the plenty of literature on the subject the present book is unique which categorically explains the long march of education in India. All crucial issues are discussed. Reports of different education Commissions and Committees are discussed. The entire information is organised under fourteen chapters. The information gathered from all secondary sources—books, abstracts, reports, articles from different journals etc. As such no claim for originality.

The book is intended to serve as a text-cum-reference work for students, researchers, teachers, teacher-trainers and trainees at different universities and other pedagogical institutes.

We are deeply beholden to all erudite scholars, and educationists whose views and research findings are used for authentication of facts. We are equally indebted to the Editors, publishers and copyright holders of different publications. Finally, we are thankful to our publishers for publishing this book in superb way that too within a short span of time.

—Editor

1

Education System in India: An Analysis

If the act or process of imparting knowledge at a school college or university is education, it is the social responsibility of the State (i.e. Government) to ensure education for all subjects. To attain education may be a personal privelege or achievement but make everybody educated (or literate) is collective responsibility of society as a whole.

Education and society are intrinsically related. And yet educational reformers, in their desire to achieve progressive changes in education, tend to give the impression as if it existed in a social vacuum. The subsystem cannot exist outside the system. Although education is a part of the larger social aggregate, its independent dynamism does not get curtailed. In fact, it generates and sustains progressive social change. Evidence of the contributions made by education to the development of human societies and to the making of civilisations is available in abundance. But not all the hypotheses on which the above faith is based are equally tenable. The fact that education function and has functioned as a double edged weapon goes to prove the operation of social purpose which give it specific twists and turns. Depending on the nature of social organisation and the propensity of the ruling elite, education through the mediation of suitable technologies has been used for war and peace, for murder and self-defence, for subjugation of people and for releasing them from bondage.

It is an accept fact that a wide range of analysis has been made of system and system with theories of culture saturation, cultural production, reproduction, socialisation and transmission. In making such analysis there is an increased interest in understanding the implied or explicit ways in which culture and education may act on each other. In nearly all the analytical models, the powerful role of education in modifying human behaviour and in reshaping the human environment is admitted.

Education—and particularly its tertiary segment may have played only a marginal role in the early years of the Industrial Revolution with an endless series of innovations acquired through intensive R & D endeavours. Moreover, the role of education as an essential input in the re-organisation and modernisation of societies in the developed countries of today has been even more far reaching. Education played a crucial role in the acquisition of the knowledge base of their people and in the setting up of their exceedingly efficient communications network.

Education and socio-economic development are inseparably interlinked. They feed, support, sustain and strengthen each other. The fact is that this obvious relationship needs to be often reiterated, particularly in the developing countries, either to the persisting naivete of the misguided or the consistent efforts of those in this unequal world who have a vested interest in keeping the poor societies poor. Therefore, educational policies must be intrinsically intertwined with the basic structural changes without which the new international order would remain an idle dream.

Since the East India Company accepted the responsibility for ensuring education to all Indian subjects in 1818, a large number of incidents and developments have occurred in the arena of Indian Education. Many commissions and committees have been set up to shape and mould the Indian education from different angle. Many conferences and seminars have been held to steer the Indian education in right direction and to fulfil the national ideals and goals with some achievements sometime or failure some other.

Here an attempt is being made to focus the opinions of the commissions and committees appointed so far and consider the valuable opinions expressed by erudite educational experts. The present state of modern Indian education has a chequered career which originated through the vicissitudes of divergent socio-economic and political factors. On the whole, an attempt has been made here to give an account of the educational system and point out crucial educational problems with suggested solution.

Education and Role of Central Government

The Central Government expected to play a significant role in the fields of education as per the constitutional provisions. Though Ministry of HRD, Department of Education, Government of India, discharges the major responsibility in the field of Education on behalf of the Government of India, yet there are other Ministries of the Centre which also perform functions in the field of Education. The following are the major functions performed by the Ministry, Government of India.

At the apex, the Central Government determines targets and prepares the educational plan to be implemented by the country as a whole, because educational planning is a part and parcel of the total planning.

— For carrying out educational plans, Government of India has set-up institutions like All-India Council of Technical Education (AICTE) and the National Council of Educational Research and Training (NCERT) which provide guidance to the States in the field of Education.

- The Central Government directs and guides the State Government, local and private enterprise so as to encourage education on right lines. This is being done by the Ministry through the Central Advisory Board of Education.
- The Government of India has set up Commissions which have gone into the various aspects of Education at different levels and have provided valuable recommendations and suggestions. These recommendations have further been considered by the experts and the states requested to implement the recommendations of the expert bodies.
- Government of India is entrusted to the establishment of an egalitarian society and therefore has taken many steps to provide equal education opportunities to the weaker sections of the society.
- The Central Government allocates suitable grant to the states, local bodies and private agencies.
- A large number of pilot projects have been undertaken by the Union Ministry which aims at providing enlightened leadership.
- The Central Govt. is directly responsible for education in various union territories and other central administered areas.
- From time to time it brings out useful information on various aspects of education. The Ministry also publishes a few educational journals/statistical informations which have proved to be very helpful in disseminating information in the country.
- It carried out some programmes in cooperation with UNESCO and other international bodies.
- The Ministry is directly responsible for the running of a few universities, national libraries, museums, art galleries and central schools.
- Besides the above, the following more steps are to be taken at the Central level:

— To expand the Central and centrally sponsored sectors in education.
— To establish institutions of scientific and technical education as well as of social sciences and humanities. Such institutions are to be established in close collaboration with the universities and are to be an integral part of university system.
— To undertake a measure for talent in different fields and to make this talent available to the states;

Education and State Governments

It worthwhile to reproduce here the observation of the Education Commission observes, "As we visualise, the responsibility for school education will rest squarely on the State Government. The local authorities will, no doubt, have a good deal of initiative and we should like the State Governments to encourage them by adopting flexible policies. But, by and large, they will act as agents of the State Governments and exercise delegated powers." Therefore, the State Education Departments which are the nodal agency of the State Government take following steps:

— Prescribing the standards to be maintained in schools in consultation with professional bodies.
— Periodical revision and upgrading of curricula, preparation of textbooks, teachers guide and other teaching and learning materials, and improvement in methods of teaching and evaluation.
— A Statutory Council of Education should be created at the state level with the State Education Minister as the Chairman. Its members should include representatives of the universities in that state, all Directors of Education and some educationists. Its main function will be to advise the State Government on all educational matters upto the school level, to review the progress of education and evaluate such programmes from time to time.

— Supply of teachers, for fixing their remuneration, retirement benefits and conditions of work and service and for organisation teacher preparation both pre-service and in-service on proper lines and for establishing, conducting or aiding training institutions of high quality with adequate intakes and outputs.
— State management of education implies that the educational institutions in the state are brought into existence by the state, are financed by it through the government offices and are also administered by persons directly appointed by government. There is no educational institutions other than government ones. However, State Control of education means overall control exercised by the State over educational institutions. There are educational institutions financed and managed by bodies other than the government. These bodies may be educational trusts, religious bodies, local boards, etc. The private institutions have greater chances of going in for educational experimentation for the heads of these institutions and their masters are always ready to appropriate, quick and prompt decision taking.

Education System in India: Organisational Setup

Since independence the Central Government, the State Governments, local authorities and the voluntary organisations have been providing educational facilities in the country, the role played by these agencies in the administration of education has been changing from time to time. The Indian Education Commission 1964-65, viewing the administration as an element in the improvement of standards, laid stress on the co-ordinating functions of the Central and State Governments. The Commission pointed out the following perceptible trends in the Indian education administration.

— A pyramid-type organisation is gradually being replaced by a flat organisation;
— Administration is being academicised day-by-day;
— There is no end to the improvement of the administrator nor to his specialisation. So he needs periodical orientation, in-service education, resulting in more and more of decentralisation; and
— Democratic attitudes are developing, may be slowly, in the participants in the administrative process.

Usually, the general educational policy and is responsible for the educational development in the Union Territories and the area governed by it. The Central Government has the following structure of educational administration:

1. Minister of HRD (i.e. Education Minister)
2. Minister of State for Education
3. Deputy Minister of Education
4. Education Secretary
5. Advisor, Deputy Advisor, Programme Department
6. Director
   (i) Project; (ii) Adult Education (iii) Statistics and Information
7. Joint Secretary
   (i) Programme Controller; (ii) Education Advisor (iii) Deputy Secretary (School Division); (iv) Deputy Secretary (UNESCO Division); (v) Assistant Educational Advisor (Publication unit).
8. Director(Internal Finance)
9. Joint Secretary
   (i) Director (Administration); (ii) Deputy Secretary (Book Improvement); (iii) Deputy Secretary (Hindi Section) (iv) Special Officer (Sanskrit); (v) Sub-

Education Advisor; (vi) Deputy Secretary (Youth Services).

10. Joint Educational Advisor

(i) Sub-Advisor (Higher Education); (ii) Deputy Secretary (Foreign Scholarship); (iii) Sub-Advisor (Union Territories)

11. Educational Advisor (Technical)

(i) Sub-Advisor (Technical Education Division).

The administrative setup for education in the states was proposed by the Secondary Education Commission.

The Education Commission did make several other proposals for the strengthening and reorganisation of the Ministry at the Centre and States. Among the proposals that the posts of the Secretary to the Ministry and the State Education Secretary should be filled but educationists rather than from the Cadre of IAS officers was also turned down. The creation of District and Municipal School Boards was one of the most important proposals made by the Education Commission regarding decentralisation of authority in educational administration. The other recommendations of the Commission were really minor, because of the assumption that the creation of the IES cadre would take care of most problems. Consequently, the present position is that the Education Commission has not been able to make any contribution to the improvement of the educational bureaucracy, either at the Centre, in the States or local level.

Structural Pattern

As is well known during British period education in India was colonial, imperialistic and bureaucratic in character. It served the purpose for which it was intended. It served to the advantage of the upper and middle strata of the society. The common people were not benefited by it. But emphasis we laid on the importance of mass education based on the tradition of the nation and its needs and aspirations. Education was regarded as a tool for national emancipation. The Indian Education Commission (1882-83), the first in the series, was set up under the chairmanship of William Hunter to enquire into the manner in which effect had been given to the principles of the Dispatch of 1854 with particular emphasis on elementary education. The second and the third commission, viz., the Indian Universities Commission (1902) under the chairmanship of Mr. Releigh, a member of the Viceroy's Executive Council and the Calcutta University Commission (1917) under the chairmanship of M.E. Sadler, Vice-Chancellor of Leeds University education. With the recommendations of the first Education Commission of 1881-82 education expanded at all levels quantitatively at the cost of quality. Its weaknesses and defects were exposed with the rapidly growing consciousness particularly after the birth of the National Congress in 1885. The national leaders laid great stress on national education under national control and based on national ideals and tradition. As a result National Education movement originated. It had sure impact on the development of primary, secondary and collegiate education.

A landmark development in the field of education was the National Council of Education (NCERT) which was set up in June, 1906. The curriculum of the National Council of Education was broad-based and comprehensive.

(a) Primary—3 year Course (6-9)
(b) Secondary—7 year Course (9-15)
(c) Collegiate—4 year Course (16-19)

Both Literacy and Scientific education was to be given including rudimentary technical education at the Primary stage. Teaching at this stage was mostly oral. The scientific and technical subjects included the use of simple tools, clay modelling, cardboard modelling, paper cutting, vernacular, object lessons, drawing, Geography, Arithmetic, Health Education and English Primer.

In the Secondary stage also literacy and scientific education was imparted with some technical subjects vocationally biased. Education at this stage was both theoretical and practical. Workshop practice and laboratory experiments were introduced. At this stage education was truly three dimensional—Literacy, Scientific and Technical and the course was obviously a mixed course. The subjects included Arithmetic, Workshop Practice, Drawing, Object lessons, Classical languages (Sanskrit, Arabic or Persian), Vernacular, Geography, History, Mathematics (from 3rd year), English (from 1st year), Physics, Chemistry and Biology from 5th year).

While at higher level i.e. at in the collegiate stage (4 years) education was also Literacy, Scientific and Technical. Both theoretical and practical subjects were taught with more proficiency. The literacy course included Indian languages, English language and literature, Comparative Philosophy, History, Economics, Political Science, Philosophy, Comparative Religion etc. The scientific and technical courses included both theoretical and practical subjects such as pure Mathematics, Mixed Mathematics, Physics, Chemistry, Agriculture, Forestry, Mining, Medicine, Engineering, Pedagogical Science, Botany etc. These subjects were taught for higher technical education.

This system of education was condemned as academic and too literacy. Therefore, after independence it was felt that in the field of education a change in pattern and content of the educational setup is must.

Post-Independence Educational Scenario

All the five earlier commissions (two in pre-Independence and three in post-independence) could not deal with education as a while but focused attention on different levels of education. The first dealt with some aspects of primary, secondary and college education (excluding university education), the second, third and forth with university education and the fifth with secondary education. The unique feature of Education Commission (1964-66) (Kothari Commission) was to limit its enquiry to specific sectors or aspects of education, but to have a comprehensive review of the entire educational system. And then unique feature of the commission was its conviction that education is the most powerful instrument of the national development. The crucial role of education in national development appears in all its vividness on every page of the report. The report concludes: 'We must either build a sound, balanced, effective and imaginative educational system to meet out developing need and respond to our challenging aspirations or be content to be swept aside by the strong currents of history.' Never before was it conceived aspirate of national honour and the prosperity as revealed in the pages of the Commission's Report.

In the field of modern Indian Education one of the novel experiments is the restructuring of the educational set up or pattern. Pattern and content are the two most important components or ingredients of education. The new structural pattern as proposed by the Education Commission and as it exists in India has tremendously affected the entire field of education— secondary, higher secondary. A change is made in the expectation of progress but every change does not produce desirable progress. The present experiment has not been introduced all of a sudden but it is the product of historical developments. Rather it is the result of successive experiments.

The prevailing education system in India comprised of both recognised and unrecognised institutions and includes formal education. According to the constitution, education is a state subject. The Union Government functions only as a coordinator of educational activities and helps to maintain uniformity in pattern and standards of education. It also act as clearing house in respect of the educational statistics.

The C.A.B.E. in 1974 strongly recommended the introduction of the uniform 10 + 2 + 3 pattern of education all over the country during the fifth plan period. The National Education Policy was announced in April, 1979 and has suggested 12 years school education and 3 years undergraduate course. Where a university desires, it could have a two-year Pass course and three years Honours course. By 1980 this pattern had been introduced in 15 States and 8 Union Territories. However, the entire period of formal education has been divided into two main stages, viz., school education and higher education. Education is further classified into two major categories, namely (a) General Education and (b) Vocational/Technical/Professional Education.

General Education

The educational structure reorganisation is provided through school education and college/higher education, according to the stages.

(1) Elementary Stage I to VIII

The education at school state is divided into pre-primary and secondary. This is based mainly on two considerations. Firstly, the three stages of education are regarded as corresponding to the three stages in the development of a child—infancy, childhood and adolescence. Secondly, from the social point of view, primary education is meant for the masses and secondary education for the selected few. The primary or elementary stage of general education with eight years duration covers mainly the primary stage with five years of schooling and middle stage with VI-VIII years of schooling in total.

(2) Secondary Stage (IX-XII)

The recommendations of the Secondary Education Commission resulted in the development of a national pattern of school education covering eleven years—five years of lower primary, three years of upper primary and three years of higher secondary to be followed by a three years course for the first degree and further two years course for the second degree. The Education Commission placed highest emphasis on the transformation of education system with radical changes in content and structure in such a manner as to make it a powerful instrument of social and economic changes and relating it to the needs of development and aspirations of the people. The system of education that is now emerging is likely to be on uniform pattern throughout the country. The minimum age at the entry into the present educational system is 5 years. The first ten tears of schooling, of the present education, "are treated as an integrated unit of general undifferentiated education which would emphasise, inter-alia, the use of socially useful productive work (SUPW) as the medium of education, the development of scientific attitudes and temper among the children and the freedom of the child and a living contact with nature". A significant feature of this higher secondary stage is the provision of a separate stream of vocation education providing a large variety of vocational courses to meet the development needs of the economy and the youths' varied needs and aptitudes.

(3) University/Higher Education

Commonly, the Higher education starts after senior secondary education comprising of three stages of university (i) graduate (ii) postgraduate, and (iii) research/doctorate degree. According to the new pattern of secondary education, the higher education now starts from 13th class and the duration of graduate and post-graduate courses remains the same.

Vocational/Technical/Professional Education

The second stream of education prepares the students for vocational/technical/professional courses. It starts at the school level and is followed by courses upto graduation, post-graduation and research. At school levels after VIII and X classes, vocational/technical education of certificate/ diploma courses of one to two tears duration is given to students in the branches of industrial trades, teachers' training, engineering, medicine etc. The post-secondary vocational/ technical education starts from XI class with two to three years duration of studies in relevant subjects. This type of education is imparted in Industrial Training Institutes and Polytechnics. The graduate and post-graduate courses are provided in technical and professional colleges. Parallel to the above formal system of education, the non-formal system of educational/training also exists in the country. There are a number of institutions providing skill development in vocational/technical trades, like engineering, agricultural extension paramedical services, crafts etc. and their training is recognised by the respective departments/ministries of Centre/State Governments.

Education has to be related to the life. It must fulfil the needs and aspirations of the people and become a powerful instrument of social, economic and cultural transformation. With this end in view, the Education Commission has recommended the prevailing structural pattern.

No doubt the present educational structure has been introduced after a much thought, discussion and deliberation in different meetings, conferences and seminars at national level yet the system has inherent loopholes.

Now we will discuss some other salient aspects of educaiton.

Women's Education

As is much stressed by educationists and sociologists, Education is needed for a cultural revolution as brought out by Iran Illich. According to Bane and Jancks, and Colemen, schools provide equal opportunities for children from unequal groups. Wynee has observed that it is through education alone that better socialisation take place. Freire says that education is essential for creating awareness among the people. However, much of rural women's education depends upon the general conditions in the villages. Mridula, Ahuja and Bhatty have made certain useful comments on women's education in Indian situation. The education of girls and of women was regarded as the legitimate responsibility of Indians: it neither suited nor interested the rulers to take much initiative in this area.

Education is one of the most important factors which determines the status (both social and economic) of a person. For the purpose of getting any job the level of education plays a very significant role in determining one's suitability or otherwise. Literate women force constitutes and important input in the process of socioeconomic development of a nation; but the literacy among women in India still appears like a far fetched cry.

The literacy amongst females in rural areas in only 17.9 per cent as against 47.8 per cent in Urban areas. This indicates that more efforts in regard to increasing the literacy are required in the rural areas. However, a comparison of the sex ratios of literates in the age groups will indicate that the gap between the literacy rates of males and females is being steadily bridged. In the rural areas the sex ratio among literates, or the number of females per 1,000 males who are literates steadily increase towards the younger ages.

In view of the above discussions, it can be stated that the women lag far behind so far as the educational achievements of the women force in India are concerned. Here, we will review the progress of education made by both man and women at different levels of education i.e. elementary, secondary and higher education as well as in professional education and try to identify the tasks ahead.

Social Education

Conventionally, in India social education corresponds to adult education. But in the progressive countries it is more than adult education. In those countries, even the educated receive social education. For fullest development of an individual, social education is essential, Education is a life long process. At the end of formal education, social education can make an individual a true dutiful and responsible citizen.

Social Education can be defined as education for the complete man. It gives him literacy, so that the knowledge of the world may become accessible to him. It will teach him how to harmonise himself with its environment and make the best use of physical condition in which he subsists. It is intended to teach him improved crafts and modes of production so that he can achieve economic betterment. It also aims at teaching him the rudiments of hygiene both for the individual and community, so that our domestic life may be healthy and prosperous. Lastly, this education should give him training in citizenship in ideal way.

The Central Ministry of Education defined social education in 1963 in the following ways:

— Social Education is adult education. It means functional literacy.

— Social Education is education for desirable social changes.

— Social Education is education for the betterment of the individual's social economic, political and moral life.

— Social Education is education which enables a community to assure direction of its own development.

— Social Education is education for better work, better rest, better use of leisure and recreation.

UNESCO named Social Education as fundamental education and defined it as—"The only means to elevate mankind emotionally, intellectually morally and materially'.

The Indian Education Commission (1964-66) has given three essential ingredients of social education:

(i) It must be work based and aimed at creating attitudes and interests and imparting skills and information for efficient doing of a work.

(ii) It must create interest in the illiterate to participate actively in vital national problems and in the social and political life of the country.

(iii) It must impart such skills in reading, writing and arithmetic as would enable him, if he so wishes, to continue his education either on his own or through other available avenues of informal education.

Social Education Agencies in India

— Youth Clubs: These clubs organise community living, games and sports etc.

— Literacy classes: They impart knowledge in SR's only.

— Community Centres: They organise social survey, information processing, group discussion, crafts, hobbies etc.

— Mahila Samitis: They undertake such work as tailoring, knitting, child care, maternity welfare, nutrition, balanced diet, household skills.

— National Social Service (NSS) Scheme: Universities and colleges undertake this scheme. Various social service activities are organised under this scheme such as Adult Education, Population Education, Social Survey, Cleaning. Health Programme etc.

— Janata Colleges: These are like popular colleges in Denmark. There are such colleges in Tripura,

Manipur and Kalimpong. They train people in SUPW (socially useful productive work).

- Youth Festival and Film Festivals: They play a great role in promoting social education.
- Mass media of communication like Radio and T.V. also impart social education.
- NCERT: It has a department of Adult and Social Education which undertakes a large number of Social Education programmes.
- National Institute of Adult Education.
- Directorate of Adult Education attached to the Ministry.

The Union Ministry of HRD (Dept. of Ed.) initiates social education schemes in cooperation with the Planning Commission of India. The different Central Ministries like Labour, Industry, Defence, Railway have their own social education programmes. The function of the Education department is mainly that of co-ordination, guidance and financial assistance. These works are conducted on the basis of the Reports of the State Governments and through the Central Advisory Board of Education which conducts conferences and meetings. The Union Ministry also gives financial assistance to voluntary organisations and State Governments for their social education work. It normally gives grants to run social education programmes for the production of books and teaching materials for adults and to conduct seminars etc. Each State Government has organisations at the state level as well as at the district levels. Most of the State Governments have either Directorates of Social and Adult Education or Social Education Boards. Each district has a District Officer and an Advisory Committee.

Adult Education

Literacy is a must for all, as a literate person has greater access to knowledge, which will assist his personal improvement, than an illiterate one. From the national point of view the existence of a substantial proportion of illiterate adults in the manpower potential of a given country can be a bottleneck in its development. Therefore, Adult Education is one of the most important and formidable issues in Indian education. The most urgent national need to our country today is the education of the adults who form the bulk of the population. More than 60 per cent of the fellow countrymen still live in the darkness of ignorance and illiteracy. In 1947, literacy in India was about 14 per cent and according to 1981 census it was 36 per cent. That means 64 per cent of Indians wereilliterate. This is the highest percentage of illiteracy in a country in the world. Though illiteracy has come down in 2005 yet it is for from satisfactory.

An adult falls within the age group of 15-45. But for all practical purposes importance is given to the age group 15-35. The term adult education is defined in different ways in different countries. Adult education also refers to some other connotations such as adult literacy, functional literacy, social education etc.

Adult education is imparted in two ways: Adult literacy and continuing education. Adult education is education for those adults who never had schooling before. Continuing education is education for those adults who have had some schooling or education before. Whereas in adult education, more stress is given on personal enrichment, in social education, social and civil efficiency and community development are emphasised.

The Government of India has given a top priority to adult education. A National Adult Education Programme was launched in October, 1978 to cover 65 million (650) illiterate persons, in the age-group 15-35. About 7 lakhs adult education centres have been set up throughout the country.

A very high priority has been given to adult education

in the sixth plan proposals. The total allocation proposed is Rs. 200 crores or 10 per cent of the total educational outlay. It was only 1.4 per cent in the fifth plan (18 crores). Different participating agencies employer group and project authorities are also expected to finance adult education programme.

Non-formal Education in India

Non-formal education has been defined as organised and systematic education activity carried on outside the framework of the formal school system to provide selected types of leaving situations to particular subject groups in the population, adults as well as - children. Non-formal education includes programmes such as agriculture, extension, farming community development, technical and vocational training etc. Such programmes are meant for youths, adults and for whom formal school education has either been inappropriate or unavoidable.

The main objective of non-formal education is to ensure life oriented basic literacy and skill for the children of the age group 6-14 who are either unschooled or drop outs. Non-formal education aims at building up awareness, competence and confidence in the learners not only to solve their own problems but also to develop an attitude of critical thinking to be in a position to face life situation problems with necessary solution.[12] However, non-formal education is not a substitute for formal education. It supplements and reinforces formal education. It removes the rigidness inherent in the education system. For successful implementation non-formal education requires prior careful planning.

A number of agencies are at work in non-formal education programmes. These include both formal educational institutions like schools particularly, primary, colleges and universities, and special institutions for non-formal education. The former have tremendous potential for non-formal education. The latter ate unique in character and specially suited for non-formal education.

Since the sixth plan there is a central sponsored scheme for running of non-formal education centres in the nine educationally backward states, viz., Uttar Pradesh, Jammu & Kashmir, Rajasthan, Madhaya Pradesh, Andhra Pradesh, Bihar, Orissa, West Bengal and Assam. In addition to the nine educationally backward states it is proposed to extend this scheme on the above pattern to all states in urban slums, hilly, desert and tribal areas and in projects for education of working children. The expenditure pattern in the scheme has been revised keeping in view the emphasis in the Education Policy on upgradation of the quality of NFE and the deficiencies observed in the evaluation of the programme undertaken by the Ministry.

The success of non-formal education programmes depends to a great extent on the degree of motivation on the part of the learners. Crores of illiterate people with some amount of education are to be educated through non-formal channels. Only the government in a developing country like ours with its limited resources cannot do this enduous task within a specified time.

Student unrest is basically a social problem. Many causes are responsible for this. Understanding psychology of youth, prompt redressal of genuine grievances and such other determinations can check this problem. With changing character of society the gravity and dimension of student unrest have also changed. Currently it is seen that general student mass is misguided by socalled student leaders, as most of student unions are now youth wings of various political parties. As we know the shrewd and corrupt politicians and other vested interest, spoil the educational atmosphere by using students.

Problems of Student Unrest

Since the 1960s, the effect of education explosion has been felt seriously, with the result that much has been written on various aspects of education. Student unrest being the most important problem has attracted the attention of the educationists and many seminars and symposiums have been held on this vital subject during this decade.

Education in the sense in which it is commonly understood is rarely imparted. The only concern of students is to pass their final examinations because without a piece of paper that entitles them to some mystic alphabets after their names, there is usually not even the prospect of a clerk's job. The piece of paper is usually granted not on fair test on intelligence but of memory, an yet assumes an importance that is totally unrelated to its real worth. To obtain that piece of paper—a passport for a job—it would be seen students are willing to rob, cheat and kill. As the Education Commission recognised a long time ago, this is a problem that cannot be tackled without a radical overhaul of the entire educational structure and the social values that go with it.

Student unrest is seen, had grown out of petty causes. Personal disputes of one student with some shopkeeper in Orissa turned into a violent student unrest as a result of which the then Chief Minister has to step down.

A variety of causes has been suggested for student unrest since independence. Some of these are historical and are related with the events preceding independence, it is difficult to assign any one key cause to student agitation in the post independence period. In most of the cases the local grievances stimulated a demonstration or protest.

1. Academic

(i) Lack of proper academic atmosphere

(ii) Defective examination system

(iii) Bookish and un-inspiring curriculum,

(iv) Raise in tuition fees

(v) Lack of individual contact between the teacher and student,

(vi) Defective admission and attendance rules
(vii) Lack of amenities
(viii) Lack of hostel facilities
(ix) lack of library facilities
(x) Lack of motivation among students.

II. Administration

(i) Double standards of the authorities and corruption at the highest echelons of administration.
(ii) Lack of sympathy for students
(iii) Non-involvement of students on university affairs.

III. Political

(i) Political interference in admissions, appointments etc.
(ii) Political interference in Union elections.

IV. General

(i) Lack of ideals in the society
(ii) Lack of commitment on the part of university teachers
(iii) Teachers in-fighting
(iv) Ideological frustration
(v) Lack of respect for authority—parental, governmental and educational
(vi) Increase in bus fare etc.
(vii) Inadequate transport facilities and lack of mutual understanding between the bus crew and the students and the police
(viii) Lack of employment opportunities.

In solving the student problems the following remedial measures may be discussed under the following heads:

— students participation in administrative and other matters
— curriculum reform
— examination reform
— employment opportunities and other related problems
— role of student advisory bureaus
— national services scheme
— role of student organisations in university life.

However, we need to treat the students as adults, give them respect and channelise their latent potentialities for the reconstruction of the nation. Student's involvement in matters relating to welfare activities, hostel management, sports and union affairs should be encouraged. But in academic matter teachers should help them and guide them. We should treat the university as a unit. Any attempt at polarisation and conflict between teachers, students and the administration should be avoided. What is needed at this critical juncture is to generate a climate of fraternity among students, teachers and administrative staffs based on mutual respect and understanding.

Summing Up

During colonial period education served to advantage to the upper and middle strata of the society. But emphasis was laid on the importance of mass education based on the tradition of the nation and its needs and aspirations. The National Council of Education (1906) was broad-based and comprehensive. Its scheme of studies was to be imparted in three stages, viz. (a) Primary—3 years course (6-9), (b) Secondary—7 years course (9-15) and (c) collegiate—4 years course (16-19). On the whole this system of education was condemned as academic and too literary.

After Independence it was felt that in the field of education a change in pattern and content of educational set-up is must. The present experiment has not been introduced all of a sudden but it is the product of historical developments. Rather it is the results of successive experiments before and after independence. However, the entire period of formal education has been divided into two main stages, viz,. school education and higher education. Education is further classified into two major categories, viz., (a) General Education and (b) Vocational/Technical/Professional Education. The C.A.B.E. strongly recommended the introduction of the 10 + 2 + 3 pattern of education all over the country during the fifth plan period. The National Education has suggested twelve years of school education and three-year undergraduate course. Where a university desires, it could have a two-year pass course and three-year honours course. By 1980 this pattern had been introduced in almost all states and Union Territories of India. This structural pattern of education has tremendously affected the entire field of education—secondary, higher secondary, collegiate and university education.

At the end of formal education social education can make an individual a true, dutiful and responsible citizen. For fullest development of an individual social education is essential; however, the Union Ministry of HRD (Department of Education) initiates social education schemes in co-operation with the Planning Commission. The different Central Ministries like Labour, Industry, Defence, Railway have their social education programmes.

To ensure life oriented basic literacy and skill for the children of the age group 6-14 and to supplement and reinforce formal education, non-formal education has been initiated in the nine educationally backward states since the sixth plan. In this scheme, assistance has been given to state governments and voluntary agencies for setting up about 150 lakh centres. Later on, it is proposed to extend this scheme to ten more educationally backward states.

However, the success of both, non-formal and social education programmes, depends to a great extent on the degree of motivation on the part of the learners.

Problems and Suggestions

The pattern of education which India inherited at the time of its independence did not suit its need. Each state in education is linked to the next one without any terminal stage. As a consequence there has been as ever increasing pressure for the provision of university education. A developing country like India can ill afford expansion of expensive university education when it has not been able to provide universal primary education to its children in fulfilment of the constitutional provisions.

The products turned out by the educational system are not in tune with needs of the country. The educated persons have looked down upon manual work and held white collar jobs in greater esteem; they have preferred wage employment to self employment. Consequently expansion of educational facilities has been accompanied by an increase in educated unemployment which the government is finding it difficult to solve by creating more white collar jobs and wage employment opportunities.

Therefore, instead of solving unemployment problem the educational system is accentuating it. The change in attitude of the students, the dignity of manual work and a preference for self-employment can be brought about though introduction of vocational bias in education.

Another question is whether education should be narrow based vocational education in secondary schools or be balanced between theoretical learning and practical experience in all branches of educational system.

In order to provide education and training and developing skills, provision of vocational education is essential. Besides the development planning envisages an increase in productivity of labour engaged in different sectors of the economy. This can come about only by providing vocational education to the people engaged in work or who are to join the work.

To conclude, it can be safely inferred that Education in India has had a chequered career. While in the beginning it was social accountability of the Govt., now in the age of globalisation it has become an industry. Capitalists and vested interest are reaping the harvest and with pity one can admit that the dream of universal education for all is going beyond the reach of common people, particularly in India. And education is gradually going to private hands.

REFERENCES

Aggarwal, J.C. (1982), *Development and Planning of Modern Education,* Vikas Publishing House, New Delhi.

Ahuja, Y.L., Kulkarni S. & Sharma H. (1988), *Active Education Policy for Skill Development,* Theme Paper of the Seminar, IAMR, New Delhi, Unpublished.

Govt. of India, Min. of HRD, Dept. of Education, *Nonformal Education,* New Delhi, 1988.

Purkait, B.R. (1987), *New Education in India,* The Associated Publishers, Ambala.

Report of the Education Commission, 1964-66, *Education & National Development,* Ministry of Education, Govt. of India.

Status Report of Non-formal Education from some states in India, Dept. of School Education, NCERT, 1978.

2

Kothari Commission

Education Commission 1964-66, popularly known as Kothari Commission under the name of its Chairman Prof D. S. Kothari, the renowned physicist was appointed by a Government Resolution in July 1964 to advise the Government of India on the national pattern of education and on the general principles and policies for development of education at all stages and in all aspects. The Commission began its work on October 2, 1964 and submitted its report on June 26, 1966. Shri J.P. Naik was the member-Secretary of the Commission. The publication of the report is an epoch-making event in the history of Education in India. The report was entitled 'Education and National Development':

Why Education Commission?

India attained Independence from the Britishyoke in 1947 and after this it was hoped that the traditional system of education would undergo a great change. But, in spite of a number of Committees and Commissions on education, much change could not be achieved. Very naturally, a comprehensive policy was needed. Hence, the Commission was appointed.

Secondly, in the post-Independent period, a good deal of expansion took place in the field of education, but all this was at the expense of quality. This needed a detailed study.

Thirdly, the Commission was appointed to bring home to the people that they should also have a share in the reconstruction of the country through education, the government of course shouldering the main responsibility.

Moreover, there is an explosion of knowledge, particularly in science and technology. The appointment of a Commission was consequently felt to meet this challenge.

Fourthly, in the past, several commission and committees examined sectors and specific aspects of education. The new Commission was to survey the entire field of educational development as the various parts of the educational system strongly interact with and influence one another. Education needs to be considered as a whole and not in fragments. Hence this Commission.

Fifthly, the system of education could not be strengthened with out eliciting the co-operation of teachers. The teacher community had hitherto been altogether neglected. All these years, the teacher had been subjected to great economic hardships. A positive approach to the problems of the teacher was, therefore, badly needed.

Kothari Commission was the sixth commission in the history of Education Commissions in India. The Indian Education Commission (1882-83), the first in the series, was set up under the chairmanship of William Hunter to enquire into the manner in which effect had been given to the principles of the *Despatch of 1854* with particular emphasis on elementary education. The second and the third commission, viz., the Indian Universities Commission (1902) under the chairmanship of Mr. Releigh, a member of the Viceroy's Executive Council and the Calcutta University Commission (1917) under the chairmanship of M.E. Sadler, Vice-Chancellor of Leeds University dealt with the problems and prospects of university education. The next three commissions were appointed in the post-Independence era. The University Education Commission (1948-49) set up under the chairmanship of Dr. Sarvepalli Radhakrishnan and the Secondary Education Commission (1952-53) appointed under the chairmanship of Dr. Lakshmanswami Mudaliar were the fourth and the fifth respectively, in the series of commissions on educations on education. Mention may also be made of the Sanskrit Commission (1956-57) appointed to consider the present state of Sanskrit education.

All the five earlier commissions did not deal with education as a whole but focused attention on different levels of education. The first dealt with some aspects of primary, secondary and college education (excluding university education), the second, third and fourth with university education, and the fifth with secondary education. The unique feature of Education Commission (1964-66) was to limit its enquiry to specific sectors or aspects of education, but to have a comprehensive review of the entire educational system. The Government of India realised that, "It is desirable to survey the entire field of educational development as the various parts of the educational system strongly interact with and influence one another. It is not possible to have progressive and strong universities, without efficient secondary schools and the quality of these schools is determined by the functioning of elementary schools. What is needed, therefore, is synoptic survey and an imaginative look at education considered as a whole and, not fragmented into parts and stages."

Another unique feature of the Commission was its conviction that education is the most powerful instrument of the national development. Educational and national reconstruction are intimately interlinked. The crucial role of education in national development appears in all its vividness on every page of the report. Standing at the critical cross-roads of history, India has to make a choice. The choice lies between education and disaster. The report concludes: "We must either build a sound, balanced, effective and imaginative educational system to meet our developing need and respond to our challenging aspirations or be content to be swept aside by the strong currents of history." Never before education was given such a niche of national honour, and never before was it conceived as a pivot of national honour, and never before was it conceived as a pivot of nation's progress and the prosperity as revealed in the pages of the Commission's Report.

The international composition of the Commission is also significant. Education for India must necessarily emerge from Indian experience, thought, culture and local conditions. But as education remains the common quest of mankind inhabiting a world closely knit together, it was found profitable to draw upon the experiences and thinking of educationists and scientists from other countries and to take advantage of the latest developments in the educationally advanced countries. The Commission included seven Indian members and five others; one each from Japan, France, UK, USA, and USSR. Besides, 20 consultants from different countries of the world were available. It is of historical interest to note that the first commission namely the Indian Education Commission (1982-83) had 7 Indians and 14 Englishmen, but in 1902 Curzon omitted to put any Indian on the Indian Universities Commission (1902) though a Hindu and a Muslim were added later when the harm had already been done. The Calcutta University Commission (1917) had some Indian members including Asutosh Mukherji. The University Education Commission (1948-49) and the secondary Education Commission (1952-53) had educationists both from UK and USA.

Three Facets of Educational Revolution

The Commission identified three important facets of the big programme that would bring about the desired 'educational revolution.'

— Internal transformation so as to relate it to the life, needs and aspirations of the nation;

— Qualitative improvement so that the standards achieved are adequate, keep continually rising and, at least, in a few sectors become internationally comparable; and

— Expansion of educational facilities broadly on the basis of manpower needs and with an accent on equalisation of educational opportunities.

Educational Programme

This is a four-fold Educational Programme. For the internal transformation of the system of education the following programmes urged high priority:

1. Work experience as an integral part of general education; vocationalisation of education at the secondary level; improvement of professional education and research, promoting national consciousness;
2. Introducing a common school system; making social and national service compulsory; developing all modern Indian languages;
3. Making science education an integral part of all school education and developing scientific research;
4. Inculcation of high values—social, moral and spiritual—at all stages of education.

Objectives of Education

The transformation was considered necessary for achieving the four national objectives: increasing productivity, achieving national integration, accelerating the process of modernisation and cultivating social, moral and spiritual values.

Programmes for Improving the Quality of Education

The quality of education is crucial for national development and the nation must be prepared to pay for the quality. According to the Commission's recommendations, the major programmes for qualitative improvement include raising the economic, social and professions status of teachers and improving the quality and scope of teacher education and in-service programmes, radical reform especially in Science and Mathematics, vigorous improvement in the method of teaching and evaluation, and providing quality textbooks and other teaching material, search for introduction of a nationwide programme of school and college improvement where each institute finds congenial conditions to strive continually to achieve the best results of which it is capable, the establishment of 'quality' schools to act as pace-setters in their districts and the creation of 5 or 6 'major' universities; revitalising the system of supervision and reorganising the State departments and the reorganisation of the educational structure on the 10 + 2 + 3 pattern.

Expansion Programme

The Commission hopes that 5 per cent of the 3-5 and 50 per cent of the 5-6 age-groups will find places in nursery schools or classes by 1986. It recommends five years of good education for all children by 1975-76 and seven years of such education by 1985-86, and places the highest priority for free and compulsory education up to the age of 14. The problems and policies of expansion at the Secondary stage would differ from those in primary education because on the one hand it would not be financially possible for several years to come to have universal secondary education and on the other hand it would be essential to enlist half the enrolment at the higher secondary stage in vocational education. It is an important recommendation that the expansion of higher secondary and collegiate education should be related to manpower needs and must be selective. The programmes of equalisation of educational opportunities visualised by the Commission include the reduction of the regional imbalances to the minimum, increased provision of free education and scholarships, paying special attention to the education of girls, placing adequate emphasis on the spread of education among backward classes including the Scheduled Castes and the Scheduled Tribes. It is also recommended that a nationwide campaign should be launched for complete liquidation of literacy within 20 years.

Recommendations of the Kothari Commission

Education and National Objectives

The most important and urgent reform needed in education is to transform it, to endeavour to relate it to the life, needs and aspirations of the people and thereby make it a powerful instrument of social, economic and cultural transformation necessary for the realisation of the national goals. For this purpose, education should be developed so as to increase productivity, achieve social and national integration, accelerate the process of modernisation and cultivate social, moral and spiritual values. 1.20 (Chapter 1, Para 20).

Stress on Science Education

Science Education must become an integral part of school education and ultimately some study of science should become a part of all courses in the humanities and social sciences at the university stage (1.23).

We lay great emphasis on making science an important element in the school curriculum. We, therefore, recommend that Science and Mathematics should be taught on a compulsory basis of all pupils as a part of general education during the first ten years of schooling (8.50).

Every primary school should have a science corner or a room to keep specimens, models and charts with the necessary storage facilities. A minimum of one laboratory-cum-lecture room should be provided in every higher primary school (8.56).

Work Experience

Work experience should be introduced as an integral part of all education, general or vocational (1.25).

Vocationalisation

An other programme which can bring education into closer relationship with productivity is to give a strong vocational bias to secondary education and to increase the emphasis on agricultural and technological education at the university stage (1.32).

Common School System

A common school system of public education should be introduced (1.35).

Social and National Service

Social and national service should be made an integral part of education at all stages (1.35).

Ten Years of Schooling of General Education

The first ten years of schooling should cover a primary stage of seven or eight years and a lower secondary stage of three or two years providing a course of general education without any specialisation (2.17).

Specialisation in Classes XI and XII

Classes XI and XII (and during the transitional period class XI only) should provide for specialised studies in different subjects at the higher secondary stage (2.18).

Two Years Duration of Higher Secondary Stage

The Higher Secondary stage should be extended to cover a period of two tears and to be located exclusively in schools (2.29).

Steps to be taken to implement this reform through a phased programme spread over the next 20 years 1965-85 (2.29).

Instructional Days in Schools

The number of instructional days in a year should be

increased to about 234 (or 39 weeks) for schools and 216 (or 36 weeks) for colleges and pre-primary schools (2.35).

Holidays to be Minimised

There is no need to close an educational institution on a religious holiday. Nor is it necessary for instance to close it on birthdays or death anniversaries of great Indians; the time could be better utilised in working hard for national development (2.37).

Academic Year to Begin on the Same Day

It is desirable to begin the academic year on the same day throughout India (2.34).

In an academic year, the hours of instruction at the secondary stages should not be less than 1,000, and preferably raised to 1,100 or even 1,200 if conditions are favourable.

Maximum Utilisation of School Facilities

The libraries, laboratories, workshops, craftsheds etc., should be open all the year round and should be utilised for at least eight hours a day (2.43).

College to be Related to a Number of Schools

Each college can be functionally related to a number of secondary schools in the neighbourhood and enabled to provide attention services and guidance to them to improve their standards (2.49).

Free Textbooks at the Primary Stage

At the primary stage a programme of providing free textbooks should be given very high priority and introduced immediately (6.16)(1).

Adequate Numbers of Scholarships

The top 10 per cent of the students in education institutions should be given small grants annually for the purchase of books which need not necessarily be textbooks (6.16)(3).

Steps should be taken to ensure that at the end of the lower primary stage no promising child is prevented from continuing his studies further on account of non-availability of a school or of socio-economic difficulties and to this end scholarship of an adequate amount will have to be provided to every child that may need it (6.19).

The main object of the scholarship programmes to be developed at the secondary stage would be to ensure that under any circumstances the top 15 per cent of the children in the age-group do get transferred to secondary schools and their further education is not prevented by poverty (6.29).

Identification of Gifted Students

Steps should be taken immediately to devise suitable techniques for identifying talent at this stage. Each State should organise a testing service at the net of the primary stage (class VII or class VIII) and also at the end of the lower secondary stage (class X) and make the assistance available to all the schools (6.22).

Residential Facilities in Schools

One good secondary school with adequate residential facilities should be developed in each community development block and about 10 per cent of urban schools should also be similarly covered (6.20)(2).

Provision of Day-Study Centres

For students who do not have adequate facilities for study at home; it is necessary to provide a large number of day-study centres at the secondary and university stage. Some institutions have tried to provide this facility by adopting an unorthodox approach i.e., by using class-room for residential and study purposes before and after school hours at night. Experiments of this type should be encouraged (6.39).

Learning While Earning

Facilities for students to earn and pay a part of the expenses should be developed on as large a scale as possible as supplement to the programme of scholarships (6.39).

Education of the Handicapped

It should be possible to have at least one good institution for the education of handicapped children in each district (6.46).

The NCERT should have a cell for the study of the handicapped (6.49).

Education of the Backward Classes

The education of the backward classes in general and of the tribal people in particular is a major programme of equalisation and of social and national integration. No expenditure is too great for the purpose (6.75).

State-level Centres for Pre-primary Education

There should be a State-level centre for the development of pre-primary education located in the State Institutes of Education (7.07).

Developmental Plan for Each District

A development plan for secondary education should be prepared separately for each district after taking into consideration the existing and prospective needs of expansion (7.46).

Enrolment Between 360 and 450 in a Secondary School

In order to be well-equipped and efficient a secondary school should have at least three divisions in each of the three classes of the secondary stage i.e., a total of nine division and an enrolment between 360 and 450 (7.60).

Freedom to Schools for Experimental Curricula

Schools may be permitted to try out experimental curricula (8.06).

Two Sets of Curricula

The State Boards of Schools Education should prepare two sets of curricula—advanced and ordinary (8.07).

Schools need not adopt the advanced curricula in all the subjects (8.08).

Three or Four Textbooks for Each Subject

No useful purpose is served by having only one textbook in a subject for a given class—this is almost invariably the position under the existing programme of nationalisation. It should be an important objective of policy to have at least three or four books in each subject for each class and leave it open to the teacher to choose the book best suited to the school. This is necessary even if there were to be common syllabus for all the schools (9.20).

Moral and Religious Education

Conscious and organised attempts be made for imparting education in social, moral and spiritual values with the help wherever possible of the ethical teaching of great religions (8.94).

Co-curricular Activities

Every school should organise a variety of such programmes that every child in it may be able to take up something suited to his tastes and interests (8.10).

Guidance and Counselling

Guidance and counselling should be regarded as an integral part of education, meant for all students and aimed at assisting the individual to make decisions and adjustments from time to time.

Evaluation

Evaluation is a continuous process, forms as integral part of the total system of education and is intimately related to educational objectives. It exercises a great influence on the pupil's study habits and the teacher's methods of instruction and thus helps not only to measure educational achievement but also to improve it.

The new approach to evaluation will attempt to improve the written examination so that it becomes a valid and reliable measure of educational achievement and to devise techniques for measuring those important aspects of the student's growth that cannot be measured through written examinations (9.65.68).

Establishment of School Complexes

The school complex should be established. Each higher primary school should be integrally related to ten lower primary schools that exist in its neighbourhood so that they form one complex of educational facilities. The headmaster of higher primary school should provide an extension service to the lower primary schools in his charge and it will be his responsibility to see that they function properly. The second tier would be a committee under the chairmanship of the headmaster of the secondary school (all headmasters of the higher and lower primary schools in the area being members) which will plan the work and give guidance to all the schools in the area (2.51).

The Neighbourhood School

The present social segregation in schools should be eliminated by the adoption of the neighbourhood school concept at the lower primary stage under which all children in the neighbourhood will be required to attend the school in the locality. This plan should be implemented in a period of 20 years.

State Evaluation Organisation

To assist the State Education Department in this programme of prescribing, maintaining and revising standards, a State Evaluation Organisation should be set up in each State, as an independent institution, preferably autonomous, and its service should be available to all concerned (10.59).

State and National Boards of Education

In order to secure continuous improvement in standards, an adequate machinery should be set up at the State and national levels (10.54).

Correspondence Courses

An immediate beginning should be made to develop a wide range of vocational and technical courses through correspondence. However, before this medium could be adopted extensively, very careful preparation and testing would be required (15.74-75).

Minimum Scales of Pay for Teachers

At the school stage, the Government of India should lay down the minimum scales of pay for school teachers. The States and Union Territories should then adopt equivalent or higher scales of pay to suit their local conditions (3.08).

Same Pay in Different Managements

The scales of pay of school teachers belonging to the same category but working under different managements such as government, local bodies or private organisations should be the same (3.09).

The minimum salaries of primary, secondary and university teachers should be in the ratio of 1:2:3 (3.10)(4).

Liberal Assistance to States

Liberal Central assistance should be given to State Governments for improving the salaries of school teachers as recommended by us (3.28).

Retirement Age

Normal retirement age for teachers be 60 years and there

should be a provision for extension up to 65 years provided the person is physically fit and mentally alert to discharge his duties efficiently (3.30).

The Indian Education Service

The creation of the Indian Education Service is a step in the right direction and if organised on proper lines, such a service would help the progress of education (18.44).

Education Acts

Education should be given a statutory basis everywhere and in all sectors and that an Education Act should be passes in all the States and Union Territories (1857).

Duration of Degree Courses

The duration of the first degree course should not be less than three years (2.29).

Apart from this, there should be no rigidity about the duration of courses in higher education (2.29).

These may vary from university to university and even in the same university from subject to subject (2.29).

Graduate Schools

In some universities strong graduate schools providing three year M.A./M.Sc/M. Com. degree course should be established in certain subject (2.29).

A beginning should be made with the organisation of four-year special courses for the first degree, in selected subjects (2.29).

A more liberal provision of scholarships should be made for these longer courses for the first and second degree (2.29).

Experimental Schools and Universities

The Universities can conduct experimental secondary or primary schools to evolve improved techniques of teaching and organisation (2.49).

Talented Students and the Role of the Colleges

The Universities and colleges could select talented students for the schools in different subjects at an appropriate stage, say in the age-group 13-15 and help them to develop their knowledge through individual guidance, provision of laboratory facilities etc., over and above regular school work (2.49).

Favourable Comments on the Report

1. ......A unique report—Mr M.C. Chagla, the then Union Education Minister.
2. ......bold and pertinent—the *Indian Express,* 1 July, 1966.
3. ......a comprehensive, critical and constructive review of the education system prevailing in the country—*The Hindustan Times,* 1 July, 1966.
4. ......a good document—Mr Chanchal Sarkar in *The Hindustan Times,* 14 July, 1966.
5. ......bold categorical and realistic—*The Hindustan Standard,* Calcutta, 12 July, 1966.
6. ......a historical document—*The Educational India,* Masulipatam, July 1966 (Monthly).
7. ......revolutionary recommendations—*Awaz-i- Ustand,* Chandigarh (Weekly), 7 July, 1966.
8. ......revolution in education—*National Solidarity* (Weekly), 7 July, 1966.
9. ......original and significant contribution—Dr D.S. Reddi, *Deccan Chronicle,* 17 July 1966.

Critics of the Report

1. ......death certificate of basic education—M.N. Acharya in *Blitz,* 9 July, 1966.
2. ......intellectual discipline ignored, Sensible in parts but often platitudious—the *Statesman,* 3 July, 1966.
3. ......Confusing *Amrita Bazar Patrika,* 13 July, 1966.

Conclusion

Education Commission's report is an achievement, a mine of information and wisdom. The report is a synoptic survey of the entire educational situation in all its complexities. It reveals in imagination sweep not found in the excellent report of the past. The achievement was possible partly because the Commission had faith in the keyrole of education in national development implying economic growth and social transformation and partly because it was knowledgeable in the strategy and techniques of prospective planning. The Education Commission naturally hopes that the nation would be willing to pay for reforms leading to the transformation of education so that fullest possible development of human resources might be possible. The Commission boldly assigns to education the task of transforming and modernising existing social order so that the desired goal of a socialistic pattern of society might be realised within the foreseeable future. While it may not be possible to engineer the educational revolution envisaged by the Commission with our present resources, we shall have achieved a marked advance even if half the recommendations are implemented.

A survey of such a large magnitude is bound to have omission here and there. The Education Commission, for instance, is not clear and definite enough on the content and courses for elementary stage. A redefinition of basic education and an examination of the merits of the earlier eight year composite basic school would have been worth-while. The division of the primary stage into lower and higher, the nature of work experience, the qualities, aspects of the elementary stage are issues which need explaining. It is doubtful if a teacher can efficiently work with a class of 50 children and still more doubtful if there are rooms in most of the schools which can seat 50 children.

The concept of work experience and vocationalisation of education have been left nebulous. Higher education has received a disproportionate emphasis. Probably, there is anxiety to produce executives, managers, technicians of calibre for the emerging industrial society.

The creation of pace-setting schools and six major universities is a disturbing recommendation. It is bound to create a new caste and deprive the common schools of the few good teachers working in them. The recommendation does not seem to be in harmony with those relating to school complexes and neighbourhood school.

Educational Structure Proposed by the Kothari Commission

1. The new educational structure will consist of:

(a) One to three years of pre-school education.

(b) A primary stage of 7 to 8 years divided into a lower primary stage of 4 to 5 years and a higher primary stage of 3 or 2 years.

(c) A lower secondary stage of 3 or 2 years.

(d) A higher secondary stage of two years of general education or one to three years of vocational education.

(e) A higher education stage having a course of three years or more for the first degree and followed by a course for the second or research degree of varying durations.

2. Age of admission to class I ordinarily not to be less than 6.

3. First public examination to come at the end of first ten years of schooling.

4. The system of streaming in school of general education to be made beyond class X.

5. Two types of secondary schools, high schools providing a ten-year course and higher secondary schools providing a course of 11 or 12 years.

6. Bigger schools and more efficient schools—about one-fourth of the total number to be upgraded and attempts to upgrade every secondary school to the higher secondary stage to be abandoned.

7. New higher secondary course beginning in class XI, to be instituted and classes XI and XII to provide specialised studies in different subjects; existing higher secondary schools with integrated courses in classes IX, X and XI and running satisfactorily to continue until class XII is added.

8. Transfer of the pre-University course from the universities and affiliated colleges to secondary schools by 1975-76 and the duration of the course to be lengthened to two tears by 1985-86; U.G.C. being responsible for effecting the transfer of all pre-university or intermediate work from university and affiliated colleges to schools.

9. Starting of Higher Secondary class or classes in selected schools by State Education Departments, as self-contained units, and assisted with adequate recurring grants.

10. Reconstituting Boards of Secondary Education to accept the responsibility for the higher secondary stage also.

11. Vocationalisation at the secondary stage at two points at the end of Class VII (VIII) and at the end of Class X and provision to be made for the introduction of different types of vocational courses at the lower and higher secondary stages, the duration of these courses to vary from one to three years which would prepare young persons for employment.

General Observations

Favourable Comments

The proposed education structure is more scientific. "The proposed system of one to three years of pre-school preparation, a 7-8 year primary stage, a lower secondary stage of 2-3 years, higher secondary of two years, and higher education beginning with a three-year course, will no doubt be considered more scientific than the present system, but unless the proposals are uniformly applied, the existing confusion and imbalance as between State be cannot removed."

Twelve-Year Course—A Very Practical Integrated System *(National Solidarity,* 7 July 1966). "The Commission has suggested a very practical integrated system consisting of a twelve-year course of Higher Secondary stage, followed by a three-year course of degree and another two-year course for the final degree."

Two-Year Higher Secondary Stage—An Important and Constructive Recommendation. Dr. D.S. Reddi, the Vice-Chancellor of the Osmania University observed, "The Commission has shown great wisdom in keeping the first degree stage at the present 3 years."(Deccan *Chronicle,* July 17, 1966).

"It has been categorical in attempting to strengthen and enlarge education by spreading it over 12 years and in retaining English." *(Hindustan Standard,* Calcutta, July 12,1966).

Criticism

"Dr. Anil Chandra Banerjee, veteran educationist and a former President of the Board of Secondary Education, wondered how by merely adding one more year to the present education structure, the quality of education could be improved. This would mean fresh financial burden on the shoulders of the overburdened guardians who would have to foot the bills for their wards in schools." *(Amrit Bazar Patrika,* July 3, 1966).

Mr. G.N. Acharya states: "The period from the primary school to the first Arts or Science degree has been 15 years for a long time. Many variations of intermediate stages have been tried; but eleven years of schooling for matriculation or its equivalent has remained constant."

Now the Commission has proposed a ten-year, common, undiversified, lower secondary, and a two-year higher secondary course, followed by a three-year degree course. This merely combines the lost year of the present secondary course and the existing pre-University or First year.

This has the startling effect of lowering the standard of the general course equivalent to matriculation by one year, when the real need is for raising the standard. Secondly, as the upper secondary course examination is to be in the charge of another Board, this will result in a needless multiplication of such bodies. *(Blitz,* 9 July, 1966).

Dr P. Parja (a veteran educationist of Orissa) felt, "The schooling period was recommended as 11 or 12 years with a primary stage of 4 or 6 years. Who will decide whether the period should be 11 or 12 years? Such indecision is prejudicial to uniformity, he said."

Then the Commission has suggested two types of schools, one providing 12-year course and the other 11 or 12-year course. This is likely to create difficulty. If the students leaving the 10-year school intend, as they certainly will, to enter colleges, will they be debarred or made to come through 11 to 12-year schools? *(Amrit Bazar Patrika,* 17 July, 1966).

Implementation of the Recommendations of the Education Commission

National Policy Resolution (1968)

Recommendations of the Education Commission 1964-66 were considered by various educational organisations and institutions. These were also discussed by educators all over the country. Many educational conferences were held to think over these recommendations. Meetings of Vice-Chancellors, State Education Secretaries, Directors of Education were convened. All these discussions and debates resulted in the adoption of a Resolution on the National Policy on Education in 1968.

Introduction of the New Pattern of Education

On the recommendations of the Education Commission and in accordance with the National Policy on Education (adopted by Parliament in 1968) the Central Advisory Board of Education adopted a resolution in its meeting held in November 1974 recommending the introduction of the 10 + 2 + 3 pattern of Education all over India during the Fifth Plan period. This resolution followed widespread consultation with several educational bodies and other concerned agencies throughout the country. By the end of the year 1978-79 this pattern had been introduced in 2 States/Union Territories, namely, Assam, Andhra Pradesh, Gujarat, Jammu & Kashmir, Karnataka, Kerala, Maharashtra, Sikkim, Tamil Nadu, Tripura, West Bengal, Andaman and Nicobar Islands, Arunachal Pradesh, Chandigarh, Dadra and Nagar Haveli, Delhi, Goa, Daman and Diu, Lakshadweep and Pondicherry.

Vocationalisation of Higher Secondary Education

A Centrally-sponsored scheme for vocationalisation was formed during 1976-77. Under it the State Governments were provided with Central assistance during the Fifth Five-Year Plan period and thereafter the programme was run on a regular basis as a State scheme.

Vocational surveys of 150 districts in a phased manner during the Fifth Plan Period were conducted. Out of the districts so surveyed, 40 districts were selected for the introduction of vocational courses at an average of 16 courses per district. On the basis of the recommendations of National Conference organised by NCERT on 5th June 1976, a document entitled 'Higher Secondary Education and its Vocationalisation' has been brought out by the NCERT. The Central Board of Secondary Education Delhi introduced a large number of vocations at the higher secondary stage from the academic session 1977-78. Two other Committees namely Ishwar Bhai Patel and Adiseshiah Report (1978) also made recommendations regarding vocationalisation.

Work Experience

As recommended by the Education Commission, work experience has been made an integral part of the new scheme of studies under the pattern 10 + 2 + 3.

Book Banks

About one lakh books banks have been established in educational institutions which provide books to the students belonging to the weaker sections of the society.

Two Levels of Courses

Under the new pattern of education, provision has been made for the students to select courses in some subjects at two levels, i.e., ordinary and advanced, depending upon their capacity to work and comprehend.

Revised Pay Scale of Teachers

The pay scale of teachers working in schools were revised almost in all the States as a result of the recommendations of the Education Commission.

National Institute of Educational Planning and Administration, New Delhi

The Working Party on Educational Planning, Administration and Evaluation in the Fourth Five-Year Plan set up by the Planning Commission reiterated the recommendation of the Kothari Commission for the setting up of the National Staff College. The Government of India accepted this recommendation and accordingly initiated at the Asian Institute an Indian Programme in Educational Planning and Administration as a precursor to the National Staff College. The National Staff College for Educational Planners and Administrators began to function on 1st January, 1971 after it was registered under the Indian Society Registration Act, 1860 on 31st December, 1970. With the expiry of agreement with UNESCO under which the Asian Institute of Educational Planning and Administration was functioning, the staff and activities of the Asian Institute were taken over by the Staff College from 1st march, 1973. The Staff College is located at the premises of the NCERT. Its main function is to provide pre-service and in-service training and professional guidance to the senior educational officers of the Central and State Governments and Union Territories. Staff College was renamed as National Institute of Educational Planning and Administration in 1980.

Follow-up of Recommendations

Following areas have remained ignored by and large. They have not received the due attention they deserved:

1. Development of a 'streak of quality' programme.
2. Creation of school complexes.
3. Development of 'neighbourhood' concept of educational institutions.
4. Establishment of suitable organisations for assessing manpower needs and of employment opportunities at the national and state levels.
5. Provision of part-time education on a large scale.
6. Evolving integrated plans of development.
7. Development of a large programme of scholarships at all stages and in all sectors.
8. Creation of Indian Education Service.
9. Creation of District School Boards.
10. Strengthening of the Offices of the District Educational Officers.
11. National Education Act.
12. Creation of a National Board of School Education.
13. Establishment of a Farm University in each State.
14. Recognition of autonomous educational institutions.
15. Freedom to Headmasters.

16. Making Institutional Plans as an integral part of District, State and National Plan of Education.
17. Developing partnership between educational authorities and industry.
18. Discouragement to public schools.

3

Adiseshiah Report

In October 1977, the then Union Education Minister, Dr P.C. Chunder, in his capacity as President of the NCERT, appointed a National Review Committee under the Chairmanship of Dr. Malcolm S. Adiseshiah, the then Vice-Chancellor, University of Madras, to review the curriculum of the +2 stage of school education with special reference to vocationalisation of education. The Committee submitted its report in February 1978.

Terms of Reference

The terms of reference of the National Review Committee for the Plus Two curriculum were as follows:

(i) To review the NCERT's Document "Higher Secondary Education and its Vocationalisation" and to suggest modification therein, if any.

(ii) To study the syllabi and courses of the CBSE and a few State Boards with special reference to a few selected vocations and to recommend appropriate syllabi.

(iii) To recommend a plan of action for introduction of Vocationalisation of the Secondary/Higher Secondary Stage.

It was further desired that the Committee in formulating its recommendations may also keep in mind the need for providing vertical mobility to students completing the +2 stage with Vocational courses and recommend ways and means for promoting such mobility.

The Need for Review

Three Important Considerations

The documents entitled *Higher Secondary Education and its Vocationalisation* published by the NCERT in September 1976 contained many important and forward looking features such as flexibility on the choice of vocation, determining vocations with reference to a district or a group of districts, need for district-wise survey of economic activities and potentials and consequent opportunities of work, micro-planning at the district level and assessment of manpower needs, special attention to be given to raising the facilities and quality of life in the rural areas, provision for guidance and counselling for careers and courses to the students, etc. which required rethinking.

2. Review was also needed in the light of the Report of the Ishwar Bhai Patel Committee on 10 year school curriculum.

3. The National goals and priorities that have been formulated for the country's development for the coming Sixth Plan had to be taken into account in this exercise relating to higher secondary stage of education.

The Main Recommendations

The main recommendations of the Report may be listed as under:

Work-based Learning

Learning must be based on work either through what the Ishwar Bhai Patel Committee calls socially useful productive work or through vocationalised courses.

Agriculture-oriented Vocational Courses

Vocational courses should be in agricultural and related rural occupational areas and in managerial, commercial, health and para-medical vocations and not through opening vocational courses at this level in the manufacturing, industrial and engineering occupations.

Flexible Streaming

There should be no rigid streaming of courses into the General Education and Vocationalised Educational Spectrums. Each school should be allowed to offer such General Education and Vocationalised Courses in accordance with the facilities available and the demand in the region.

Two Spectrums of the Higher Secondary Stage

The Higher Secondary Stage should comprise of a General Education Spectrum and a Vocational spectrum.

Curriculum

The curriculum should be so structured that the courses lend themselves to imparting instruction in terms of well connected modules to enable the students to choose and combine them according to their needs.

Suitable Text-books

In order to impart instruction in vocational courses, in agricultural and related subjects, books be written on a priority basis to suit local conditions and made available to the schools. In some general education and commercial subjects where textbooks produced in other countries are suitable, these books may be adapted and translated in Indian languages.

Semester Pattern and Credit System

In some States where the Universities have already adopted the semester system the same may also be introduced in classes XI and XII. The other States may study the experiences of the States which have already introduced the semester system and take suitable steps for the orientation of teachers, and preparation of modules of learning and textbook for adopting the semester pattern, at a later and appropriate time.

Counselling and Placement

As vocationalisation is extended Counselling and

Placement Officers be appointed in clusters of 3 or 4 schools, particularly in rural areas to start with.

Teachers for Vocational Courses

At the start there should not be insistence on post-graduate qualification in respect of teachers of vocational courses. What is needed is means of developing the required skills and competencies in particular vocations and for this, services of persons who have had actual experience of on-the-job may be fruitfully utilised to teach vocational courses. Part-time teachers may also be appointed wherever necessary.

Pre-service and In-service Training of Teachers

Both pre-service and in-service teacher education should be so organised as to bring about the proposed changes at this stage of education. The Universities, the Teachers Training Colleges, State Councils of Educational Research and Training (SCERTs), State Institutes of Education, State Institutes of Science Education, NCERT, Boards of Secondary Education, Agricultural Universities, institutions like ICAR and all others who are engaged in the preparation of orientation of teachers should be actively involved in this task.

Vocational Survey

With regard to the offering of vocationalised courses in rural or urban schools, a vocational survey of the area—metropolitan, block, taluk, district or State—be undertaken, such surveys being done even in cases where the vocational courses have started.

Location of Schools in the Rural Sector

In the selection of schools, it is recommended that the location of schools in the rural sector be given priority. Since little or no vocationalised education facilities are readily available for rural students, it is recommended that all the new schools should be constructed in rural areas and should be adequately.

Use of Available Facilities

To economies on the financial investment on infrastructural facilities, it is recommended that the spare capacity in all these schools be used and the enrolment be increased through running double shifts wherever it is feasible and whenever further demands for technical skills and competencies arise in neighbourhood, including as necessary (adding) new courses and strengthening the existing facilities.

Apprenticeship Facilities

Apprenticeship facilities should be extended to all the students who complete education in vocational streams if they desire to benefit from such training.

Recruitment Policy

The recruitment policy of the government as well as public sector organisations should be revised and job requirements should replace the university degrees as essential qualifications. Vocationally qualified persons should be preferred to graduates, and be entitled to the pay scales available to the graduates as long as the job performed are the same or similar. Also such persons should be eligible for the higher positions in the ladder, either on the basis of departmental tests or improvement of qualifications through correspondence or evening courses or block-time training.

Verticle Mobility

The apprenticeship and recruitment policy are part of a package recommended to improve the prospects of the majority of those who enter the plus 2 stage and terminate their formal schooling after acquiring some vocational skills.

Organisation of National Council of Vocational Education

One of the most important prerequisite for the successful implementation of the vocational spectrum of the plus 2 stage is to bring about cooperation and coordination for the purposes of employment and recognition, among all agencies and departments of the government. Such co-ordination will also economies on our scarce financial resources by preventing replication of efforts in various departments offering vocational education and making a well-planned effort possible to achieve the National goals more effectively and cheaply. A National Council of Vocational Education should be set up and all the agencies such as the Indian Council of Agricultural Research, All India Council for Technical Education, the Nursing Council, the Dental Council, the Pharmacy Council and the National Council for Training in Vocational Trades should be members of this apex body.

State Council for Vocational Education

At the State level, State Councils for Vocational Education be created to perform similar functions under the general guidance of the National Council of Vocational Education.

Local Support

The programme of vocationalisation of education requires constant support of local community and other agencies. Agencies, such as Panchayat Unions, Agricultural and Rural Cooperatives, the Small-Scale Industries Corporation, Khadi and Village Industry Commission, local branches of Nationalised and other banks, Financial Corporations, Krishi Vigyan Kendras and various voluntary organisations, help in identification of vocations and in training of pupils and teachers of vocational courses, as also in training for entrepreneurship, provisions of loans and credit facilities, marketing of product and services.

Evaluation of the Programme

It is not only adequate planning and preparation but also a continuous process of evaluation of the programme that is necessary for the success of the plus 2 stage and its vocationalisation sector. There should be an in-built machinery for such evaluation of the programme at various levels i.e., the National, the State and the local and appropriate follow-up action taken.

Financial Resources

(1) No large scale of ambitious expenditure be incurred on equipment, unless it is ascertained that it will be needed for a long period and even so not in the area of manufacturing, industrial or engineering skills which are left to existing vocation/technical education institutions.

(2) In fact with the short-term emphasis in the report on agriculture, managerial and health and para-medical vocations attempts should first be made to identify and exploit locally available resources.

(3) In view of the immense stakes in the programme of vocationalisation and in the interest of national economic development and social transformation, some additional resources will be needed. Any expenditure on vocationalisation should be considered as a national investment for the future. Where necessary, provision for additional financial resources must, therefore, be made ungrudgingly. Such an expenditure will generate new capabilities in the human wealth of our country, which will in its turn return the investment multiplied over the years.

CURRICULUM OF HIGHER SECONDARY EDUCATION

The Review Committee has suggested two broad learning components of the Higher Secondary stage. These have been termed as:

(i) The General Education Spectrum

(ii) The Vocationalised Spectrum.

The General Education Spectrum

According to the Committee the General Education spectrum of the Higher Secondary School is for the general information of the person and personality through learning centred around languages, socially useful productive work and a combination of the starting phases of natural, social or human science disciplines. Its aim is essentially to prepare the students for university education in the arts or sciences or for professional studies. This is the bridge facet of the plus 2 stage. This is also the phase of the educational system in which there is a built-in continuity with the past, the main innovation being learning acquired from socially useful productive work.

General Education Spectrum: The Course Pattern

The committee has recommended as:

Course	*Time Allocation*
1. Language(s)	15%
2. Socially useful productive work	15%
3. Elective (three)	70%

It is recognised that this general scheme must be applied with a certain amount of flexibility, allowing individual States and Union Territories and even individual schools to adopt the courses and the distribution of time to local conditions and pedagogic perceptions.

The Vocationalised Spectrum

The Committee observes that the Vocationalised Spectrum of the Higher Secondary Schools is learning of skill or a range of skills through study of technologies, related sciences, and farm or other practical work. This vocationalised training must be distinguished from technical/vocational education imparted in the I.T.I.s technical high schools, agricultural or industrial polytechnics, where a certain level of skill as craftsman or technician or extension agent is aimed at and attained. The Vocationalised Spectrum that is referred to embraces in the UNESCO language "those aspects of the educational process involving, in addition to general education, the study of technologies and related sciences and acquisition of practical skills, aptitudes, understanding and knowledge relating to occupations in the various sectors of economic and social life. Such an education would be an integral part of general education and a means of preparing for an occupational field and an aspect of continuing education. This spectrum refers back to the terminal character of formal schooling that it represents for 50 per cent of its entrants."

Since the content and scope of vocationalisation must be in conformity with national goals and the specific needs of the local community at every given point of time, the vocationalisation of higher secondary education recommended aims for the next five years at increasing the employment potential of the people through education for self-employment, with emphasis on agricultural and related occupations including tiny, small, cottage and agro industries and through preparation for specific competencies in different vocations.

The Vocationalised Course Pattern

The Committee has recommended that the pattern of the course and the allocation of time for the Vocationalised Spectrum be:

Course	*Time Allocation*
1. Language(s)	15%
2. General foundation course	15%
3. Elective vocational subjects	70%

General Foundation Course

The objectives of the course are to enable the student to:

1. become aware of the need for rural development and self- employment;
2. understand the place of agriculture in the national economy;

3. develop skill and managerial abilities to run small-scale and cottage industries;
4. gain insight into the problems of unemployment, underemployment and economic backwardness of India.

Two Parts of the General Foundation Course

The course is meant to be taught for 2 years, 4 to 5 hours per week.

Part *A* of the course is common to all vocations. From Part B, the unit most related to the particular vocational may be chosen.

Part A. This includes five heads: (1) Gandhian concept of education; (2) Agriculture in the national economy; (3) Rural development; (4) problems of urban slums; and (5) Health, hygiene and sanitation.

Part B. Any one of the 9 sections to be chosen: (1) small scale and cottage industries; (2) Entrepreneurship; (3) Co-operation and credit facilities; (4) Marketing; (5) Sales promotion; (6) Unemployment, underemployment and man-power utilisation in India; (7) Human relations; (8) General exposure to world trends and changes; and (9) Environmental protection and development.

Elective Vocational Subjects

These are to be selected from among the following groups:

1. Agricultural and related vocations (15 in all)
2. Business and office management (8)
3. Para-medical (13)
4. Educational service (9)
5. Local body and other services (4)
6. Journalism (2)
7. Home science related vocations (6)
8. Other general services (7).

Advantages of the Recommendations

Learning to Do

The report has been aptly entitled 'Learning To Do—Towards a Learning and Working Society'. The scheme proposed by the National Review Committee (1978) admirably fits into the economic and social programme of the Government with its emphasis on agriculture and rural oriented educational programmes. The Committee has specially recommended that location of schools in the rural sector be given priority.

Learning to be Based on Work

Dr. Malcolm S. Adiseshiah, the Chairman of the Review Committee in his letter of 'transmittal' to the Minister of Education and Social Welfare has stated, "the central finding of the Committee is that Learning must be based on Work, either through what the Ishwar Bhai Committee calls "Socially Useful Productive Work which has been woven into the general education courses, proposed in the report or through the vocationalised courses, that we have recommended." This recommendation fully meets the needs of the present situation.

General Education Course in Place of 'Academic Course'

The Review Committee has very apatly used the term General Education and eschewed the term Academic Course because of its peculiar connotations.

Vocational Course to be Agriculture Oriented

The Review Committee has given special attention to the fact that India is, by and large, a rural country and accordingly agriculture and rural-based vocational courses have been recommended. To quote, The Chairman of the Review Committee in this regard:

"For the immediate future, i.e. for the 6th Plan, the vocational courses to be offered at the Higher Secondary level should be in agricultural and related rural occupational area and in managerial, commercial, health and para-medical vocations, and not through opening vocational courses at this level in the manufacturing, industrial and engineering occupations. Given the larger scale unemployment of the product of the I.T.I.s and to a lesser extent of the Polytechnics and Engineering Colleges as set forth in official reports these offerings at the +2 stage are not needed. There was also the need for this stage of education to conform to the National Priority to Agriculture, rural development and adult literacy that had mean sadly neglected to-date by the formal school system. In fact, we recommend opening or locating of higher secondary schools in rural areas with vocational courses in agriculture and related occupations partly to make for this lacunae."

Flexibility

The recommendations of the Review Committee provide for a flexible approach to the provision of various courses. It has been recognised that General Scheme must be applied with certain amount of flexibility, allowing individual States and Territories and even individual schools to adapt the courses and distribution of time to pedagogic perceptions and local conditions.

Need for Sufficient Preparation in Vocational Courses

Further Dr. Adiseshiah, in his letter of transmittal has observed, "A final consideration that I would like to bring to your attention is our plea for careful preparation to ensure that the many facets of the reform of Higher Secondary Education are thought through, planned for, and provided against as the country's stakes in this educational stage are high. One problem here is that almost all States as well as the central agencies have already launched on the plus 2 stage. Hence for most agencies the recommendations in this report will have to be used as guide posts and lead points to review what has been embarked upon, and make such corrections and changes in the future as they may deem necessary and appropriate. In fact such a system of continuous evaluation should be built into our entire educational system, and for this steps should be undertaken by the Central and State Boards and the National and State Vocational Councils of Education that have been recommended. To err may be human, but to persist in it is inhuman."

Recruitment Policy

All will fully endorse the recommendation of the Review Committee that job requirements should replace the university degrees as essential qualification. There is a great weight in the argument that vocationally qualified persons should be preferred to graduates and be entitled to the pay scales available to the graduates as long as the jobs performed are the same or similar.

A Comprehensive Document

The report has given a critical analysis of the situation and has suggested valuable guidelines for embarking upon a countrywide programme of vocationalisation of higher secondary education. The magnitude of the problem has been outlined scientifically and statistically. Many valuable suggestions have been given for popularising vocational courses.

Defects of the Recommendations

'Learning to be' instead of 'learning to do'

The title of the present report taken from the title of the International Report 'Learning to be' suggests that the primary function of education is 'doing' and not making 'a man or a woman'. In other words the title gives the impression that a man merely exists for bread and butter and he has very little regard for higher values of life. It is true that by laying emphasis on 'doing' the report has highlighted the special need for vocationalisation. But the report suggests that education is meant for the satisfaction of the needs of an

'Economic Man'. Basically, the aim of education is the complete fulfilment of man, in all the richness of his personality, the complexity of his forms of family and of a community, citizen and producer, inventor of techniques and creative dreamer.

Financial Implications of the Scheme

It is to be noted that the National Review Committee like the earlier Ishwar Bhai Patel Committee has failed to work out the implications of the introduction of the vocational courses and the socially useful productive work in educational institutions. Unfortunately, our educational experts usually indulge in platitudinous talk ignoring financial matters with the result that most of the reports cannot be put to practice. It must always be remembered that, however an ideal a programme, it cannot be implemented without the establishment of farms/workshops in a large number of schools. It also requires enormous raw material and appliances and appropriate training and guidance to the students. One fails to appreciate as to how these problems are to be solved.

Defective Method of Working of the National Review Committee

It appears that the review committee has not made its recommendations on any scientific and adequate data. It has also not tried to assess the views of the students and their parents. Questionnaires on the various aspects of the vocationalisation of education should have been administered not only to the students and their parents but also to various other persons connected with educational reform. Interviews should also have been held with different categories of persons. It must be borne in mind that an objective assessment based on scientific and reliable data is absolutely essential. It is most desirable that educational organisations like NCERT and SIE conduct action research on the various issues concerning the worthwhileness and implementation of the new courses.

Vocational Courses vis-a-vis Academic Courses

Generally it is seen that vocational courses provided in the institutions imparting General Education have not given the desired results. Definitely, a second thought is needed on the issue whether it is not uneconomical to provide for vocational courses in the institutions meant for General Education. It is also to be experimented if by expanding facilities in the polytechnics and vocational schools we can train personnel for the middle level occupations. If we glance through the vocational courses, we find teacher training as one of the courses. It is very doubtful if the products of the higher secondary schools in this area can compare with the teachers training colleges which specialise in this field and which have the requisite facilities. Similar may be the case with many other vocational courses. This is not to dispute the necessity of vocationalisation of higher secondary education. Vocationalisation of higher secondary education is something on which all are agreed but there appears to be very little consensus on the 'How' and 'When' of it. It is true that there can be no perfect model for the entire country. However, the moot point is—Are our schools which have been primarily designed for catering to general education capable of providing adequate facilities for the vocationalisation of higher secondary education?

It is very much intriguing that the terms like socialism, secularism, democracy and egalitarian do not find any place in the Adiseshiah report. Similar is the case with values like moral and spiritual training which are conspicuous their absence.

Involvement of Students in Adult Literacy Programmes

It is very doubtful if the students can be effectively involved in running functional literacy programmes in the villages or urban slums of their neighbourhood.

Undue Emphasis on the Principle of International Sharing

Perhaps there was no need to devote a paragraph to stress the importance of this principle.

Unrepresentative Composition of the Review Committee

Out of the twenty-seven members, thirteen were Delhi and one may be tempted to remark that it was a Delhi Based Report and not an All India Report. Representatives of the private sector engaged in trade and industry were not associated with the committee. There were four representatives of the public school system and none from the schools catering to academic or general education. Similarly rural schools were not adequately represented. The committee was almost a 'man's world'. Coming to gender basis there were only two female members against 25 males in the Committee.

Much Emphasised Flexibility

It is felt that it is very dangerous to go on harping on the 'flexibility' of the pattern of education, curriculum and the contents of the various courses. We must bear in mind that excess of every thing is bad. Flexibility must always be within limits. There is every possibility that flexibility may result in the emergence of the classical policy of 'laissez faire' which will be hardly conducive to national and emotional integration. Flexibility may mean anything and everything.

Plus 2 Stage

There appears to be no need of introducing 'U.P.W.' in the general education course at the plus 2 stage in view of this being a stage of diversification and specialisation. Moreover students of classes XI and XII would have got adequate experience in this area during their secondary education i.e. classes IX and X. The entire time at the plus 2 stage should be utilised for the electives and languages.

Problems for Implementation

The situation as is prevailing today indicates that response to the introduction of vocational courses at the higher secondary stage in higher secondary schools has not been very encouraging. The number of students opting for these courses as stated earlier is very meagre. Some of the important problems are as under:

Selection of Suitable Courses by the Students

Usually no scientific method is used for selecting candidates for a particular course with the result that students fail to choose courses in accordance with their abilities and aptitudes. This causes frustration to the students on several occasions. It is, therefore, suggested that a comprehensive programme of educational and vocational guidance should be organised in all the higher secondary schools and specially those providing vocational courses.

Guidance and Counselling

It is obvious that higher secondary institutions will have to provide guidance and counselling for careers and courses to the students both at the point of entry and at the end of semesters.

Reservation

It is only just that for some time reservation of at least 20 per cent of seats in prestigious courses may be made for students who have been deprived of suitable educational opportunities.

Admission Tests

In the case of reserved as well as unreserved seats there should be admission tests amongst candidates for ensuring eligibility. The tests themselves need not be too elaborate, running into several papers, for a number of days, they may consist of one or two suitable papers of two hours duration.

Choice of Vocations Surveys

A survey of activities of the districts would lead to the

kind of vocations which are likely to have relevance, and to the identification of numbers which would be needed.

District and State Vocational Committees

District and state vocational committees having representatives of productive activities and services, trade and commerce, administration, planning and educational institutions would be most useful not only in deciding upon the vocations for which facilities should be provided from year to year, but also in deciding on the content of the vocational courses and more than this, the manner of facilitating training in these vocations by the cooperative participation of the above mentioned agencies.

Opportunities for On-the-Job Training

On-the-job training would be a must, in almost all the vocations and the school time-table would have to be so designed as to meet this situation.

Adoption of Higher Secondary School

The government could consider involving large public undertakings and workshops, such as those belonging to the railways to take positive steps to adopt higher secondary schools for teaching and training in certain fields so that the costs of vocationalisation do not mount, at least in part, owing to the duplication of facilities. The laboratories and workshops of these institutions should be made available during the vacations and during holidays. It is in a sense a partnership programme between education and other sectors of the economy and the services between the school and the factory.

Lack of Further Training Opportunities

One of the main drawbacks of the present vocational courses is that there is little opportunity for the students to further improve and update their qualifications and skills in suitable higher vocational institutions. If such opportunities are assured them from the very beginning they will opt the vocational courses readily.

Vocational Education

For making the vocational programme a success, a proper directional and supervisory machinery will have to be created at various levels.

Evaluation

Suitable evaluation tools will have to be developed immediately to assess the performance of the students in the vocational courses. Subjective element will have to be reduced to the minimum.

Reorientation and Training

The introduction of vocational courses has created enormous problems of training of teachers. As a matter of fact only bonafide vocational experts can impart vocational education effectively. Ways and means will have to be devised so that such trained vocational experts come forward for working in our educational institutions. Proper qualifications will have to be prescribed for teachers teaching vocational subjects.

Suitable measures will have to be adopted speedily for equipping the teachers for shoul-dering the new responsibilities imposed upon them by the introduction of vocational subjects.

The instructors from the ITI may be invited to assist the teachers in order to raise quality of instruction imparted by them.

The teachers training colleges and departments are required to recast their curriculum so that it is in accordance with the new requirements.

Recognition of Diplomas/Certificates and Degrees

A student will not go in for a vocational course unless

he is sure that a particular course will lead him to a specific job. This points to the need of a more centralised system for identifying the courses which are acceptable to the organised sector and whose equivalence is already determined.

Similarly proper arrangements will have to be made for those students who wish to go in for higher education after completing a two-year vocational course.

Preparation of a List of Good Schools

A list of good schools doing useful work in the field of vocational education at the higher secondary stage may be prepared and teachers, principals and others connected with vocational education deputed to see the work of such institutions.

Co-ordination with the Finance Department

It has generally been observed that there is no proper co-ordination between the educational administrators and the officials of the Finance Department of the states with the result that there is an undue delay in getting financial sanctions for the requisite staff, equipment, etc. Suitable ways and means will have to be devised so that the officials of the Finance Department appreciate and sense the urgency and significance of educational reforms in their real perspective and give up their traditional attitude of putting unnecessary obstacles.

Now, in the year 2005 the entire scenario has undergone a tremendous transformation. Vocational courses are much rough after area of education at the secondary and higher level. Thus the critique on Adiseshiah Report can be considered a contemporary appraisal. In nutshell, the report was a milestone at least to initiate a most desirable debate on vocational education.

4

Basic Education

Buniyadi Talim or Nai Talim, as Gandhiji used to name it, ushered in a new era in the arena of education in India. In the opinion of Dr. Zakir Husain "this new scheme which we are advocating will aim at giving the citizens of the future a keen sense of personal worth, dignity and efficiency, and will strengthen in them the desire for self improvement and social service in a co-operative community."

"This basic education," according to a pamphlet published by the Ministry of Education, "is not only a valuable and integral part of the priceless legacy that Mahatma Gandhi left to the nation, but embodies certain educational ideas and principles of greater significance that have been welcomed and endorsed by distinguished and discerning Educationists in India and abroad." "Economically considered, carried out intelligently and efficiently, the scheme will increase the productive capacity of our workers, and will enable them to utilise leisure advantageously," reported the Zakir Husain Committee.

University Education Commission has stated, "At this fateful moment in our history, we have the extreme good fortune to have had presented to us a pattern and philosophy of education of such universal and fundamental worth that it may well serve as the type for bringing into being the new India which is the desire of many of us. We have no sympathy with here worship and feel that there should be no withholding of criticism of an educational plan because it was presented by our great leader. With some details of Gandhiji's programme of basic education we may not agree. However, taking his concept as a whole it presents the seeds of a method for the fulfilment and refinement of human personality, the wisdom and excellence of which will become more apparent through the years, and will stand the test of time and of criticism. Years of time and vast effort will be required to insure this movement against warped and mistaken expression and to develop effective skills and methods; yet inherently the concept is one of the world's great contributions to education.

Gandhiji has stated the essential elements of a universal method of education, from the time a little child shares in its mother's work, through the whole process of growth of personality to the time when the mature man of disciplined mind and character works at the side of the master in the achievement of a great design. The essence of this philosophy is that education should combine practice in the every day processes of living and working with more formal training. This is a fundamental concept which is steadily gaining support and application in the field of education.

Gandhiji was not the first to have this vision. Aristotle, Francis Bacon, Milton and Louis Agassiz were among the world's great men who specially expressed a similar conviction. But in one important respect he differed from most of the others. While their minds caught the vision of a new way, the bookishness of their lives held some of them captive. Therein is Gandhiji's pre-eminence. No sooner was a conviction matured in his mind than he acted on it.

Basic education conference 1937

In October 1937, at a conference of national workers at Wardha under the chairmanship of Gandhiji, his ideas were considered and the following resolutions passed which became the fundamental features of the scheme:

(i) That in the opinion of the conference free and compulsory education be provided for seven years on a nation-wide scale.

(ii) That the medium of instruction be the mother-tongue.

(iii) That the conference endorses the proposal made by Mahatma Gandhi that the process of education throughout this period should centre round some form of manual productive work, and that all the other abilities to be developed or training to be given should, as far as possible, be integrally related to the central handicraft chosen with due regard to the environment of the child.

(iv) That the conference expects that this system of education will be gradually able to cover the remuneration of the teachers.

Zakir Husain Committee on Basic Education

A Committee was appointed under the chairmanship of Dr. Zakir Husain to prepare a detailed syllabus on the lines of the above resolutions.

Since the publication of the Zakir Husain Committee report, there have been long and continuous debates on the utility of basic education system, the duration, the nature and contents of the syllabus. At long last it has been decided that the Basic Education is the most appropriate pattern of education for the whole country.

The fundamental features of the scheme, having undergone a lot of change, are as follows:

(a) A school of say 5½ hours could roughly be divided on the following basis:

   (i) Physical activities
   20 Minutes

   (ii) Mother Tongue
   40 Minutes

(iii) Social Studies and General Science
60 Minutes

(iv) Art
40 Minutes

(v) Arithmetic
20 Minutes

(vi) Craft work including study of
2½ Hours
correlated subjects

Thus, the craft work will have 2½ hours instead of 3 hours and 20 minutes.

(b) Free and compulsory education to be given in 8 years (from 6 to 14 years) in two stages, instead of 7 to 14. The junior stage will cover five years and the senior 3 years.

(c) The medium of instruction is to be the mother tongue.

(d) Education is to centre round some form of productive work. The social and physical environment should be used for correlation in addition to craft.

(e) The self-supporting aspect is not to be overemphasised. The sale-proceeds of the finished goods should be able to help the school to cover some parts of its expenditure.

(f) External examinations are to be abolished. The day-to-day work of the students is to be the determining factor.

(g) Text books to be avoided as far as possible.

(h) Cleanliness and health, citizenship, play and recreation are to be given sufficient importance.

Needs of Basic Education

It is admitted by everybody that the system of education introduced by Macaulay is outmoded and outdated. Gandhiji realised fully that the traditional system is unreal and artificial.

He said, "I am convinced that the present system of education is not only wasteful but positively harmful. Most of the boys are lost to the parents and to the occupations to which they were born. They pick up evil habits, effect urban ways and get a smattering of something which may be anything but education." Gandhiji again feels, " The present system of education does not meet the requirements of the country in any shape or form. English has been made medium of education in all the highest branches of learning, has created a permanent bar between the highly educated few and the uneducated many." He further adds, "We have up to now concentrated on stuffing children's minds with all kinds of information without even thinking or stimulating or developing them. Let us now cry a halt and concentrate on educating the child properly through manual work not as a side activity but as a prime means of intellectual activity."

A number of defects were clearly visible in the system of education introduced by the British in India. These may be categorised as:

1. It was an un-Indian system of education.
2. The system neglected citizenship training.
3. It was an urban system of education in a rural country.
4. The curriculum was English dominated.
5. The system was too literary and bookish.
6. The system was very wasteful.
7. The system followed a single track.
8. The system was unplanned.
9. The system was very expensive.
10. The system was not in accordance with the needs of a secular democratic country.

Basic education aims at removing the defects. Gandhiji wanted to make education self-sufficient, otherwise the teeming millions of India could not be educated.

Salient Characteristics of Basic Education

"This Basic Education," according to pamphlet published by the Ministry of Education, "is not only a valuable and integral part of the priceless legacy that Mahatma Gandhi left to the nation, but embodies certain educational ideas and principles of great significance that have been welcomed and endorsed by distinguished educationists in India and abroad." "Economically considered carried out intelligently and efficiently, the scheme will increase the productive capacity of our workers, and will enable them to utilise leisure advantageously," reported the Zakir Husain Committee.

The Basic Education has the following certain distinctive merits:

1. Child-centred Education

In the words of an eminent educationist, "The Basic Education regards the child as the educational consumer whose needs must be studied and understood, catered to and fulfilled." All the great educationists like Rousseau, Pestalozzi, Froebel, Herbart, Dewey, etc. emphasised that top priority should be given to the child—his nature, needs and interest.

2. Craft as the Core of the Basic Plan

Craft is the medium of education in the Basic system. Gandhiji writes, "The core of my suggestion is that handicrafts are not to be taught, not merely for productive work but for developing the intellect of the pupils." According to his view "stress should be laid on the principles of cooperative, activity planning, accuracy, initiative and individual responsibility in learning." Gandhiji has further observed, "The process of education should be imparted through some handicraft or industry."

3. Self-supporting Aspect

"Earn while you learn" is another feature of the plan.

The idea of a self-sufficient basic school has a special significance in a poor country like India. Without self-sufficient schools it is very doubtful if we could fulfil the obligation to our Constitution of providing free and compulsory education to all the boys and girls of school-going age. In the absence of such schools we may have to wait for many, many decades to provide education to such a group.

4. *Integrated Knowledge*

Basic education treats knowledge as an integrated whole. Curriculum is built round three integrally related centres: (1) Physical environment, (2) Social environment, (3) Craft work.

5. *Learning by Doing*

Learning by doing sums up the educational methods of Basic Education. It is absolutely wrong to think that true education is acquired from books alone. There are other methods and sources which are more helpful in acquiring true knowledge. 'Chalk' and 'talk' lessons are also not very useful. All educationists have condemned bookish knowledge. Gandhiji believed that school must be a doing thing. In basic system of education children acquire the knowledge of the formal school subjects as a bye-product of purposeful activities.

6. *Relationship with Life*

A Basic school must become an active environment where teaching is not cut off from the life of the community. There is to be a constant two-way traffic between the miniature community of the school and the community itself. Education is to be directed to the needs of life. It is not to pursue an ideal which has no relation with or is totally isolated from the real situations of life.

7. *Training in Citizenship*

Basic education aims at developing ideas of mutual understanding and habits of co-operative and mutually helpful living among the students through its various practical and constructive programmes. The new education aims at giving the citizens of the future a keen sense of personal warmth, dignity and efficiency. It is likely to strengthen in them the desire for self-improvement and social service in a cooperative community.

8. Free and Compulsory Education for Seven Years

The free and compulsory education means an education for which parents will not have to pay any fee and for which they must send their children to school. Gandhiji writes, "Primary education extending over a period of 7 years or longer and covering all the subjects up to the matriculation standard except English, plus a vocation used as a vehicle for drawing out the minds of boys and girls in all departments of knowledge should take the place of what passes today under the name of primary, middle and high school education."

9. Greater Freedom for the Teacher and the Taught

Discipline does not mean order and external restraint but an intelligent use of Freedom in Basic education.

10. Emphasis on Mother-Tongue

Gandhiji stressed that proper education can only be imparted through the mother-tongue. Foreign tongue as the medium of instruction makes us unfit for original work. It makes us crammers and imitators. Zakir Hussain Committee observes, "The proper teaching of the mother-tongue is the foundation of all education. Without the capacity to speak effectively and to read and write correctly and lucidly, no one can develop precision of thought or clarity of ideas. Moreover, it is a means of introducing the child to the rich heritage of his people's ideas, emotions and aspirations and can, therefore, be made a valuable means of social education, whilst also instilling right ethical and moral values." Also, it is a natural outlet for the expression of the child's aesthetic sense and application and if the proper approach is adopted the study of literature becomes a source of joy and creative appreciation.

11. Basic Education is not a Class Education

The ultimate objective of Basic education was to create a social order in which there is no unnatural division between 'haves' and 'have-nots' and every one is assured of a living wage and the right to freedom.

12. Basic Education in the Rural as well as Urban Areas

It is a wrong notion that Basic education is intended to be imparted in rural areas only. To quote Dr. K.L. Shrimali, "In fact, in one sense there is a greater need for Basic education in urban areas. In rural areas the children who participate in the life of the farm or allied occupation of their families have certain types of further education. In performing their jobs the children come into direct contact with actual life and the experiences they get from the basis of further education. On the other hand, in large towns and big industrial cities the children miss the opportunities of rich experiences and direct contact with life". Basic education is a plan of national education for the whole country including both rural as well as urban areas. Keeping in view the educative possibilities of a craft in relation to local needs, curriculum may differ from region to region. There is no rigidity in the curriculum of Basic education. However, it will be wrong to think that rural children should have altogether a different type of education from urban children. Difference will be of a degree and not of kind. Basic principles of life are the same everywhere.

The word 'Basic' is derived from the word 'Base' which means the bottom or the foundation of a thing upon which the whole thing rests or is made.

It is basic because it is based on ancient Indian culture.

It is basic because it lays down the minimum educational standards which every Indian child is entitled to receive without any distinction of caste or creed.

It is basic because it is closely related to the basic needs and interests of the child.

It is basic because it makes use of the native potentialities of the child.

It is basic because it is intimately related to the basic occupations of the community.

It is basic because it is for the common man of the country, who is the foundation and the backbone of our national life.

It is basic because it comes first in time i.e., it is the primary period of one's education.

Criticism of Basic Education

1. Unsound Psychological Foundation Basis

Dr. R.S. Naidu observes," The delicate but inexorable laws governing the development of the tender mind of the child have been completely ignored. The child is treated just as a policeman or a soldier, merely as a unit in a homogeneous mass. His precious individuality ignored. He is viewed merely as a means to an end—the end being earning capacity and citizenship of sorts. In the Wardha scheme of training for teachers child psychology is conspicuous by its absence.

"Play is the only means by which creative energy can be released. Enlightened and informed educational opinion all over the civilised world is decidedly against forcing the child to learn a craft before he is twelve plus. It is nothing short of cruelty to make the child earn an anna or half an anna per hour during the stage when he ought to be playing and enjoying himself.

"There are three aspects of human nature—cognitive, affective and conative. The Wardha scheme emphasises the last aspect piously hoping that the student will willy-nilly get trained in the first through his training in the last. The middle aspect is completely ignored."

2. Craft as the Only Basis of Correlation

P.S. Naidu has stated, "It is impossible to establish any natural association between craft and all the subjects of cultural value which any sane system of education should cover through its curriculum. Teaching should be concrete and should be based on the child's active experience in his environment. But it is absurd to hang all knowledge from the beg of a single craft."

On the hand, it is apt here to quote the Editor, *Educational Review*, "The essence of Basic education is that it is learning by doing, that it is activity centred, that it is craft-centred, everything cannot be taught through crafts or practical activities."

3. Ignores National Genius

Again P.S. Naidu said, "Education suited to our national genius should have a definite religious bias, with contempt of worldly pursuits in its core. Craft-centred education is decidedly alien to our ancient ideals."

4. Basic Education not Suited in an Age of Industrialisation

In the opinion of S. Natrajan, "The policy of the Govt. of India as a whole is concerned with industrialisation of the country. It is not necessary to labour the point that Basic education is a concept which runs counter to such a policy. As ours is a system of education which claims to produce an integrated individual, the emphasis on craft is out of place in a community which has its face turned towards developing its economy to the full. So far discussion on Basic education has failed to relate to the economic policy of the State. But if this point is ignored we shall find ourselves burdened with an educational system which turns out misfits ever more rapidly than the one with which we are so dissatisfied."

Editorial, *Educational Review* has mention it as, "With rapid industrialisation of India knowledge of science and mathematics may become more desirable than skill in handicrafts."

5. Ruinous Competition

In the view of P.S. Naidu, "This scheme will hit the professional artisans hard by creating ruinous competition."

6. Deficient Working of Basic Schools

In this connection J. Lahiri says, "There is some loss in mechanical arithmetic and spelling lack of sufficient intensive and repetitive drill."

"Two types of Basic education have ultimately crystalised: The orthodox Wardha type of eight years craft-centred Basic schools and the more liberal craft-biased but activity type of Basic schools in two stages, *viz.*, Junior Basic stage of 6 to 11 plus and Senior Basic stage up to 14 plus with the result that at the moment we find two types sponsored by the different stages."

7. Neglect of Child

Anath Nath Basu has said, "In a hurry to pay more attention to craft, it has neglected the child."

"Basic education is looked upon more as a social and economic duty than as a joyful adventure."

While in the opinion of R.K. Singh, "Craft is only a slogan, a fiction, which is practised on ceremonial occasions for the benefits of visitors."

8. Faulty Time -table

To cite R.K. Singh, "In a Basic School only two-thirds or half the normal time is given to academic education; the rest being taken up by crafts. And further since on the time-table academic subjects generally come after the craft work, mostly agriculture, students are sometimes too tired to take to academic work kindly."

9. Secondary Importance to Literacy and Know'edge

Again R.K Singh says, "Literacy and knowledge of subject matter are considered to be of secondary importance."

10. No Dexterity in any Craft

While R.K Singh says, "Students spend one-third or half the time for craft work without acquiring any dexterity worth speaking of in any craft."

The Editorial, *Educational Review* opines, "A careful study of what is taking place in the Basic schools today has revealed that the teaching in such schools has less emphasis on the quantum of knowledge stipulated to be conveyed to the children during particular periods."

Thus it can be said about Basic Educaiton.

1. Basic Education is a *Fad.* It has no sound psychological and pedagogical basis.

2. Basic Education is a *Fallacy.* The very fundamentals are wrong and not properly conceived.

3. Basic Education is a *Farce.* The scheme is impracticable. Traditional methods are still followed. The craft materials are just stored and a show is put up, whenever there are visitors.

4. Basic Education is a *Fraud,* which is being committed on the nation by those who are in power. It is a sort of political stunt to play with the sentiments of the people.

Future of basic education and the education commission

The Commission believed that the essential elements of Basic Education were fundamentally sound, but some modifications were needed.

"The movement of Basic education launched by Mahatma Gandhi more than 35 years ago, proposing a new type of elementary education for the nation which would centre round some from of manual and productive work and have intimate links with the life of the community, was a landmark, in the history of education in India. It was a revolt against the sterile, book-centred, examination-oriented system of education that had developed along traditional lines during several decades of British rule. It created a national ferment which may not have transformed the quality of education at the primary stage, but which has certainly left its impact on educational thought and practice on a much wider sphere. We believe that the essential elements of the system are fundamentally sound, and that with necessary modifications these can form a part of education, not only at the primary stage but at all stages in our national system. These elements are (1) productive activity in education; (2) correlation of the curriculum with the productive activity and the physical and social environment; and (3) intimate contact between the school and the local community."

The Commission popularised the concept of 'work experience' and saw that the two ideas—work experience and basic education—were essentially similar.

"In the curricula of most contemporary school systems, particularly in the socialist countries of Europe, a place is found for what is variously called 'manual work' or 'work experience'. In our country, a revolutionary experiment was launched by Mahatma Gandhi in the form of Basic education. The concept of work experience is essentially similar. It may be described as a redefinition of his educational thinking in terms of a society launched on the road to industrialisation."

The Commission gave a call for the reorientation of Basic education programme in view of the changed character and need of the new society. It is not difficult to miss the clear shift of emphasis in terms of a new science-oriented social order in the following words:

"The programme of Basic education did involve work-experience for all children in the primary schools, though the activities proposed were concerned with the indigenous crafts and the village employment patterns. If in practice Basic education has become largely frozen around certain crafts, there is no denying the fact that it always stressed the vital principle of relating education to productivity. What is now needed is a reorientation of the Basic education programme to the needs of a society that has to be transformed with the help of science and technology. In other words, work-experience must be forward looking in keeping with the character of the new social order."

5

Secondary Education in India

At the time of Independence in 1947, India took over a simple, single-track and small system of secondary education which was not directed towards development of the country. This had to be so, because the system had been established by British East India Company, which was primarily interested in preparing some personnel to continue its own officers in India rather than the education of the Indian people for any social, cultural or economic betterment. Briefly speaking, secondary education at that time like other stages and aspects of education, was facing mainly three types of problems. The problem of expansion, the problem of making secondary education relevant to social, economic and other needs of the country and the problem about raising the standard and quality of education generally. Continuous effort at resolving these problems has been made all through the post-independence period. While reasonable good progress has been achieved in expanding secondary education facilities, the other two problems continue to face us. Education being a sub-system of the larger social system, the problem of relevance may perhaps never be solved. Thus perennial efforts are compulsory for resolving this.

Before the Independence, secondary education was mainly confined to cities and towns, and the rural population, which constitutes about 80% of the total population, was bereft of secondary education. Through the successive five-year plans, we have made considerable progress in expanding the facilities. The middle schools have been up-graded to secondary and higher secondary levels, new such schools have been established, where needed, and more and more students have enrolled. Physical facilities like school buildings, hostels, playfields, libraries and laboratories have also been created to the extent the limited financial resources permitted. Some lee-way, however, remains to be made up in this regard. Also, the enrolment of girls and that of children from the tribal, scheduled caste and other backward communities is still to be pushed up.

One important fact to be mentioned here is that secondary schooling facilities have become available within a reasonable distance of most of the habitations. For the rest and for the benefit of employed persons, housewives and others, the secondary and higher secondary schooling facilities have been made available through correspondence and distance education. On consideration of equity, the tuition fees have been completely abolished in the case of scheduled tribes and castes. In a few states, such fees have been dispensed with in respect of all students upto the end of the high or higher secondary singe. The various state governmerits have been expanding secondary education with an aim that no student seeking admission to that stage will be denied the admission.

Science Education

Many measures have been taken during the post-independence period to make secondary education more meaningful and relevant to the needs of time. One such measures relates to the introduction of science teaching. Before independence, science was taught as an optional subject at the secondary stage of education. Due to the optional character and limitation of seats, very few students could take advantage of science education. Taking into consideration and importance of science in our lives, the facilities for science education were expanded in the secondary and higher secondary schools, thanks to the boost given to this subject by the first Prime Minister of India, Pandit Jawahar Lal Nehru. During the sixties, when Shri M.C. Chhagla was the Union Education Minister, a crash programme for science education was launched by the central government. It was directed to increase the facilities for science education, improve science laboratories and appoint science teachers in the schools. The scheme was financed on 100% basis by the central government. Later, as a follow-up of the report of the All India Education Commission of 1964-66, science was made a compulsory subject right from class I upto the end of high school all over the country. It occupies that position today. It is likely to continue to have the same position in future too.

Computer Education

With the emergence of the use and importance of computers are emerging in a big way, courses in computer education are being introduced in more and more secondary and higher secondary schools of the country. This programme has expanded in an increasing measure in present time.

Multipurpose Schools

The first effort at Vocationalisation started in mid-fifties through implementation of the All India Secondary Education Commission of 1953-54. The commission recommended an 11-year higher secondary school with the provision of 7 streams in classes IX, X and XI. These streams were Humanities, Science, Technical Stream, Commerce stream, Agriculture, Fine Arts and Domestic Science. Those higher secondary schools, which provided three or more of these streams, were called Multipurpose schools. We gave these schools a curriculum with bias towards practical work in the hope that it would provide employment-oriented secondary education. But we did not succeed. The school leavers were not acceptable to industry and other sectors of employment because of their insufficient training for work. They were also not given any preference in admission by the professional colleges, the argument being that they were weak in the basic sciences. Further, we started the Multipurpose schools around 1955, but we thought of training special teachers for them through the Regional Colleges of Education of NCERT much later. I think we lacked, at the time, experience. In any case, the whole philosophy and planning of the Multipurpose schools were defective.

Vocational Education

Vocationalisation has become an integral part of the our education as a process today. Some students can learn best through work only. What they learn through work by hands or on a machine can be of equal value as compared to the intellectual work. Vocationalisation also becomes necessary to give employment to the school leavers on one hand and to provide middle-level manpower to the various sectors of development of the nation on the other. Turning out unemployed and unemployable educated persons not only implies a wasteful system of education but it also causes tension and unrest among the youth. The latter may create political turmoil or law-and-order situations. General education has continued to be bookish, academic and insulated against practical concerns inspite of some efforts to change this character. There is considerable mismatch between the requirements of the economy and education.

Post-Basic Schools

Based on Gandhian concept the post-basic schools had been started from about the year 1950 onwards as the secondary stage of the then nationally accepted Basic System of Education. They were only 66 in number and located in rural areas. Most of them were run by established voluntary organisations, which had done notable work in the field of basic education with considerable zeal and conviction. But these schools also could not organise practical courses of a type that would ensure successful employment of the students. Efforts were made to integrate these and the Multipurpose schools without success. Gradually, the post-basic schools also disappeared along with the basic education system.

Vocational Stream

The diversification of secondary education is being emphasised in continuous way. The first (1968) national policy on education introduced the 10 + 2 + 3 structure with the stipulation that at the +2 stage there would be two stream; Academic and Vocational. The latter stream was to provide courses, largely terminal in character, leading to effective self-employment or service in agricultural, industrial, commercial or other types of establishments. It was desired that 50% of the students would get diverted to the vocational courses. Tangible results have not yet emerged in this area too, but the efforts are continuing.

In view of a felt need to provide middle-level trained man-power, some vocational institutions had already grown up in the country. A survey conducted by the Indian Institute of Applied Manpower Research (IIAMR) in 1977 revealed that there were at that time 6052 technical, vocational and training institutions, where the admission requirement ranged from a pass at the middle or secondary or higher secondary examination. The suggested vocationalisation of the +2 stage has, therefore, to be taken to supplement the existing facilities for vocational education. This will strengthen general education and make the social-leavers, who do not wish to go in for higher education, or are not capable of making full use of that education, more employable.

It has been continually advocated ever since the scheme of vocationalisation of the +2 stage was launched that, (i) the duration of the courses should vary from 1 to 3 years, depending upon the requirements of the particular courses, (ii) The course-content and practical experience should be such as to equip the student fully to get a job or to establish himself as a self-employed person; and towards that end, the syllabus and the on-the-job training should be determined in collaboration with the potential employers of the students and some part-time teachers also secured from them, and (iii) Every vocational courses should be locality oriented and mostly non-engineering in character. The country has accepted the last suggestion. It is trying to implement the second suggestion.

Started in 1976, the scheme of vocationalisation of the +2 stage, has so far been introduced by about 15 states and union territories only. The programme is slow. I think the factors responsible for lack of adequate success include these: (i) The selection of the vocational courses is largely ad-hoc. It is not based on any survey of the employment of the area around the school, (ii) Involvement of the potential employers of the students is not adequate, (iii) Non-existence or inadequacy of text and reference books for the courses, (iv) Poor or no emphasis on entrepreneurship training as an integral part of the vocational course, (v) Absence of a follow-up programme for the vocational students to help them secure financial and other assistance in order to settle down as self-employed persons, (vi) Poor facilities of vertical growth of the vocationally trained persons, (vii) Insufficient stress, in the recruitment rules in the government and other sectors, on specialised training, (viii) The Department of Education in the Union Ministry of Human Resource Development which guides and monitors the programme in the country, does not have even one specialist in vocational education. The NCERT, as an autonomous body, cannot discharge that responsibility effectively, and (ix) Traditionally, intellectual work in India has had better social status than physical, manual or machine work. The 1986 National Policy on Education (NPE-1986) has reinforced reorganisation of secondary education through introduction of the Vocational Courses. It may be hoped that a more serious and systematic effort at vocationalisation of secondary education will now be made so that notable results accrue. This is important for both the present and the future.

The Teacher

The teacher is the most important one. He is the delivery

agent for all that is desired to be done in the schools and, therefore, special attention needs to be paid to him. It has been a deliberate and wise policy on our part that with the perennial shortage of funds for education, we have given priority to the teacher, his economic and social status, his preparation and his professional refreshment. The salaries of the school and college teachers in India have been raised four or five times since the independence. As a consequence, the average emoluments of a secondary school teacher has risen from about Rs. 100 p.m. to about Rs. 3000 p.m. Although the purchasing power of the latter amount is not much, yet it compares well with the employments in many other comparable services. It is not enough to keep the teacher above want. He should be offered the highest possible wages in-order to attract the best talent to the teacher profession. That alone will contribute to build the future generation. The teacher is also being helped, to some extent, with facilities like housing, medical aid and travel. The outstanding among them are also being honoured through national and state level awards. The national awards are presented personally by the President of India at a ceremonial function. Such teachers are also given an extension of two years in their service.

The minimum qualification for a secondary school teacher is a university degree with a professional training. The same for a higher secondary school teacher is a post-graduate degree and professional training. A controversy has been going on for many years whether in the case of a higher secondary school teacher the regular one year's professional training was essential or preference should, instead, be given to better achievement in the concerned academic subject. Many Public schools in India prefer a first division Post-graduate teacher to one who is professionally trained but has secured a third division in the academic subject of his speciality. I also favour this view with the provision that a short duration orientation, say of three months, should be given to the untrained teachers. About two decades back, an opinion was pressed that every one cannot be a good teacher and, therefore, the pupil-teacher should be selected after the higher secondary schooling and given a longer duration training in both the academic and professional subjects simultaneously. An experiment conducted in a special institute set up at Chandigarh about two decades back is reported to have failed. A similar integrated course given in the regional colleges of NCERT also does not appear to have created any distinguishing impact. But the programme is continuing with continuous efforts at re-organisition.

Every person needs professional and intellectual re-orientation with the knowledge explosion. The need of the teacher in this regard is apparently the greatest. Accordingly, large scale programmes of refresher courses for the school (and college) teachers have been lunched in the country. Effort is also being made to make use of educational technology in the conduct of this programme. In this regard, worth mentioning is the contribution of the organisations like, State Institutes of Education, State Institutes of Science Education, NCERT, and UGC.

The huge backlog of untrained school teachers has been cleared and today there is ho dearth of trained teachers. There is, however, some shortage of trained teachers in subjects like English and Mathematics. Some of our secondary and higher secondary school teachers have been selected for appointment by the various countries in Africa and Asia and they are working there successfully.

Many concerted efforts were made to reorganise and improve the quality of our pre-service training of teachers in the recent past. But not much could be achieved. As a result, many of the teachers continue to say that a good deal of what they learnt during their training is of no avail in their teaching work.

Medium of Instruction

The medium of instruction is another parameter affecting standard of education and achievements of the students. In India, the general policy is to use the mother tongue or the regional language as the medium of instruction at the school stage. The government and the aided school system is mostly following this policy. There are, however, a small number of public schools and convent schools which continue to teach through English, which is neither the mother tongue of most of their students there nor the regional language of the area. Such schools are generally located in big cities and towns. They charge heavy fees and are thus exclusive in character. Some of them, however, show good result in the public examinations. Some of them also have better physical facilities and programmes for co-curricular activities. The medium of instruction in the colleges of engineering, medicine and management, which provide higher potential for employment to their students, continues to teach through English only. For these considerations, the English medium schools are popular among the parents. As a result, English medium schools are getting opened in smaller towns and even in villages too. All of them are financially self-sufficient, and some of them make good earnings. And school are now being treated as industry

Three-Language Formula

This formula was conceived soon after the Independence by the CABE the supreme advisory body for education. It was an attempt to compromise the positions of the mother tongue, the national language and English, each of which is important in its own way in a multi-lingual country, like India.

The formula provides for the study of the just mentioned three languages in the non-Hindi speaking states and of English, Hindi and another modern Indian language, preferably a south Indian language in the Hindi states. These three languages, preferably a south Indian language in the Hindi states. These three languages were to be studied compulsorily by all children during the middle and high school stages. This arrangement equalises the load of language-study on the students all over the country. The education policy of 1986 has reiterated this same formula. The above formula was adopted by all the states. After some years, however, it acquired a political overtone. Some opposition was expressed against the study of Hindi, and in one state only two languages, namely the regional language and English are taught in the state system of education. It has also been complained that the Hindi states have not been implementing the formula correctly. It is true that in these states, Hindi, English and Sanskrit have mostly been taught. It must, however, be mentioned that in the Hindi areas, say in Uttar Pradesh, intermittent efforts have been made to arrange for the teaching of a south Indian language in some schools; and for that purpose, some school teachers were got trained in language-teaching in the concerned states. But the progress in these regard has not been significant. In modern times, the more languages one knows the better it is for him.

Due to its special position in Indian culture, Sanskrit too should be accepted as one of the three languages under the formula. This will also be in harmony with the importance given to the teaching of Sanskrit in the NPE, 1986. This will also introduce greater elasticity and feasibility in the formula. In the Hindi belt, encouragement should be given to the study of a south Indian language by as many students as possible; and for that purpose, all necessary facilities should be made available in the school system. But if we take a realistic view, these states should not be criticised if many children there do not offer to study a south Indian language because (i) most children in these states have little opportunity to use the south Indian languages and therefore, they have little motivation to study them, and (ii) it is not reasonable to equate Hindi, the constitutionally accepted national language with other languages of the country although it is true that every Indian language is equally important is also a national language, language of the nation deserve to be developed and popularised in every possible manner. In the Hindi areas language combinations like (a) Hindi, English and Bengali, or (b) Hindi, English and Punjabi or (c) Hindi, English and Oriya, or (d) Hindi, English and Gujarati, or (e) Hindi, English and Marathi, or (f) Hindi, English and Kashmiri may also be fully acceptable and convenient.

Thus it is necessary that we should treat the language and its script as two separate entities. For example, Urdu, which was born and developed in India only, has traditionally been written in the Persian script, but now it is written in Devanagari script as well. Similarly, Sindhi is largely written in Devanagari script, but some persons continue to write in the persian script. It is possible to write any language in any script. It seems worthwhile to suggest, therefore, that the third modern India language under the formula should be taught through the script of the mother tongue of the student or that of the regional language, whichever is known to him. This will reduce to about half the strain on the student to study the third language. Through this arrangement, the student will also start speaking the third language earlier than before. The concerned script can be learnt later in life by those students who feel the need for it or are interested in learning it because of their linguistic aptitude or otherwise.

No doubt English has become the international language. It has also established itself as an important library language in the sense that bulk of literature on specialised and other important subject is available in English only. As a consequence, the teaching of English has been gradually introduced even in countries like Japan, Germany, France, China and Russia, when it was never taught in any big way and where all work, including teaching, was done through the concerned national language alone. The treasure of English language, which India has acquired through its long contact with the British should, therefore, be preserved; and wherever English is taught as a subject of study, it should be done properly.

Text Books

With the large-scale expansion of educational facilities and the consequential enrolment, need was felt to make available good text books at low prices, which all the students could afford. Earlier, such books were written by individual authors and published by private publishers, which were commercial establishments and worked mainly for profit. These books were costly and they were sometimes selected on considerations other than the quality. Government hand, therefore, to nationalise the text books. As a consequence, there were some teaching troubles in the beginning like delayed supply and the publication of spurious editions. But these were gradually resolved. The contents of the nationalised books are good and their prices very low. In this field, NCERT has made a praiseworthy contribution through the production of model text books which have been willingly adopted or adapted by the various state governments and other organisations running the schools. So also the production of the Central Institute of English and Foreign Languages, Hyderabad in respect of the English language series of text books. Mention in this regard may also be made of the National Book Trust (NBT), the Children's Book Trust and a number of private publishers who have brought out supplementary reading material for the secondary and other stages of education.

Curriculum

Concerted efforts to reconstruct the secondary education curriculum have been made from the dawn of the Independence. The object has been to modernise the curriculum, to make it more meaningful and relevant to the needs of the students, to equip it to meet better the social and other needs of the country, and to raise the standard of education generally. This work has largely been done by the boards of secondary education, which are generally autonomous in character and are not an integral part of the government secretariat. The Central Board of Secondary Education (CBSE) has been playing a leading role in this field. The Council of Boards of Secondary Education, popularly known as COBSE and born in 1970, has contributed to coordinate the work of curriculum reconstruction in various states and pass on the best experience from the board to the other boards.

CABE introduced in 1963-64 an All India syllabus for its member schools, which were spread all over the country and abroad. In fact, introduction of this all India syllabus could be considered to be an educational reform. Previously, the boards or universities, conducting the secondary school examination had laid down their own curricula for the schools in their jurisdiction. The proposal for an all India Syllabus, with suitable variations in each state, was then incorporated in the 1968 national policy on education. This was reinforced by the 1986 policy. The latter policy has actually visualised the introduction of a national curricular framework in the schools all over the country. Such a curriculum is desired to fulfill certain important requirements. In its preparation, the socioeconomic considerations are to include principles of equity, strengthening of national identity, and development of scientific temper, art and creativity. Other elements like explosion of knowledge and the appropriate technology to cope with its interface between work and education, value education, and global perspective are also to be duly emphasised. Centrality of the student, professional role of the school, and focus on learning instead of teaching are to be the pedagogic concerns.

The national curriculum also visualises a common core as an essential feature. The core is to include elements like history of India's freedom movement and constitutional and other elements which are essential to nurture national identity. This component is also to be centered around certain learning outcomes, which are the same for all learners.

Examination Reform

The colonial system of education in India has been examination-ridden as well. Accordingly, various measures were taken during the post-independence period, to reform the examinations and make our system of evaluation more scientific in character. They should also minimise the impact of change factor and the subjectivity of the examiner and contribute tc raise the standard of education. The efforts made in these regard have brought about the following reforms in Indian examination system:

1. The evaluation procedure have been bettered by (a) supplying outlined answers and marking schemes to the co- examiners, (b) providing the latter with detailed instructions to ensure uniformity in evaluation, and (c) introducing central evaluation.
2. Increasing emphasis is now laid on internal evaluation, for the teacher is the best evaluator of his pupils.
3. The questions and question-papers have been improved by (a) basing the questions on appropriate objectives of education so as to secure their validity, (b) ensuring their reliability, (c) controlling options in the question papers to the extent of abolishing the over-all options, (d) introducing short answer questions in a fair proportion, leading to greater coverage of the syllabus, (e) making both essay type and short answer type questions more specific and pointed in scope, and (f) requiring the paper setter to submit outlined answers and the marking scheme.
4. Introducing grades in place of percentage of marks.
5. Adding oral examination to evaluate oral expression as well.

Scheme of School Classes

The first attempt at changing the on-going structure or scheme of school and college classes and introducing a broad uniformity in the same all over the country was made in mid- fifties with the introduction of the 11 year higher secondary school and the 3 year degree course in arts, science and commerce. But for various reasons, these attempts further complicated the on-going scheme. In the mid-sixties, therefore, another attempt in the same direction was made by introducing the 10 + 2 + 3 pattern of education. The same pattern has been reiterated by the NPE-1986 education policy. In fact, this policy has moved a step further in the direction of uniformity by breaking the first 10 years of schooling into 5 years of primary education, 3 years of middle education and 2 years of high school education. Thus the suggested structure should become (5 + 3 + 2) + 2 + 3 all over the this structure provides for a clear stage of 2 years, the +2 stage, in which the traditional general education should be supplemented with vocational courses. A uniform structure all over the country also strengthens national and emotional integration. It makes it easier to produce textbooks and other reading material for the students and price them low, it also facilitates improvement of our programmes of pre-service and in-service training of teachers as also their mobility and employment. The inter-regional movement of the people for trade, commerce, industry and other purposes is also made easier through a uniform pattern of education all over the country.

Kendriya and Navodaya Vidyalayas

Following the recommendations of the 2nd Central Pay Commission, the government of India decided to set up, in mid- sixties, a network of schools called Kendriya Vidyalayas in different places where there was concentration of central government employees. These schools were intended to provide schooling facilities to the transferable central government employees, including the defence personnel. The balance of the seats, if available in any vidyalaya, could be given to other categories of children in a specified order of priority. This was a kind of welfare measure for the central employees; because with the adoption of regional language as media of instruction at the school stage, the education of their young children suffered when they were transferred from one state to another. All the Kendriya Vidyalayas, therefore, provided the same curriculum and activities and adopted the same media of instruction, namely Hindi for social studies and English for science and mathematics. They provided classes I to XII and were affiliated to CBSE Gradually, these Vidyalayas have become very popular and they are in great demand. They are administered by an autonomous organisation which is presided over by the Union Minister of Education and which has sixteen regional offices located in different parts of the country.

In order to accelerate the growth of talent among the children, which have been neglected in the past, launching of a special scheme of model schools, one in each district, was incorpo-rated in the 1986 policy on Education. About 250 such schools have already been established. These vidyalayas are to have classes VI to XII and the students to be enrolled in class VI are to be selected from out of those passing out from class V in the district. 75% of the seats in class VI are reserved for children from rural areas. Each of these schools is residential and fully financed by the Central Government. The medium of instruction, as announced at that time, was to be the same as in the Kendirya Vidyalayas. Both the Kendriya and Navodaya Vidyalayas have been planned as pace-setter institutions. In this manner, apart from serving the specific causes, for which they have been established, they are also to contribute to raise the standards of school education in the country. Whereas the Kendriya Vidyalayas have created a good impact, the Navodaya Vidyalayas have also made good start.

But now in the year 2005 we can observe that Kendriya and Navodaya schools all over the country falling on the line of all government institutions. Barring few exceptions, if any, these elite schools (in the sense of quality education) are gradually proving while elephants to the public exchequer. It inducted dedicated teachers and staff with strict discipline, let us hope for better.

6

Higher Education: Growth and Development

Of late, Higher education has emerged as a significant component of national education system in India. Its potential has been realised in the context of socio-economic and political development in the society. Simultaneously, its development has been influenced by several intricate factors related to social, cultural, political and economic aspects of life. To quote Prof. Adiseshiah, "while education can be a pace setter for society, equally and even more, education including the university, is also a faithful mirror of society." In the Indian context, with a view to bring about further development of the system, it becomes essential to study the future of higher education in coming decades taking into consideration both the trend of this system since independence and projection of a desirable future.

TABLE 1: COMPARATIVE GROWTH OF HIGHER EDUCATION INSTITUTIONS AND ENROLMENT

	1950-51	*1984-85*
Universities	27	125
Deemed Universities	—	15
Institutions of National Importance	—	10
Colleges	800	5482
Enrolment (in lakhs)	1.74	35.4

Expansion of Higher Education in India

During the post-independence period, the demand for

higher education has increased 20 times in relation to its position during 1950-51. The post-independence era has exhibited higher education as a means for social mobility, especially for the downtrodden masses. Various facilities, in accordance with the constitutional provisions, provided for lower sections' entry into higher education have encouraged the growth trend. Establishment of new colleges and universities in different parts of the country, particularly the growth of higher educational institutions in rural areas, has facilitated to some extent the democratisation of enrolment policies in higher educational institutions. As a whole, the fifties and sixties showed the trend of rapid expansion, may be for another significant reason of accommodating large number of products of higher education in the employment market. The growth rate came down in seventies. Further, the eighties made an upward trend. However, the rates is quite small as compared to the percentage in the sixties of the last century.

The eastern zones of the country in addition to their neighbour states of Andhra Pradesh and Bihar have maintained the earlier trend of expansion of all India level till date. However, there are mismatches of rate of expansion of enrolment with the rate of expansion of institutions, especially in the context of Maharashtra, Karnataka, Orissa and Madhya Pradesh. In such cases, there is every possibility of problem of increase of non-viable institutions which may result in the disfunctioning of the institutions. As a whole, it can be visualised that, with a view to meet social and individual needs, the higher education system would follow the positive trend of growth in the coming decades, of course, accommodating necessary structural changes expected from time to time.

Structure of Higher Education

The special feature of higher education in India is that around 88 per centof the total enrolment remains in undergraduate courses, whereas around 10 per cent students enroll in post-graduate courses, and around one per cent students go for research. The position of the percentage of total enrolment during 1984-85 does not show any marked deviation from the average position of enrolment at different stages during the last three and half decades.

Continuation of this trend of higher education, concentrating on undergraduation does not reflect an ideal feature of higher education. The crisis goes on increasing, as undergraduate education is treated as some kind of compensatory education. In general, at undergraduate stage, teaching has taken the form of imparting knowledge without generating scope for questioning about the validity of the information which is being transferred to the students. A degree holder 'is sometimes treated as having finished his schooling and sometimes as having done only a part of the degree course' (Singh, 1985). The static structure of higher education over a period of three and half decades has not been responsive to the ideological issues, and developmental needs of the society. Especially the persistence of the low share of post graduate and research involvement restricts the efficiency of higher education system in research and development activities. Further, it proves its inability to keep pace with structural changes that take place in the field of economy. It is apprehended that continuation of low share of post graduate and research would reflect the weakness of human resource system to adapt to the increasing complexities of the process of modernisation and change. With a view to strengthen the functioning of university education, every effort should be made to expand postgraduate and research activities in proper direction.

In the post independence period it was realised that the qualified and technically skilled manpower would be of immense value in a developing economy. During this period, in spite of high rate of expansion of economic system, major share of enrolment in higher education remained with non-professional courses as compared to professional courses.

Social Accountability of Higher Education

With a view to attain egalitarian values of the society, it is expected that the phenomenal growth in educational facilities would lead to a balanced development of human resources. However, the lion's share of available educational facilities goes to the advantaged sections of the society.

Still, we have to go a long way with regard to equal distribution of educational opportunities for SC and ST and weaker sections of the our society who remained oppressed for ages. Even though, a positive trend is marked with regard to women's enrolment, attainment of their equal share with men population remains a far fetched goal. Especially, women's enrolment has reflected under achieving position with regard to Science, Engineering and Technology, Law, Agriculture, and Veterinary Sciences. Further the problem of enrolment of women among SC and ST groups can be treated as the problems of weakest among weaker ones. There is a hunch that in a stratified society the rapid rate of expansion in enrolment may corroborate the possibility of increment of entrance of students from weaker sections of the society. While the rate of growth of enrolment comes down to a very low level, there is every possibility that the ratio of enrolment position of such groups may not increase further. Keeping this in view, while efforts are made to stabilise the enrolment position in higher education, special efforts must be made for encouraging the upward mobility among weaker sections, by providing financial assistance, hostel facilities and extra coaching to them and establishing colleges/universities in rural and tribal zones of the country.

Indian higher education system has not matched to the manpower requirements of the country. While the problem of unemployment has been acute for the products of all the faculties, there have been instances of existence of shortages of manpower. The former category problem is in vogue with regard to the products of general education. On the other hand, higher level skill shortages are noted in technical and professional occupation, craftmanship, and production workers. There are instances, where vertical mismatches have taken place because of availability of over qualified persons on the labour market.

The empirical studies quote the large gap in availability of higher educated manpower between India and developed countries. In the process of economic self-sufficiency, India is still in need of large number of trained manpower. The real problem as witnessed today "is not in the expansion of higher education or with the products of higher education but with its unplanned expansion, the type of expansion which has not matched with the type of manpower demand and the country's level of absorption of technology and management" (Agarwal, 1985). In this context; it can be presumed that in the absence of identification of appropriate approaches of manpower planning, educated unemployment phenomena will have its strong hold in the country. Vocationalisation of secondary education may solve the problem of faster expansion of higher education. Still, the problem of unemployment of products of vocational streams would persist, as it is witnessed in the cases of states like Maharashtra, Karnataka and Gujarat which have already vocationalised the +2 stage of education (CASE, 1985).

Future Perspectives and Quality Improvement

Time and again it has been emphasised that appropriate measures must be taken to check the expansion rate and to improve the standard of higher education. With a view to maintain egalitarian norm in the functioning of the system, compromising steps are taken between academic performances and popular demand for expansion of education. As UGC (1985) statement reads, "although there is need to regulate expansion in view of the limitation of resources, it is not easy to deny expansion altogether as weaker sections of the society have looked for Higher Educations as a means of social and economic mobility; the demand for education should not be judged purely from the point of view of the labour market alone, but due consideration should also be given to the social, cultural and humanistic aspects of education". Thus, a conservative stand cannot be taken to attain quality at the cost of quantity. The expansion of higher education system will continue further with an imbalanced rate of growth in different zones of the country. Keeping in view the popular demands of higher education, efforts should be made to provide appropriate infrastructure to all the institutions for the maintenance of quality and standards. The autonomy of the universities must be secured while granting affiliation to new colleges according to the guidelines provided by the UGC from time to time. Appropriate measures should be taken for teacher training programmes and upgrading research endeavours of teachers of higher education.

Moreover, stable policies should be evolved for academic and professional incentives to devoted and effective teachers. Use of modern methods of teaching, validated learning materials, and electronic equipments must be encouraged to stabilise higher education teaching programmes. With a view to improve research activities, the university teaching departments and leading post graduate departments of affiliated colleges should be provided with appropriate physical and human resources.

The existing schemes of Centre of Advanced studies, special assistance and post graduate teaching and research grants must be upgraded and expanded to a larger number of institutions of the country. Along with the UGC, the State Governments should extend similar facilities for upgradation of research schemes of universities and post-graduate institutions.

Higher Education in Divergent Forms

With a liberal outlook, certain social scientists opine that within a long range perspective, equity and efficiency are complementary to each other "if educational resources are not being put to the best use, it is inefficient; if those who can profit and who have to profit are not able to do so, it is inefficient". (Raza et al., 1985). A country following democratic ideals will have to democratise the higher education system. All care must be taken for providing educational opportunities for those eligible students who desire to study further. In this context, the Education Commission (1964-66) had recommended for a dual practice, viz. (i) selective admissions can be done for full time institutions only for ensuring the quality of higher education and (ii) part-time courses like Correspondence Courses and own-time education can be encouraged for meeting the popular demand of education. However, looking at the socio-political influences, the National Policy of Education of 1968 was silent over the issue of selective admission. But, it is well understood that education can be both efficient and equitable if the majority of the people, the disadvantaged having proportionately more opportunities, are able to benefit from it. Further, looking at the total university enrolment in relation to population in the age cohort of 17-23 years, it can be expected that the situation is not that much alarming from the point of view of rate of expansion in a highly populous country.

Due to several influential factors like change of structure of secondary education, introduction of vocational education, rapid progress of science and technology, fast changes taking place in knowledge etc. the level of demand for higher education would take a different turn in future.

Especially, the need for continuing higher education would increase in future among the technicians, semi skilled labourers, professionals, scientists, engineers and others. Accommodation of clients of diversified groups into higher education would be possible through identification of different suitable means of non-formal education in addition to the age old structure of formal system. Hence the need for popularising continuing education programmes; Distance Education System functioning inside the frame work of formal system and outside the traditional universities.

Distance Education System in the form of Correspondence Courses has been in existence in Indian Universities since 1962. Of late, two open universities, viz., Andhra Pradesh Open University and Indira Gandhi National Open University have added a new dimension to the existing structure of higher education in the country. The success of correspondence system of instruction can be recognised in the Indian universities, as around 40 universities are offearing as many as 50 courses in general and professional fields and at undergraduate, post graduate, Research, Diploma and certificate courses. These institutions have been gaining ground by annually enrolling around 1.5 lakh students constituting 5 per cent of total enrolment in all the universities of the country. The enrolment position at different stages reveals that unlike formal streams, the correspondence system has accommodated a very high percentage (33%) of post graduate students. Among all post graduate course several Arts courses, in total have been enrolling highest number of courses. However, the courses like M.Com. and M.Ed, have attracted very high number of students. The trend shows that popularisation of non-formal/Distance Education streams would bring a change in the existing structure of enrolment in different stages.

In all, courses offered by correspondence institutions have been mostly traditional degree-oriented ones and have been limited in number. The innovative courses which have been restricted to a few institutions have attracted around 2 per cent of the total enrolment. Till date, it seems the distance education system has remained a sub-component of traditional university structure. It is high time to realise the significance of this system to meet the specific requirements of target group learners. These institutions are supposed to follow flexible approaches in offering much multi-disciplinary courses, which may be very much different from traditional courses. In the meanwhile, it would be essential to maintain parity between distance system and regular system of education. Further, establishment of open universities in different zones of the country would enable strengthening the scope of higher education among the needy group of learners. Use of advanced educational technology in both software and hardware forms would enrich the efficiency of self learning system with appropriate guidance from the distance education institutions.

Higher Education's Multiple Roles

It is often criticised that the higher education system must come out of its conservative functions of teaching and research activities which may be indifferent to social development. The social responsiveness of higher education can be directly realised through appropriate use of its own resources for integrated rural development activities, removal of illiteracy and awareness development programmes, application of research findings in developmental activities and policy formation, training of planners and teachers, preparation of learning materials and use of innovative communication strategies for extension programmes. In this context, while encouraging these activities there will be a shift from dominance of individual disciplines to inter-disciplinary and multi- disciplinary approach in the pursuit of meeting diversified developmental needs of the society. A handful of teaching departments and independent institutions have already made a breakthrough in this line. It can be hoped that the traditional institutions of higher learning will adapt their roles in carrying out interacting activities with the developmental programmes. Further, there is every possibility that new forms of higher educational institutions would come up to concentrate on developmental programmes through inter-disciplinary research activities; on-the-job training activities for labour forces, and management personnel; policy oriented evaluation activities; community service camps; and performing via-media roles between the traditional university resources and outside community. The nature of functioning of such institutions would be non-formal, innovative and participatory.

The present day activities of universities are directed towards two major dimensions (i) producing, conserving and diffusing knowledge and (ii) grading and certification. The latter has dominated the scene to such an extent that the entire management of the university is mostly occupied with it at the cost of the former basic functions. The implication of national policy (1986) of delinking degrees from jobs may bring "are-fashioning of job specific courses and afford greater justice to those candidates who, despite being equipped for a given job, are unable to get it because of an unnecessary preference for graduate candidates". In addition to these implications, if implemented properly, this would promote learning and competitive atmosphere in the educational institutions. Major concentration of the universities would remain on the basic functions of teaching, research and extension activities, with due emphasis on continuous evaluation of learners' performance in curricular programmes. Of course, the success of implementation of this scheme would solely depend upon the co-operation of public.

Summing Up

In the process of socio-economic changes of the country, Higher Education system has undergone changes both at structural and functional levels. Controversial situations created in the context of social mobility among different sections of the society will continue to be reflected in the higher education system for a considerable period of time.

Of course, efforts should continue to expand and consolidate the system keeping in view sociological ideals of the country. Mostly changes in the structure of secondary education; faster expansion of technology and exposition of knowledge; and requirement of updated skills in developmental programmes would demand expansion of non-formal streams like open university system, correspondence courses, extension education-programmes and continuing education programmes. The future of higher education will demand special attention of policy makers and educationists for improvement in instructional systems of both formal and non-formal streams through appropriate use of modern educational technology. Facilities for university and college teachers training programmes; upgradation of research activities especially socially useful ones; delinking degree for jobs; and evolving appropriate schemes for preparing the youth to face the challenges of present and future would emerge as specific highlights in the future of Indian Higher Education system in India.

Currently, higher education is also coming under the grip of liberalisation. Whereas on the one hand, liberalisation has made finance easy far, it is going to be costly affair to pursue higher education for average Indian. Let us remember that that University is not an industry to gain financial profits. Universities are the factories where the new generation is prepared for the future.

REFERENCES

Adiseshiah, M.S. (1985), "Role of Universities as Agents of change" in J.V. Raghavan (Ed.), *Higher Education in Eighties.* New Delhi: Lancer International.

Agarwal, B.L. (1985), "Nexus Between Jobs and Degrees" in J.V. Raghavan (Ed.), *Higher Education in Eighties.* New Delhi: Lancer International.

Association of Indian Universities (1980), *Handbook of Distance Education,* New Delhi.

Association of Indian Universities (1985), *Higher Education and Development*. New Delhi.

Association of Indian Universities (1985), *Three Aspects of University Education*. New Delhi.

Bell, R.E. and Youngron A.J. (Ed.) (1973), *Present and Future in Higher Education*. London: Tavistock Publications Ltd.

Cantor, L.M. and J.F. Roberts (1983), *Further Education Today*. (2nd Ed.) London: Routledge and Kegan Paul.

Centre of Advanced Study in Education (1985), *Vocationalisation of Education at +2 Stage*. A Planning Commission Sponsored Project, Baroda.

Government of India (1948-49), *Report of the University Education Commission*. New Delhi.

Government of India (1964-66), *The Report of the Education Commission*. New Delhi.

Kaul J.N. (1975), *Higher Education, Social Change and National Development*. Simla: Indian Institute of Advanced Study.

Ministry of Human Resource Development, Government of India (1986), *National Policy on Education, 1986, Programme of Action*. MHRD: New Delhi.

Ministry of Human Resource Development, Government of India (1986), *National Policy of Education, MHRD:* New Delhi.

Sahoo P.K. (1983), "Higher Education in India — Certain Issues", *New Frontiers in Education*, Vol. XIII No. 4.

Singh, A. (1985), *Redeeming Higher Education*. New Delhi: Ajanta.

Singh, M.B. and Seth S.C. (1985), "Report on Teaching and Research in Futurology: A Special Report", *Indian Review of Management of future*.

University Grants Commission, (1963), *Reports on Standards of University Education*. New Delhi, U.G.C.

University Grants Commission, (1985), *Annual Reports for Years: 1960-61 to 1984-85*, New Delhi.

7

Technical and Vocational Education

During ancient times vocational education in India was central around only to education relating profession of priest and teachers, education of soldiers, commercial education, technical skills and Ayurvedic medicines

Present structures of vocational education are of relatively recent origin, but the idea, simply stated, is that man has learned how he may improve his standard of living by working more efficiently. Programmes and techniques have been developed through the ages of teach man to work more efficiently. More recently, these have been referred to as programmes of vocational education.

The ways and means of implementing this process of learning to work have grown with the passage of time. This growth has resulted in emergence of differing techniques and practices in the organisation and operation of educational programmes of vocational education. These techniques and practices have an important bearing on the degree of efficiency with which the educational programmes operate in teaching individuals to work. The study of such techniques and practices in important not only to the individual but also to the society itself in order that the highest efficiency possible may be attained in the use of these educational techniques and processes.

Technical and vocational education is the real demand of the present when tremendous and miraculous achievements in the field of science and technology have transformed the fact of earth and human life on it. Earlier notions of time, place have no significance now. As such the growing demand for technically skilled manpower.

Indian education is considered literary in character lacking seriously in vocational, industrial and technical aspects. Nearly all the Commissions and Committees appointed on Indian education from time to time, have reiterated this complaint. As a matter of fact, dominated by literary element for a considerably long period of time; its chief aim has been to produce officials and clerks for various departments of the Government. Industrial education of any sort or in any degree was conspicuous by its absence for a long time in the sphere of Indian educational system.

This system of education was brought into being during the nineteenth century due to the political slavery of the country and other circumstances arising therefrom. It naturally resulted in the inability of our country to compete successfully with other progressive nations of the world in the sphere of industrial development. The educational outlook remained backward leading ultimately to the crucial problem of unemployment among the young persons and it is still growing in its monstrosity.

Nevertheless, after Independence the attention of the country has been focussed on this deficiency and efforts have been made in the sphere of technical and vocational education. Historically, in short, we can divide the education into 4 periods: (1) 1800 to 1857; (2) 1857 to 1902; (3) 1902 to 1950; and (4) Plan-period (1950—to the present day). Below is given a brief account of the progress in this field during all the four periods.

The First Phase (1800-1857)

The educational system of this period was influenced by the policy of the East India Company. The Company needed some Indian clerks and officials for its various departments in order to manage affairs well. The company stood in need of doctors for the army, judges and pleaders for the courts, and engineers for constructing roads, canals and government building under the Public Works Department. Hence these were the chief branches of technical and vocational education in the educational system of that period.

1. *Law*

The Britishers had established the Kolkatta, Madarsah and the Sanskrit College, Banaras for the education in law, where law pertaining to the main Indian races, Hindus and Mohammedans, might be taught and whence the East India Company might draw her supply of judges and pleaders for its courts. Law was taught in the Sanskrit College, Banaras. In 1842, a professor was appointed in Hindu College, Kolkatta for law. In 1857, with the incorporation of the Kolkatta University and owing to certain difficulties of starting law college under it, the classes in Jurisprudence could not be started until 1865. Regular classes in law could be instituted only after the establishment of Mumbai and Chennai Universities.

2. *Medicine*

In the medical field, there were in vogue two systems in India, i.e., *Ayurveda* and *Unani*. But the British rulers keeping their entire educational policy in view, introduced European medical system which could be learnt only through the medium of English. As a matter of fact, a controversy had emerged about Oriental and Occidental system in the medical field as well. But the policy of westernisation enunciated by Lord Macaulay, and the announcement of Lord Bentinck considerably influenced medical education in the country. In the beginning, Indian students had an inherent dislike of the work of dissecting the corpse, but Madhusudan Gupta, a medical student, gave the lead in this field by dissecting a corpse at Calcutta.

The modern medical science was introduced in India for the first time in Bengal, Bombay and Madras. In 1822, there was established a Native Medical Institution at Calcutta. Later on, in 1826, classes of medicine were started in Banaras Sanskrit College and Calcutta Madarsah. These institution provided education in *Ayurvedic, Yunani* and *European* medical systems. But after 1835, education in *Ayurvedic-Yunani* systems was discontinued and it was decided that education would be provided only in western medical system. In 1844, four Indian students were sent to England for acquiring knowledge in the western system of medicine.

In 1845, people collected subscriptions in order to found the Grant Medical College at Bombay in the sacred memory of Roberts, the Governor of Bombay. Prior to that, the Native Medical School had been founded at Bombay in 1826 and medical classes had been started in Poona College. The Grant Medical College had been recognised by the Royal College of Surgeons in England in the year 1855. Later on, it was amalgamated with the University of Bombay. There both English and provincial languages were used as the media of instruction. In 1835, a medical school was established at Madras for the training of apprentices for lower posts. In 1851, it was raised to the status of medical college and was finally merged into the University of Madras. The medium of instruction in this institution was English.

3. *Engineering*

In 1844, at the Hindu College, Calcutta, a chair in Civil Engineering was instituted but it was not filled up for a considerably long time. Not until 1856 could there be established an Engineering College at Calcutta.

In the year 1824, the Bombay Native Society had opened classes in engineering and mother tongue was used as the medium of instruction. Engineering classes were started at the Elphistone Institute in the year 1844, and at Poona in

1854. At Madras, education in Engineering could not be inaugurated until the incorporation of Madras University. Here a Survey School had been running since 1793 which was, later on affiliated to the Madras University in 1858. In United Provinces, an Engineering College had been established at Roorkee in 1847 which was named afterwards as the Thompson College in 1854.

4. Other Forms of Vocational Education

Besides the above mentioned important branches of vocational education, the training of teachers too formed an important part of educational system of the period concerned. In this sphere, the Christian missionaries did much appreciable work in the teeth of strong indifference of the Company towards it. Bombay Province showed indications of progress in this sphere and many a normal school to train teachers were established. Besides this the subject of Art formed an integral limb of vocational education. In 1850, Dr. Hunter established a school for Fine Arts and Crafts at Black-Town, Madras. In 1853, Sir Jamshedji Jijibhai donated one lakh rupees for the development of Art in Bombay. With the help of this liberal benefaction, the J.J. School of Art was established at Bombay in 1856.

Second Phase (1857-1902)

This phase is comparatively of greater importance from the view point of industrial and vocational education, though the main objective of vocational education in this period too was to produce a number of well-trained, efficient and experienced Indian officials who might conduct efficiently the work of administration and organisation under British officials in various government departments. In 1857, with the incorporation of three Presidency universities: Bombay, Madras and Calcutta, subjects such as Law, Medicine, Engineering, Agricultural Science, Commerce and Technical Education were included in the curriculum of Universities and special teachers were appointed to teach these subjects. Also the system of conferring certificates degrees in these subjects was introduced during this period.

1. Law

Education in Law was provided in the universities according to the Educational Dispatch of 1854. Study of Law was, by and by, growing in popularity, because lawyers and judges were in great demand owing to the establishment of law-courts in the country. Both these professions were regarded as respectable and immensely lucrative. Hence educated people belonging to higher stratum were much attracted towards them. There were mainly three means of education in law, i.e., Law colleges, classes of Law in Arts and Science colleges and Law schools. There was a Law College at Madras. The Punjab University also had a Law College attached to it. These two were the only full-time Law Colleges. Otherwise, law classes were held in other colleges in the evening on part-time basis. The Government Law College at Bombay too imparted education in law in the same way. There were no separate and full-time Law Colleges in Bengal, Central Provinces, and United Provinces; but Law classes were held in Arts and Science Colleges.

Education in Law was under the control of University, Department of Education and High Court respectively. Universities set up curriculum of education in law and they held examinations. Law schools and colleges were under the control of the Department of Education and High Court prescribed certain conditions, the fulfilment whereof only could entitle a Bachelor of Law to undertake the profession of Law. Prior to this, the High Courts gave their own examinations. In some provinces, examinations of 'Pleader' and 'Mukhtar' were conducted only for Matriculate candidates. The course of LL.B. covered usually a period of two years. It was three years at some places to be completed only after graduation either in Arts or Science.

3. Medicine

Progress of medicine in this period was as follows:

(a) Human Medical Science

The trained candidates in medical science would usually be employed in Government and Municipal Board hospitals, or in some big company or factory, or would start individual practice. A medical college was instituted at Lahore in 1860. By the year 1902, there was a total number of four Government Medical Colleges in India established at Calcutta, Madras, Bombay and Lahore. Apart from these colleges, there were certain medical schools as well. From amongst these Law Schools, there were eleven Government medical schools (one in Madras, three in Bombay, four in Bengal, one in U.P., one in Punjab and one in Assam); one Municipal Medical School at Madras and ten private schools (one in Assam, one in Sindh, four in the Punjab—two for Mohammedans and one for Hindus—and four in Bengal). Medical science was gaining popularity by and by among the men but women were still under the dire clutches of superstitions, beliefs and obsolete prejudices. In 1902, the figures of students studying medical science in Medical Colleges and Medical Schools were respectively 1,466 and 2,727. These figures included 242 women students, mainly European or Christian. There were only fifteen Brihmin, fifteen non-Brahmin, fifteen Mohammedan and twenty-two Persian women.

(b) Veterinary Science

The Government diverted their attention towards verterinary science as well besides human medical science. Veterinary science occupies a very important place in an agricultural country like India. In 1832, a Veterinary College was founded at Lahore, at Bombay in 1882 and at Calcutta in 1893. Another veterinary school was opened at Ajmer, but it was later on amalgamated with the veterinary college at Lahore.

3. Engineering

Engineering and Technical education was in a great demand during the period, which was characterised mainly by industrial upheaval and development and construction work of railways, roads and canals. It was during this period that District and Municipal Boards were coming into being and sea routes and jute and cotton mills were being opened. Under such circumstances, there was an immense need of the services of expert engineers. The profession of engineering was quite lucrative from monetary point of view, attracting, therefore, a large number of able students. On account of an abnormal demand for education in engineering was tremendously expensive. Hence only well-to-do persons could afford to defray the expenses on the engineering education of their wards. These students would usually get good jobs under the Public Works Department at the completion of their education.

In 1865, the Bengal Engineering College was merged into the Presidency College. In course of time, it was shifted to Shibpur. The Engineering class and. Mechanical school which had been founded at Poona by the Government in the year 1854 developed ultimately into the Poona Engineering College. This college was affiliated to the Bombay University. During 1901-02, it imparted education in Science, Agriculture and Forestly besides Engineering.

Thus there were four important Engineering Colleges in India in the year 1902: Roorkee, Shibpur (Bengal), Poona and Madras. The number of students attending them was 865. The development of the Madras Engineering College took place between 1858 and 1862.

Besides these, a few other Technical and Vocational institutions had been established during this period. For instance, the Victoria Jubilee Technical Institute had been established at Bombay in the year 1887. In 1902, the total number of technical schools in India was eighty attended by 4,894 students. The Government of India also established some such schools on the recommendations of the Famine Commission. The ancient industries of India had completely been destroyed by the British Government. Hence in order to stem the rising tide of discontentment among the Indians, it was of paramount importance and necessity that Government should establish industrial schools. The demand for industrial education was also increasing among the people. These factors produced benign effect upon the development and progress of engineering as well as technical education in India.

4. Agriculture

In spite of the essential agricultural characteristics of the country, the Agriculture college had not shown remarkable progress. In 1880, the Famine Commission had laid special stress on the propagation of agricultural education but all to no avail. In 1890, Dr. Voilker called a conference of the representative from different provinces and laid down many valuable recommendations with regard to agricultural education for the considerations and action of the Government of India which took the following main decisions:

1. There should be more than four institutions conferring degrees in agricultural science, i.e., Madras, Calcutta, Bombay and any proper place in North-Western Province (U.P.). Other provinces should also take advantage of them.
2. The degrees, diplomas and certificates in agricultural science should be treated on a par with those in Science and Arts.
3. A special institution should be established for the purpose of conferring degrees, diplomas and certificates in agricultural science.
4. Practical training in agriculture should be treated as compulsory for certain posts.

5. Practical agricultural education on the Government farms is also important before or after the appointment of teachers in agricultural schools.
6. Certificates should be compulsory for the appointment to certain posts as teachers of agricultural science and assistant officials in the Directorate of the Department of Agriculture.

There were five institutions in British India imparting agricultural education; at Poona, Shibpur, Syedpeth (Madras), Kanpur and Nagpur in 1902. The Agricultural College, Syedpeth was established in 1864 and Poona Agricultural Branch in 1879, and at Shibpur in 1899. At Kanpur and Nagpur, education was imparted to Quanungos, teachers and peasant children. Agricultural education thus organised was quite inadequate. It totally lacked in research and practical education. Not unlike other branches of education, the chief aim of agricultural education, instead of being an increase in agricultural production of the country, was confined only to produce officials for the Department of Agriculture.

5. *Commercial education*

The Commercial education too did not shown any marked progress like agricultural education. Except the Punjab University, no other university had recognised it. At Bombay, there was a similar institution which imparted education in the subjects of Commerce of England. In 1902, there were in India fifteen commercial schools in which 1,123 students received education.

6. *Others*

Schools for education in other professions than those referred to above, were also established such as Teaching, Forestry and Art Fresh Training and Normal Schools were opened for teachers' training. During 1881-82 there were 106 Normal Schools in the country. Later on, in 1901-02 the number of these schools was 179 (133 for the males and 46 for females) attended by 4,410 and 1,292 students respectively. There existed six Training Colleges in 1902 for the training of the teachers of Secondary Schools. The most eminent institutions from amongst these were the Lahore Training College and those at Madras, Nagpur, Rajmahendri and Allahabad. The Madras and Allahabad Training Colleges conferred the diploma of L. T. upon the successful candidates. Besides these colleges, there were 50 training schools also for the teachers of secondary schools.

For Forestry education, in the year 1878, the Forest School was established at Dehradun and a branch of Forest-science was opened in the Engineering College of Poona. There were four main Government Art College in India in the year 1902 for the sake of imparting education in Art. These were: J. J. School of Art, Bombay; Mayo School of Art, Lahore; School of Art, Calcutta and School of Art and Industry, Madras. These institutions conducted education in Art, Painting and Commercial Art. In the year 1893, the Secretary of State for India suggested that the Art Schools were of no practical use and that expenditure incurred on them was nothing short of wastage; hence they should be converted into the form of technical schools. But later on no definite decision could be taken in this respect. Thus comes to a close the second period of industrial and vocational education.

The Third Phase (1902-1950)

This period bears a unique importance in the sphere of Indian vocational education. A marked success had been achieved in the field of vocational, industrial and technical education since 1902.

Earlier, the utility of such education was purely mercenary. People received this type of education mainly to secure some employment under the Government. But in modern times, the educated people got training in these branches solely for the purpose of meeting the industrial and vocational requirements of the society. There were many factors leading to its progress. In the first instance, it was an age of growing political awakening in India, which increased the urgency of the demand of a revolutionary change in the sphere of education. With the advent of Independence in the country, several laboratories and research bureaux were established with a view to bringing India on an equal footing with other progressive countries in scientific progress as well as to meeting manifold requirements of a newly freed country through the industrial and vocational upheaval. Departments of new technical and scientific subjects were opened in colleges and universities. Secondly, the attention of the Government was diverted towards it since Lord Curzon's term of office and Governmental machinery speeded the work in this direction. Thirdly, private enterprise too contributed considerably to the growth of industrial and vocational education. Wealthy people made liberal benefactions and helped the establishment of many industrial institutions. Fourthly, provision was made for sending Indian students abroad, i.e., England, America, Germany and Japan for thorough study of modern sciences, vocations, arts and crafts in these countries and they developed them in India after their return from abroad. After the independence of the country a steady progress is being made in this direction as will be evident from the following account.

1. Law

With the growing popularity of education in Law, the number of Bachelors in Law rose inordinately in the country. Lawyers overshot the mark of their need for the country. Most of the lawyers have taken to profession of law being urged merely by pecuniary interests. The net result of all this has been that various evils have into it which have vitiated the atmosphere of our society. But the country at the same time, has produced lawyers of eminent order also. As a matter of fact, lawyers have contributed immensely towards the achievement of our Independence in 1947. However, study of law during the period 1902 and 1927 was immensely beneficial for the interests of the country. But the economic crisis following this period resulted in a marked decrease in the number of students of law and this state of affairs persisted upto 1940. But taking the advantage of the improvement in the financial condition of the peasants, the pleader resumed their work of exploiting them to serve their own pecuniary interests. These circumstances led to a renewed interest in the study of law. The entire market of law is overflooded today by these professionalists.

There were 14 Law colleges in India during 1946-47, six Universities having Law Departments and law classes were conducted in six colleges affiliated to Agra University. The course of law, generally, covered a period of two years. The same course in Delhi and Calcutta Universities took the students three years to complete it. The Bombay University provided the education in law just after the passing of Intermediate examination; elsewhere study of law began only after graduation. Frequently, the professoriate was drawn from amongst the junior lawyers. Classes were held either in the morning or at the close of the day. One important defect inherent in the education of law as it was pursued by students was that they never took it seriously. They hardly paid any heed to the class lectures or consult the original books, but tried to get through the examination by simply having gone through questions and answers of the examination papers of a few past years. This tendency persists even today and perhaps more than before. The natural consequence of all this had been that there was a total lack of research work and higher studies in the sphere of education of law.

The Dr. Radhakrishnan Commission put forth the following recommendations in this connection:

1. There should be reorganisation of our law colleges.
2. A degree course covering three years in pre-legal and general studies should be required for admission to law classes.

3. The staff of the Law Faculties should be recruited and controlled by the Universities in the way similar to Arts and Science Faculties.
4. As regards special legal subjects, a three-years course should be offered and the last year should be given over largely to practical training.
5. The staff in law faculty should be both part-time and whole-time.
6. Law classes should be scheduled only during the regular hours of teaching.
7. Students pursuing study of law should not undertake the study of any other subjects.
8. There should be facilities of higher education and research work in law; and
9. Improvement should be introduced in the system of examination.

2. Medicine

Progress of Medicine in this period was as follows:

(a) Human Medical Science

Medical science showed a marked progress during this period. With the development in general education the Indian people began to realise the immense scope for medical science in the country. During 1946-47, there were 26 Medical Colleges and 25 Medical Schools in India. All India Institute of Hygiene and Public Health had been established in 1932 at Calcutta by Rockefeller Foundation. This fulfilled a great need of the country. In 1933, the Medical Council Act was passed and Indian Medical Council was founded. This provided a great stimulus to the progress of medical science in India. Besides this, in 1916, the Lady Harding Medical College was founded at Delhi for the sake of women students. Moreover in 1922, the School of Tropical Medicine was established at Calcutta. In addition to the afore-mentioned medical institutions, some other institutions were brought into being such as Dehradun

X-ray Institute and the Central Institute at Kasauli. A number of colleges for *Ayurveda,* Homeopathy and Yunani systems of medicine have been opened.

The University Education Commission has put forth the following recommendations concerning the progress in the sphere of medical education:

1. Medical colleges should admit a maximum number of hundred students;
2. All the departments of study which need hospital facilities should be located in same campus;
3. There should be the provision of ten beds per student admitted to a college;
4. Training should also be acquired in rural centres both at the under-graduate and post-graduate stages;
5. Provision of post-graduate training should be made in those colleges which have adequate staff equipment;
6. More importance should be attached to Public Health, Engineering and Nursing;
7. Indigenous medical systems should be encouraged; and
8. History of Medicine with special reference to Indian systems should be taught in the first Degree course in Medicine.

(b) Veterinary Science

The period witnessed a good progress in the sphere of veterinary science. In 1903, the Civil Veterinary Department was made available for the general public as well. Progress in Agricultural department entailed a development in Veterinary Department. During 1902-07 the veterinary schools were abolished to be substituted by Veterinary Colleges. Consequently, veterinary colleges were established at Madras and Patna in 1905 and 1930 respectively. The Imperial

Veterinary Research Institute was established at Garh Mukteshwar in U.P. in 1948, a veterinary college had been established at Jaipur. There are Research Institutes at Izzatnagar and Bangalore. The U.P. Government has established a Veterinary College at Mathura.

3. *Engineering and Technical*

The Engineering and Technical education assumed a new form after the year 1902. It was essential for the development of native industries that the study of Engineering and Technical education should not be directed to the production of clerks and officials for Stated departments but to meet the multifaceted requirements of the country. Hence this sort of education has marched progressively on these lines. In the post-independence India, many colleges and Research Institutes, as has already been indicated, have emerged gradually.

In the first decade of twentieth century, a college of Engineering and Technology had been established at Jadavpur in Bengal. In 1917, Engineering classes were started in the Hindu University, Benaras and Engineering Colleges were established at Patna, Lahore and Karachi. Thus by the year 1937, the total number of Engineering Colleges in India was eighty. Out of these institutions, Karachi and Lahore colleges went under the possession of Pakistan. In 1947, the number of Engineering Colleges in India became seventeen. The Wood-Abott Committee-Report and the Sargent Scheme helped the progress of education in Engineering to a considerable extent of which mention had been made elsewhere. In 1948, the N. R. Sarkar Committee had been appointed which recommended the establishment of four big Engineering Colleges in the East, West, South and North of the country. The University Education Commission also made valuable recommendations in 1949. The importance of technical education was realised still more after the independence of the country. The provision of this type of education was, therefore, made in the departments of Industry, Commerce, Transport, Agriculture, Public Health and Engineering. After 1947, facilities for technical education showed an upward trend so that the number of students seeking admission to technical institutions grew rapidly.

4. Agriculture

Agricultural education had invited the attention of the Government since the beginning of the twentieth century. In 1901, the Government of India had established the post of the Inspector-General of Agriculture and expanded the Agricultural Department. In 1905, a sum of 20 lakhs of rupees had been ear- marked to be spent yearly on experiments and research in Agriculture. The Central Government made plan to make various facilities available for agricultural education. Accordingly in 1908, the Central research Institute, Pusa (Bihar) had been established. A donation of thirty thousand dollars by Mr. Henry Phillips, an American benefactor, considerably helped the establishment of this institute. After the earthquake of 1934, this institute was shifted to Delhi. Besides this, agricultural colleges were established at different places, i.e., at Kanpur (1906), at Coimbatore (1909), at Sewar (1909) and that at Lyallpur in 1910. The Poona Agricultural School was raised to the status of Agricultural College. Further institutions were founded at Naini, Kanpur and Nagpur. Colleges at Syedpeth and Shibpur were abolished. Five out of these six agricultural institutes were under the control of the Government; the Naini Agricultural Institute, Allahabad was under the control of an American Mission.

The Agricultural Commission was appointed in 1928. This Commission put forth many valuable recommendations with respect to the improvement in agriculture and general rural conditions, having studied all the problems connected therewith. As a result of these recommendations, the Imperial Council of Agriculture Research was established in the year 1929. The subject of Agriculture was also included in the curricula of Secondary and Primary education. Agricultural education had been expanding continuously since 1903. The number of agricultural colleges was on constant increase and maximum facilities were being provided in the sphere of agricultural research. Many students were sent to England and U.S.A. for higher studies in agriculture.

5. *Commerce*

The commercial education made satisfactory progress during this period. During 1901-02, there was not even a single commerce college in the country, but by 1936, the number of these colleges became eight. The first commerce college was founded at Bombay in the year 1913. Later on, the facilities of Commerce were instituted in Calcutta, Dacca, Allahabad, Delhi and Lucknow universities. During 1946-47, the number of commerce colleges was 14 and that of schools 296. Commerce Faculties had been established nearly in all the universities upto 1950. Besides, in many degree colleges, commerce department had been opened like Arts and Science ones. Education in this subject was introduced in Middle, High School and Intermediate classes also.

(6) Others

There were certain other branches of it which prepared students for the economic aspects of their lives, i.e., Teaching, Forestry, Art and Cottage Industries etc. Many colleges and schools had been established for the training of teachers. During 1946-47, there were 33 Training Colleges which provided training to 2,747 students. There were training colleges for women candidates as well. Some universities were running classes of B. Ed. and M. Ed. The Institute of Education, Bombay and Central Institute of Education, Delhi provided facilities in research work.

There were fourteen Art Schools in India in 1947 for the education in Art, attended by 1,693 students. There existed institutions for the education in fine arts like music and dancing. The prominent in this respect were Bhatkhande Sangeet Vidyalaya, Bombay; Morris School, Lucknow; Sangeet Vidyalaya, Calcutta and Kala Kshetra, Adiyar. After 1947, many Art institutions emerged into existence. For the sake of education in Forestry, there existed two institutions, one at Dehradun and the other at Coimbatore.

The Fourth Phase (1950-1980)

The technical and vocational education made an admirable progress during five year plan period.

The All India Council for Technical Education (AICTE) had appointed a Technical Man-Power Committee in order to find out the number of technically trained persons needed by the country. The Committee drew up a comprehensive programme with respect to expansion in technical education. Besides this, two more Committees, i.e., the Scientific Man-Power Committee and the other, Overseas Scholarship Committee had been appointed in 1947. The duty of these Committees was to express their views on the problems of and facilities about Scientific and Technical education inside the country as well as abroad. The Overseas Scholarship Committee recommended that students should be sent abroad for the training only in those subjects for which our country had no provision. Moreover, the condition of the existing institutions should be improved and fresh ones be established so that Indian students might not feel the necessity of receiving technical education in foreign countries. According to these recommendations, scholarships were awarded to the students inside the country or those who intended proceeding abroad for further studies in technical and industrial branches of education. Besides, liberal grant-in aid was sanctioned to universities and other educational institutions conducting the particular sort of education referred to above. This produced a salubrious affect in the sphere of education, and universities expanded their work by reorganising their Research Faculties.

The Scientific Man-Power Committee observed in 1947, describing the facilities then existed, that they were almost non-existent in respect of post-graduate education. There were only five established institutions in the whole country which imparted education upto postgraduate standards; and even then the range of subjects was limited. Only one institution offered post- graduate courses in aeronautical engineering, metallurgy, internal combustion engineering and power engineering; two institutions in chemical technology; one each in ceramics, glass, sugar, technology, pharmaceutics and oil technology and two institutions in Applied Physics.

As regards the degree colleges and under-graduate courses, there were over 23 first grade engineering colleges in the country offering courses in Civil, Electrical and Mechanical Engineering. As regards technological subjects, there were only 8 first grade institutions teaching technological subjects upto degree standard. In the matter of junior engineering and technological education upto the diploma standard, there were over 45 institutions distributed all over the country in 1950.

The Scientific Man-Power Committee, therefore, recommended that "the first approach to the problem of development of engineering and technological education should be to strengthen the existing facilities in the institutions by equipping and staffing them adequately for the present intake of students and to bring up the standard of training to the desired level." The First Plan also agreed that "it would be advisable to consolidate the work in the existing institutions and not embark upon new ventures, except in certain specialised fields." Therefore, it was decided by the Planning Commission in 1951 that "The improvement of institutions and reorientation of training are, therefore, the needs of the hour rather than any expansion in numbers."

As a result of the Government's policy to encourage technical education continuous and vigorous efforts have been made since 1950 in these directions. Impetus was given to it by the Engineering Personnel Committee (1956) and the Committee for Post-graduate Engineering Education and Research (1961). The development of technical education with respect to the growth of industries was promoted through the Apprenticeship Act (1961), the Industrial Training Institutes and junior technical schools at the skilled worker level and the spread of polytechnics at the technician level, assistance received from friendly countries and International Organisations in the form of equipment and experts have gone a long way in promoting the technical education during the recent years. During the recent years the rapid growth of technical education has severely strained the resources of existing institutions. A survey in 1964 had indicated that engineering colleges and polytechnics had an overall shortage of 35 per cent in teachers, 53 per cent in equipment, 51 per cent in instructional buildings and 55 per cent in hostels. The result of these shortages is that there is high rate of wastage particularly in the polytechnics. It will therefore, be more advisable to make up these deficiencies and consolidate the existing institutions by providing physical facilities and bringing about closer integration of engineering education with the industrial needs of India.

Kothari Commission has made important observations for promoting technical and vocational education in India. In the opinion of the Commission, there is considerable scope along with the polytechnics for starting a range of interesting courses in commercial, clerical, scientific and industrial trades and in areas of special interest to girls. "Products of technical high schools and polytechnics should be encouraged to set up small enterprises of their own or to join together with other in creative small-scale workshops, industries and services needed in the community."

The Commission has suggested improvement in the standards, recruitment of well-qualified staff for selected branches of engineering, removal of the anomalies in the pay scales between staff members in science and technology faculties, reservation of seats for well-qualified persons of other faculties, practical training for full-time degree students starting from the third year, diversification of courses at the degree and diploma levels to meet the changing needs of the economy and more facilities for training for teachers and research in important fields. The Commission is of the opinion that while planning technical education, man-power needs of the country should be kept in view and there should be greater co- ordination with industries.

At the end of the Fifth Plan there existed a wide network of engineering and non-engineering institutions consisting of 32 and 22 trades respectively approved by the National Council for Training and Vocational Trades to young persons in the age-group of 15-25 years. For this purpose there are 357 ITIs with an over- all capacity of 1.55 lakhs set up in various parts of the country. There are 7 Central Training Institutes at present for the training of instructors run by the Directorate of Employment and Training. Similarly, institutions have been established for the training of advanced craftsmen in industry. In order to meet the growing need of trained man-power at middle-level 291 polytechnics with an annual enrollment capacity of 50,000 students studying for a diploma have been set up in India. About a dozen women polytechnics also exist providing specialised course to female trainees.

For professional engineers and technologists 141 Engineering Colleges leading to Bachelor Degree and Engineering and Technology with a total capacity for 25 thousand are functioning in the country, besides 65 institutions for post-graduate degree. Mention has already been made of five Indian Institutes of Technology (IITs), which provide facilities for high-level education and research. It is expected that by the end of 1985 India would meet the technical manpower requirement with levels of facilities already created.

Similarly there has been a notable advancement in the field of agricultural education, medical education, management education and scientific research. The vocational and technical education in India has developed mainly in relation to assessed future demand for manpower and has largely been responsible for the growth of our industrial structure. This is however, unfortunate that country has not been able to provide employment to all the products of technical educational system which has an annual inbuilt capacity of intake for 25,000 students for Degree courses and 50,000 for Diploma courses. This can be attributed to our tardy performance in the field of economic development during the period of planning. It is therefore desirable that during the next 10 years there should be no further expansion of institutions of engineering and technology.

According to the Draft 6th Plan also the emphasis now onward should be on consolidation and qualitative improvement. "The Plan provides for a phased programme of removal of obsolescence and modernisation of facilities on the basis of redesign of laboratory and workshop practice and of modernisation and diversification of courses with greater flexibility especially with reference to the needs of rural development, reduction of wastage and integration of curriculum development with laboratory work-planning."

In view of the above policy provision has been made in the VI Plan for completing the on-going programmes of consolidation and improvement of facilities in existing institutions. The provision, however, has been made to fully establish the five centres of advanced study and research in energy studies, material sciences, cryogenics, ocean engineering and resources survey. These centres would concentrate mainly on research in identified fields in accordance with the National Plan of Science and Technology.

The Planning Commission is of the opinion, "The technical education system represents a national resource of science and technology with specialised laboratories, sophisticated instrumentation facilities, and more importantly, teams of highly qualified scientific and engineering personnel on their faculty. These internal resources should be utilised not merely towards technological self-reliance but also to bring about progressive improvement in the quality of technical education."

Summing Up

The world of today is marching fast on the path of materialistic progress and prosperity. For a developing country like India there is no short-cut to progress but to utilise her resources in men and material for its rapid economic growth and the prosperity of the masses who are steeped in abject poverty. This could be possible through training her manpower into the higher skills of Science and Technology in an adequate manner. This will require an almost overhauling of her time-worn pattern of education and imparting it a new scientific orientation. It is a matter of satisfaction that during a short span of period after Independence, considerable progress has been made in this direction and India is marching slowly, though steadily on the path of industrial growth.

Now, the scene of Technical education has gone tremendous change. Really the Fifth Phase inhered in after 90's of the last century when Information Technology came in a big way and revolutionised all spheres of life. Now India can boast of having best institutions of technical and vocational education. All universities have schools of science, technology, medicine and law. Several special universities are set up providing exclusively these education.

REFERENCES

Draft VI Plan (1978-83), p. 224.

Govt. of India, *Scientific Policy Resolution*, op. cit., para 6.

Radhakrishnan University Education Commission, 1948.

8

Adult and Continuing Education

In an ever changing society which grows complex and mysterious at every turn of the year, professionals need guidance and illumination almost throughout their careers. With the launching of National Adult Education Programme in 1978, the University Grants Commission (UGC) has played a key role in shaping the character of University Adult Education in India. The UGC has not only formulated a number of guidelines on adult and continuing education programmes, but has also provided one hundred per cent funding support to universities to implement the programmes. Today most of the universities have set up Adult Education Departments and they have implemented a variety of programmes. University Education in India is identified with the preparation of people for professional work. Today it needs to be examined whether the initial training and preparation of young people for occupations of professional level is all that universities need to do.

This is significant to note here that the scientific and technological growth in India, and the resolve to upgrade levels of living in our rural areas have necessitated the acceptance and operationalisation of a culture of lifelong education. Individuals and groups need to be continuously galvanised into developmental action through a process of periodic updating of their knowledge and skills, a better understanding of their work environment and living and its challenges, and adaptation of innovative behavioural practices. The Educational Policy Perspective recently circulated by the Government of India visualises a lifelong learning society.

The new schemes of the University Grants Commission under its Continuing Education Programmes offer an excellent opportunity to institutions of higher education to extend their physical and technocratic resources to all segments of the community in their area in the form of short-term need-based educational programmes.

Continuing Education is thus low-cost educational provision deriving its support from the existing infrastructure in the institutions of higher education. It requires an innovative approach to target group identification, assessment of their needs, formulation of educational programmes, choice of innovative instructional methodologies, low-cost financial management strategies and ongoing feedback mechanisms. The UGC guideline on Adult/Continuing Education stresses that the universities and the colleges must become sensitive to the learning needs of the community and respond to the same through relevant learning programmes and tools.

Objectives

The programmes of Continuing Education should include objectives such as, to:

(i) enrich higher education by integrating continuing and adult education programmes and extension work in the system.

(ii) provide opportunities for disseminating knowledge in all walks of life.

(iii) enable the universities to establish the necessary linkages with the community.

(iv) cater to the self needs of all sections of society but specially to the needs of the less privileged and underprivileged sections.

(v) provide an opportunity to the faculty and the students for field experiences through faculty and student participation in extension research in selected areas in relation to major problems of development in cooperation with government.

This programme can be conceived in four major categories:

(i) awareness and development of general interest in contemporary affairs.

(ii) imparting and improving professional skills through special training.

(iii) imparting functional literacy and numeracy, post-literacy and supplementary education through non-formal programmes.

(iv) developing curricular linkages between field work and action.

Now the target groups belonging to the less privileged and underprivileged sections of the society may include women, in particular women of rural and slum areas, Scheduled Castes and Scheduled Tribes, drop-outs, unemployed and out of school youth, handicapped workers in the unorganised sectors, workers in organised sectors, teachers and handicapped children and university students from underprivileged rural groups and slums.

Thrust Areas

The UGC has suggested thrust areas to receive priority in the Ninth Plan:

(i) development of vocational skills and professional competences among technical, marginal and professional, industrial and unemployed youth through inservice programmes

(ii) arrangements for remedial and bridge courses and programmes for students from urban slums, rural areas, tribal areas, handicapped and other weaker sections

(iii) conduct of pre-examination training and entry to professional and technical courses

(iv) promotion of activities for general self-employment and self-reliance

(v) identification and organisation of needs-based instructional programmes for community development

(v) training and extension packages for functionaries of various social development programmes such as population education, legal literacy, science for the people, environmental education, rural development and peace education etc.

Operational Strategy

The following eightfold operational strategy is adopted:

1. *Programme for Scheduled Castes / Scheduled Tribes and Backward Classes*

At university level they need pre-examination coaching for various competitive examinations. The Ministry of Social Welfare is operating a number of schemes for the welfare of these sections of society.

2. Continuing Education for Women

It is for the benefit of women to cover a wide spectrum such as home science courses, nutrition, health and hygiene and child welfare, economic development and courses in contemporary social cultural awareness.

3. Workers Education

In this, workers may be of two categories: (i) Illiterate and semi-literate workers, including unskilled and semi-skilled workers like masons, carpenters, barbers, bus and taxi drivers, transport workers, paramedical staff, class-iv employees etc. (ii) Literate workers, including teachers of all categories, ministerial staff in offices, officers of all categories, and skilled technicians and administrators. They need regular staff development courses to enhance their skill and efficiency in their day to day work.

4. Continuing Education for Professionals

5. Continuing Education for Business Executives

6. Continuing Education for School Dropouts and Unemployed Youth

Continuing Education for school dropouts would facilitate their entry into the national development mainstream. The problem can be tackled by organising job oriented bridge and remedial courses and well planned career counselling efforts.

7. Programme for Slum Dwellers and Migrant Workers

The migrant workers and slum dwellers constitute the bulk of the weaker section of the society. These sections live in miserable conditions. To this section, besides basic literacy and numeracy, awareness regarding health and hygiene, labour laws, the environment, economic opportunities, social development benefits, etc. will be extremely critical.

8. Social Development Education for all Citizens

The complexity of modern urban life requires of each individual a large number of roles and skills as parents, members of a neighbourhood, residents of a city, citizens of a nation and the world, and above all as integral parts of the ecological system. Programmes for children's education, area development, environmental education, legal literacy, national integration and global brotherhood, etc., may be organised.

For this purpose the following areas are adopted in the Ninth Plan:

(i) training of personnel in each university and its colleges in the methodology of continuing education programmes with a view to their acquiring knowledge and skills

(ii) preparation of a handbook on Continuing Education

(iii) development of a course bank stating titles of courses, courses, course content, management strategy, instructional methodology and feedback mechanisms

(iv) setting up of a monitoring mechanism to monitor the growth of continuing education as related to area development and national development needs

(v) developing learning materials (print and audio-visual)

(vi) Institution of teachers' fellowships to enable teachers to devote their time to the development and management of continuing education programmes

(vii) encouragement to research in the area of Continuing Education

(viii) setting up of institution based and community based evaluation studies in this area

(ix) development of a series of films

UGC is providing financial assistance for this purpose at university, college and community level. This has been in the form of staff inputs and programme inputs and some non-recurring infrastructural inputs in the Department of Adult/Continuing Education.

To conclude, it may be said that adult and continuing education is gaining widespread popularity. With the establishment of IGNOU and a number of other open universities in the different parts of India this has made remarkable progress.

9

Population Education

Growing population at an unprecedented pace has affected the quality of life on the earth. India is the second largest country after China on account of population. As such emerged the need of Population Education.

The National Family Planning Programme, initiated in 1952 during the First Five Year Plan (1951-56), adopted a 'clinical' approach to family planning and opened a number of clinics with the expectation that the people would take advantage of the facilities. This approach was modified thereafter. The 'community extension' and 'cafeteria' approaches were followed during the Third Five Year Plan (1961-66) with emphasis on creation of motivation among the people to respond to the family planning message and to utilise the services offered by changing popular attitudes and values to family planning. The 'cafeteria approach' in which various alternative means of family limitation (temporary and permanent) were propagated from the middle of '60s, did not make much headway as the official emphasis remained on terminal methods alone.

Later, many legislations were brought out, including on abortion (medical termination of pregnancy) and the age of marriage. An 'incentives and disincentives' scheme was introduced. Women s education, population education, child nutrition, etc. and their integration with family planning programme was thought of. Consequently a comprehensive National Population Policy, integrated with the overall strategy of socioeconomic development was evolved in April 1976 with a view to promoting family planning at a faster pace by involving in the programme the other development departments of the Government both at the Centre and in the States. Also, all the organisations which commanded credibility and influence with the people and were interested in the public welfare were given importance in the task of promoting family planning.

The following are some of the important features of the National Population Policy of 1976:

- increase in the age of marriage from 15 to 18 years for girls and from 18 to 21 for boys;
- freezing of the population figures kat the 1971 level until the year 2001 for the purpose of representation in the National Parliament as well as for allocation of Central assistance, devolution of taxes, etc., to the States;
- linking of a part of Central assistance to the State for their development with their performance in family planning';
- greater attention to girls' education;
- proper place for population education in the total system of education;
- involvement of all ministries/departments of the government in the family planning programmes;
- increase in monetary compensation for sterilisation;
- institution of group awards as incentives for various organisations and bodies representing the people at local levels, including Zilla Parishads and Panchayat Samities;
- intimate association of voluntary organisations particularly those representing women, with the implementation of the programme;
- greater attention to research; and

— greater use of motivational media, particularly in rural areas, for increasing acceptance of family planning (Sreedhara Swamy, 1984, pp. 154-155).

During the period of National Emergency (1975-77) the family planning programme became a matter of grave political controversy. The Janata Government was formed at the Centre in 1977 and the revised Population Policy was announced by the then Health Minister, Raj Narain. While the new government, in its population policy statement, stressed the importance of limiting population growth, it emphasised the voluntary nature of the family planning programme. Simultaneously, the 'family planning programmes' were redesignated as 'family welfare programmes.' In addition to the items of the 1976 policy, this policy statement advocated a greater role for maternity and child health services, as expansion of the immunisation programme, improvement of women's education and population education, and the involvement of voluntary, youth and women's organisations. The major feature is the "educational and voluntary approach" to family welfare. Population Education as a part of normal courses of study was stressed for youth. Special attention was given to encourage necessary research inputs, alongside education, in the field. Thus, a multi-pronged strategy was evolved to attain the envisage demographic goals and the family planning (welfare) programme has been adopting increasingly effective approaches from time to time, i.e. from a 'clinical' approach to a 'community extension' approach and then to an 'integrated development' approach coupled with 'incentives and disincentives' to promote family planning.

In our interdependent world, it is not possible nor practicable to attempt to solve problems in isolation. Thus, matters of population must be seen in conjunction with many other factors—including health, education, employment, food supplies, housing and environment (Waldheim, 1974). In India the concern for population planning permeates all government policies and programmes related to health, environment, energy, agriculture, food, urban rural development, housing, etc. Success on the population front is considered crucial for securing national development goals (Parekh and Pandey, 1991, p. 27).

The 'incentives and disincentives' have been continued to encourage people, at least the Central and State government employees, to go for sterilisation. Presumably, the worst element of it is that a lion's share of financial incentives go to the educated-employed while a very negligible quantity of incentives is given to the poor, illiterate, uneducated and educated underemployed. When education is perceived as a tool that can promote the adoption of the small family norm, why are more attractive incentives given to the educated-employed than to the other groups? The people in high positions, most often highly educated, get an increment which is equal to or even more than what the other people get as incentive for adopting family planning. Moreover, that negligible amount of financial incentives too they get once and only once in their life, at the time of the sterilisation operation, where the incentives of the employed continue throughout their life, which in cumulative account multiplies many times more than that of the poor. Why is the same quantity of monetory incentives not incorporated in the scheme of incentives and disincentives to the other groups, particularly the illiterate, unemployed and the poor? Is it not prudent to decide incentives for the people keeping in view their socio-economic status, particularly education and income? Is it irrational to confine financial incentives only to the illiterate uneducated and unemployed poor and also to certain categories of the employed like class III and class IV employees and other lower income groups.

Instead, why is the discrimination between the educated-employed and the uneducated-unemployed people, in this regard? What are the bases for such discrimination? There are many research studies (Nag, 1982; Hussain, 1970; Ghosh 1975) on fertility which reveal the existence of inverse relationship between fertility and income and education, and positive relationship between fertility and illiteracy and poverty. Even the percentage of illiterate and poor population to the total population and their contribution to population growth/problem is tremendous, while that of educated-employed is negligible. Yet, the monetary incentives in the scheme are more in favour of the educated-employed. Is it not highly cost-ineffective? Why are the scientific changes not effected in the same? Is it because the policy is designed by the educated-employed—the high profile people? In addition, would the promotion of education with the perception that the education would promote adoption of family planning/small family norm on one hand and giving attractive financial incentives to the highly educated on the other hand not appear to be two contradictory practices of the Government?

In this context, promotion of education looks even absurd. However, the above two contrary practices-promotion of population education and unequal incentives to the educated-employed and uneducated-unemployed family planners—are continued by the Government. Such a practice is most undesirable and it can only be hoped that it is shifted in a desirable direction.

In the above given dilemma between education and incentives to the educated, can one attribute family planning solely to education or incentives? What sort of attitudinal changes do education or incentives bring in the matter of family planning? In the absence of systematic evaluation and research and in the light of the problems, is it possible to make any vogue assessment of changes in population—related attitudes and values due to population education programmes or family planning incentives? To what extent can a reduction in the fertility rate of a country or a community be attributed to population education programme? How, then, can one justify the population programme? What then are the most appropriate ways of evaluating the impact of population education on the knowledge, attitudes and behaviour of different target audiences? Until 1986, When the National Education Policy was announced, population education was part of the National Population Policy. The extension orientation to the family planning programme during the Third Five Year Plan marks the starting point of population education in the non-formal sector. Later, a number of seminars and conferences were organised by national and international organisations working in India in response to the demands of policy changes that were brought out from time to time. As a result, population education has found a place in non-formal and formal education programmes, including higher education.

The purpose of education is to prepare the young for adult life. This requires both presenting relevant information and teaching analytical processes and skills that can be broadly applied. Since population affects all aspects of modern life, important population issues and methods for analysing population problems should be an integral part of in-school education (Sherris and Quillin, 1982). While concerted and sustained efforts have been made since 1980 to integrate elements of population education in both formal and non-formal education systems, the adoption of the 'National Policy on Education 1986' has been the most significant development. The policy reflects the magnitude of the demographic situation and all the concerns related to the causes and consequences of rapid population growth. It categorically mentions that 'the growth of our population needs to be brought down significantly over the coming decades' (National Policy on Education, 1986, p. 2, para 1.13).

The policy document is imbued with issues related to the prevailing population situation. It is generally observed that 'the perception of population—related issues by an individual may vary from that desired by the community or defined by national policies. This so happens because the national policies in respect of population issues are formulated according to the needs and requirements of the well-defined national goals, whereas individuals... perceive the population phenomena in their own socio-cultural milieu shaped by the traditional norms and values patterns. Unless a perceptible social change directed towards the attainment of national goals takes place, there cannot be a commonality in the patterns of perception at individual, community and national levels. With a view to including such a social change education can play a decisive role' (Pandey, 1985, pp. xviii-xix). The policy encapsulates almost all critical concerns in respect of the national system of education. 'A common core' reflected in the national curricular frame-work includes all those issues on which rational attitude has to be developed in each individual (National Policy on Education, 1986, p. 2, para 1.10). These issues constitute more than half of the ten 'core curricular areas' mentioned in the Programme of Action of National Policy on Education (1986, pp. 144-145). These are: constitutional obligations, equality of sexes, protection of environment, removal of social barriers, observance of the small family norm, and inculcation of scientific temper. The National Literacy Mission (1988, p. 14) document has also incorporated these issues and made them an integral part of functional literacy to be imparted to illiterate adults.

For the first time in the history of the nation the 'observance of small family norm' finds a place of importance as a core element in the national education policy. This value is sought to be achieved, not in isolation, but by promoting proper attitudes, particularly in women, in respect of removal of illiteracy, interrelationship among population, environment, development and quality of life, and prevalent values and beliefs. 'Recognising the holistic nature of child development,' the policy accords high priority to 'Early Childhood Care and Education (ECCE) and suitably integrates it with the Integrated Child Development Services programmes, wherever possible' (National Policy on Education, 1986, p. 6. para 5.2). This stipulation has a direct bearing on the demographic goals of bringing down the death rate in general and infant mortality rate in particular. Towards this end is the policy commitment that 'education will be used as an agent of basic change in the status of women' (ibid, p. 6 para 4.2), on which greatly depends the hope of restricting the fertility rate. The policy has itself recognised that 'the largest single factor that could help achieve this (limiting population growth) is the spread of literacy and education among women' (ibid, pp. 2-3, para 1.1). It states that 'the whole nation must pledge itself to the eradication of illiteracy, particularly in the 15-35 age group' (ibid, p. 9, para 4.12). The policy document simultaneously assures that 'the new thrust in elementary education will emphasise universal enrollment and universal retention of children upto 14 years of age.... '(Ibid, p. 11, para 5.5).

Obviously, the National Policy on Education 1986 is imbued with the demographic concerns of the nation and committed to reorient the education system so that it can help in the attainment of demographic goals. Even while making stipulations regarding the future perspectives, it states that 'the main task is to strengthen the base of the pyramid, which come close to a billion people at the turn of the century. Equally, it is important to ensure that those at the top of the pyramid are among the best in the world'. Never before has the education policy lent such unequivocal support to the national population policy. Until the adoption of this policy in 1986, population education was a component of the national population policy; but since then it has become a truly educational programme drawing support from the education policy.'

Concisely all the above provisions provided credibility

and strength to education activities being conducted with a view to institutionalise population education in the education system. 'With a view to institutionalising population education, various kinds of educational activities are conducted in order to make it an integral part of the entire education system. "A broad strategy of integration has been adopted for development of different types of materials, incorporation of population education contents into existing syllabi and textbooks, making it a part of the on-going examination system, training of teachers and other functionaries, organising curricular and cocurricular activities and evaluation of various activities (Parakh and Pandey, 1991, p. 35) in school education by National Council of Educational Research and Training. But, population education is not treated as a separate subject or a separate educational activity. Similar efforts were also made in the field of non-formal education.

Thus, all possible attempts have been made at various levels to integrate the elements of population education in almost all aspects of school education (including teacher education) and non-formal education. In addition, efforts at institutionalisation of population education in the Adult Education sector were made by the Directorate of Adult Education government of India while such efforts in the University Education sector were undertaken by the University Grants Commission (UGC). All this has been designed to institutionalise population education in the entire education system of the country and to promote functional coordination among all the sectors of education through effective institutional arrangement. The efforts of institutionalisation of population education in all the above three sectors, school and non-formal, adult education and university education or higher education are dealt with in detail below.

(1) Population Education in Formal Sector

Population education programmes in the country owe their origin to the National Seminar on Population Education held at Mumbai on August 2-3, 1969 under the joint auspices of the Union Ministries of Education and Youth Services and of Health and Family Planning. The Seminar recommended that population education be introduced in the curriculum of schools and colleges. It further recommended that a separate Population Education Cell be established in the NCERT in order to develop suitable curricula on population education.

During the decade 1970-80 efforts were initiated to develop curricula, teaching units and to revise teacher education programmes in the country. As mentioned earlier, National Population Policies announced in 1976 and 1977 stressed the need to introduce population education in schools. The joint meeting of all the Boards of Secondary Education in the country held in New Delhi in September, 1978 unanimously decided to include population education in schools and teacher training institutions. Sri Venkateswara University, Tirupati set up a Population Studies Centre in April 1973. The Centre, the first of its kind in the country, has been organising teaching, training, extension and research activities. The concept of population education has been included in the curriculum of teacher training institutes and in B.Ed. programmes of some of the Universities of India.

The NCERT conducted a base-lien status survey in 1989-80 and organised four regional seminar-cum-workshops before embarking upon a challenging and prestigious National Population Education Project. A number of curricular, textual, instructional and source materials were developed as a preparation for launching the Project in schools and other educational institutions in the States and Union Territories. The Government of India entered into an agreement with the United Nations Fund for Population Activities (UNFPA). The National Population Education Project was launched aiming at the institutionalisation of population education in the existing education system. Since then the project has run through two cycles, each of five years duration, and its third cycle is much through its way. In the first cycle the emphasis was on expansion of project activities. During the first stage, project activities were started in M.P., Rajasthan, Bihar, Gujarat, Maharashtra, Karnataka, Tamil Nadu, Haryana, Punjab and in the Union Territory of Chandigarh in 1980. In 1981 the activities were extended to the States of Andhra Pradesh, Assam, Himachal Pradesh, Jammu and Kashmir, Kerala, Orissa, Uttar Pradesh, West Bengal and the Union Territories of Delhi. Later they were extended further to bring into the fold 28 States and the Union Territories where activities were conducted for students and teachers of primary, upper primary and secondary stages and for student teachers of elementary and secondary teacher education.

(2) Population Education in Adult Education Sector

As per recommendation of The National Conference on Population Education conducted by the NCERT in 1971 recommended that population education should be integrated into the ongoing programmes of functional literacy and the ideas of population education be systematically incorporated in the literature being produced for neo-literates. Since then, population education has found a place in all the non-formal education programmes initiated by the Government of India. But the major breakthrough in this regard happened after the launch of the National Adult Education Programme (NAEP) on 2nd October, 1978. The major aim of NAEP was the total development of the individual through education. In this context, population education was recognised as one of its vital components. Having recognised the need of Population Education in NAEP, a National Seminar on Integration of Population Education in NAEP, was organised at Mumbai jointly by the Directorate of Adult Education and the Family Planning Association of India on March 3-7, 1979 which recommended the integration of population education in the overall framework of NAEP, including training and material preparation and evaluation, by establishing systematic linkages between population education and NAEP.

Agai a National Conference on Planning and Development of Population Education in Adult Education held at Tirupati on September 17-20, 1979 paid attention to how the content of population education could be incorporated in the NAEP curriculum. It recommended participatory action research projects towards the integration of population education in adult education.

As per the recommendations the National Steering Committee on Population Education (14th May, 1984) "in the Seventh Five Year Plan suitable provision should be made for population education programmes in the school education, both formal and non-formal, university education and adult education sectors" (Directorate of Adult Education, 1984, p. 2). Accordingly, in order to take up the integration of population education in the existing adult education programme, a preparatory project on population education funded by UNESCO/UNFPA was launched by the Directorate of Adult Education from January 1, 1985 which was followed by a Five Year Project (1986-90) during the Seventh Five Year Plan in all States in a phased manner. Under this UNFPA project, the Directorate of Adult Education organised the first "Planning and Development Meting for Integration of Population Education in Adult Education Project" at New Delhi from 23-30 April, 1985, and prepared work plans for integrating population education contents in the existing basic literacy materials. Within a short period after the first meet, the second "Planning and Development Meeting for Integration of Population Education in Adult Education Programme" was held at Literacy House, Lucknow from 5-10 August, 1985 for integrating population education in the Post-literacy and follow-up materials for the learners and training materials for the functionaries-instructors, supervisors and project officers. This work was mainly undertaken with the help of the State Resource Centres and other agencies through different media.

(3) Population Education in Higher Education Sector

The UNFPA agreed to assist the UGC for strengthening population education activities during 1986-90. The extension of the National Population Education Project to the level of higher education in India provided a population education opportunity to young people in the universities/colleges and through them to those in the community.UGC decided to involve all the universities and colleges in a phased manner in the programme of population education during the period April, 1986 to March, 1990. The steps taken by UGC to promote the cause of population education through universities and colleges include the following (UGC, 1986, pp. 184-186).

- Inclusion of population education in the scheme of restructuring of courses at the undergraduate level in foundation and applied courses;
- Circulation of a set of 15-lecture series on various aspects of population education for use by universities and colleges;
- Assistance to universities and colleges for surveys/ research projects on population education with particular reference to small family norm, infant mortality, malnutrition, age at marriage, sex ratio, indigenous practices of population control, knowledge, attitude and practice (KAP), etc.;
- Strengthening of population education at the post-graduate level and provision of UGC assistance under its normal developmental programmes;
- Population education as one of the major activities under the Programme of Adult, Continuing and Extension Education through universities and colleges;
- Institution of Population Education Clubs through

universities and colleges for students and the general community.

— Promotion of television series on population education; and

The National Steering Committee on Population Education constituted by the Ministry of Education and Culture in the Government of India has the overall authority to coordinate the implementation of the project. There are advisory committees in universities and colleges for target-oriented, time-bound implementation of population education activities. These committees have adequate representation from the universities/colleges, Government departments, voluntary organisations at the National, State and district levels for ensuring effective implementation, coordination, monitoring and evaluation of the programme.

Twelve Population Education Resource Centres (PERCs), distributed all over the country have been set up to provide resource support to universities, colleges and adult education centres. Through the project document had visualised the setting up of these PERCs in three phases six in 1986, three in 1987 and three in 1988, in view of the rapid expansion of population education clubs all over the India, it was found essential to locate all the 12 PERCs in very first year. PERC is a substructure created under the Population Education in Higher Education Project. Of the 12, one PERC specialised in population education programmes for women and one for rural populations. Each PERC has been assigned a service area within which it is expected to provide resource support to the strengthening and extension of population education in universities and colleges. For that, UGC has provided staff and programme support to each PERC with a view to enabling it to promote implementation and overview the programme. Each PERC receives guidance from UGC for its work. It receives support from the six Tasks Forces which have been constituted under the project—one each in training, curricular development, learning materials (print), learning materials (audio-visual), research, documentation and dissemination, and monitoring and evaluation with a convener for each.

While the project was to see completion of its first cycle in 1991, a mid term review was undertaken in 1989. An evaluation was also undertaken by an external agency in 1992 which submitted its report with very comprehensive recommendations regarding strengthening the management structure, human resource development, population education clubs, curriculum development, learning materials, training monitoring, research and evaluation, documentation and dissemination, women's programmes, and financial aspects for strengthening the institutionalisation of population education in Higher Education in India (Ed. CIL, 1992, pp. 77-89).

Currently population education is included in course curriculum right from school level. The major intension being spreading consciousness about population explosion, health and other relevant issues.

10

Distance Education

> "Next to knowing when to seize an opportunity, the most important thing in life is to know when to forego an advantage"
>
> —*Benjamin Disaraeli*

> "Reastlessness and discontent are the first necessities of progress."
>
> —*Thomas A. Edison*

Though launched in 1962, in India, distance education did not make much headway during the sixties of last century. It started taking roots in the mid-seventies when more and more universities started institutes for correspondence courses. By 1975-76, a total of 64,210 students were enrolled for distance education. The enrolment more than doubled in three years and by 1978-79, the number of students enrolled rose to 1,33,459. During the span of next nine years, the number was more than thrice and by 1987- 88, a total of 4,02,720 students were enrolled for distance education.

It may be noted that the percentage share of distance education in total enrolment in higher education was 2.6 in 1975-76. It gradually increased and by 1980-81, it rose to 5.7 and to 8.9 in 1986-87. As part of the National Education Policy, the State intends to keep enrolment in formal education restricted. It has therefore stopped encouraging the starting of more and more colleges and universities. This explains the slow growth of enrolment in the formal system in universities and colleges. As against it, the National Education Policy intends to encourage the expansion of distance education.

It may be noted that the formal system is unable to meet it. This explains why a very large number of students take to distance education or private appearance. In areas, where strong and viable distance education institutes have developed, the number of students taking recourse to private appearance has declined. But the areas devoid of good distance education

TABLE 1: TOTAL ENROLMENT IN HIGHER EDUCATION IN INDIA

Years	*University Departments and Colleges*	*Distance education (Universities and Institutions)*	*Total Enrolment*
1975-76	2426109 (97.4)	64210 (2.6)	2490319 (100.0)
1976-77	2431563 (96.8)	79718 (3.2)	2511281 (100.0)
1977-78	2564972 (95.6)	119163 (5.5)	2684135 (100.0)
1978-79	2618228 (95.1)	133459 (4.9)	2751687 (100.0)
1979-80	2648579 (95.1)	136699 (4.9)	2785278 (100.0)
1980-81	2752437 (94.3)	166428 (5.7)	2918865 (100.0)
1981-82	2952066 (93.8)	193691 (6.2)	3145757 (100.0)
1982-83	3133093 (94.1)	197555 (5.9)	3330648 (100.0)
1983-84	3307649	n.a.	—
1984-85	3404096	n.a.	—
1985-86	3570897 (91.0)	355090 (9.0)	3925987 (100.0)
1986-87	3681870 (91.1)	357791 (8.9)	4039661 (100.0)
1987-88	n.a.	402720	n.a.

Note: Figures in parentheses indicate percentage.

facilities have a very large number of private coaching academies thriving because non-availability of a seat in the formal system is not discouraging people to acquire higher education. If distance education facilities are valuable, they are made use of, but in their absence, people make use of the provision of private appearance to satisfy their demand for higher education.

The upshot of the entire argument is that the supply constraint is operating in higher education. The moment supply is increased, demand immediately rushes to fill in the gap.

The states in which the policies of promoting distance education have taken firm roots show a very high percentage share of distance education in total enrolment. In 1986-87, about 42 per cent of the total enrolment in Tamil Nadu, 19 per cent in Andhra Pradesh, 26 per cent in Himachal Pradesh, 18 per cent in Delhi was accounted for by distance education. But a distressing aspect of the situation is that in some states e.g. Uttar Pradesh, Madhya Pradesh, Gujarat, West Bengal, Orissa, Assam and Bihar, Distance Education is practically non-existent.

Region-wise, the Southern Region in India is the most highly developed so far as distance education is concerned. Out of a total enrolment of 12.04 lakhs in higher education, distance education accounts for 2.65 lakhs or 22 per cent of the total enrolment. In the Northern Region, out of total enrolment of 11.17 lakhs, distance education accounts for 0.66 lakhs or 5.9 per cent of the total enrolment. In this region, Uttar Pradesh is lagging far behind the other states—its enrolment in distance education is just 2,500 as against 5.1 lakhs in colleges and university departments.

The Central and Western Region also indicates that only 2.2 per cent of the total enrolment in higher education is accounted for by distance education. Except Maharashtra in which some breakthrough has been made, other states viz., Madhya Pradesh and Gujarat are just initiated into distance education. The Eastern Region with a total enrolment of 7.30 lakhs in higher education has barely 3800 students in distance education. This is rather distressing.

TABLE 2 : SPATIAL DISTRIBUTION OF ENROLMENT IN HIGHER EDUCATION IN INDIA (1986-87)

	Region and States	*University Department*	*Colleges and Distance Education*	*Total*	*Share of D.E. in Total (%)*
SOUTHERN REGION					
1.	Andhra Pradesh	279822	65980	345802	19.1
2.	Karnataka	254049	7512	263621	2.9
3.	Kerala	143593	5133	148726	3.5
4.	Tamil Nadu	261413	186820	448233	41.7
	Sub Total	938877	265505	1204382	22.0
NORTHERN REGION					
5.	Delhi	103092	22741	125835	18.1
6.	Haryana	73637	4358	77995	5.6
7.	Himachal Pradesh	30250	7181	27431	26.2
8.	J&K	29455	2043	31498	6.5
9.	Punjab	136229	14533	150762	9.6
10.	Rajasthan	180412	13045	193457	6.7
11.	Uttar Pradesh	508098	2476	510574	0.5
	Sub Total	1051173	66379	1117522	5.9
CENTRAL AND WESTERN REGION					
12.	Madhya Pradesh	272458	1556	270014	0.6
13.	Maharashtra	478643	20448	499091	4.1
14.	Gujarat	213549	89	213638	0.04
	Sub Total	964650	22093	986743	2.2
EASTERN REGION					
15.	Assam	81001	—	81001	—

Table 2 cont....

	Region and States	University Department	Colleges and Distance Education	Total	Share of D.E. in Total (%)
16.	Bihar	265095	2380	267475	0.9
17.	Manipur	11046	—	11046	—
18.	Meghalaya/ Nagaland	9205	—	9205	—
19.	Orissa	73637	14834	75071	1.9
20.	West Bengal Tripura/Sikkim	287186	—	287176	—
	Sub Total	727170	3814	730984	0.5
Grand Total		3681870	357791	4039661	8.9

Source: Compiled from the University Grants Commission Report for the Year 1986-87 and the earlier reports.

In an overall sense, despite the relatively high growth rate in distance education as compared with that in the formal system, total enrolment of 3.58 lakhs in distance education in 1968-87 accounts for 8.9 per cent of the total enrolment in higher education. From the spatial distribution of distance education students, it becomes clear that it is not the demand constraint but the supply constraint which has become more powerful in restricting the growth of distance education.

Distance Education : Region-wise Change in Enrolment

The Southern Region which had a total enrolment of 23,824 in 1975-76 has grown the fastest and its enrolment stood at 2,88,004 in 1987-88. In relative terms, whereas it accounted for 37 per cent of the total in 1975-76, its percentage share improved to 71.5 in 1987-88. As compared with it, the Northern Region had an enrolment of 37,358 in 1975-76 and its enrolment rose to 82,411 by 1987-88. The percentage share, however, declined from 58.2 in 1975-76 to 20.5 in 1987-88. The Central and Western Region which had an enrolment of 1,432 in 1975-76 improved its enrolment to 23,947 in 987-88.

Its percentage share stood as 5.9 in 1975-76. The Eastern Region is an arid region so far as distance education is concerned and its percentage share declined from 2.5 in 1975-76 to 2.1 in 1987-88. In absolute terms, enrolment improved from 1,596 in 1975-76 to 8,318 in 1987-88.

TABLE 3 : ENROLMENT IN DISTANCE EDUCATION IN INDIA-REGION-WISE

Year	*Southern Region*	*Northern Region*	*Central and Western Region*	*Eastern Region*	*Total*
1975-76	23824	37358	1432	1596	64210
	(37.1)	(58.2)	(2.2)	(2.5)	(100.0)
1976-77	25818	42695	9536	1669	79718
	(32.4)	(53.6)	(12.0)	(2.0)	(100.0)
1977-78	59457	48368	8456	2882	119163
	(49.9)	(40.6)	(7.1)	(2.4)	(100.0)
1978-79	71323	46187	13941	2008	133459
	(53.5)	(34.6)	(10.4)	(1.5)	(100.0)
1979-80	83307	42844	9072	1476	136699
	(60.9)	(31.4)	(6.6)	(1.1)	(100.0)
1980-81	110038	41724	12809	1857	166428
	(66.1)	(25.1)	(7.7)	(1.1)	(100.0)
1981-82	135922	42250	12765	2754	193691
	(70.2)	(21.8)	(6.6)	(1.4)	(100.0)
1982-83	138294	42283	14615	2363	197555
	(70.0)	(21.4)	(7.4)	(1.2)	(100.0)
1983-84	n.a.	n.a.	n.a.	n.a.	n.a.
1984-85	n.a.	n.a.	n.a.	n.a.	n.a.
1985-86	265370	66146	21035	2592	355090
	(74.7)	(18.6)	(5.9)	(0.7)	(100.0)
1986-87	265505	66378	22093	3814	357791
	(74.2)	(18.6)	(6.2)	(1.1)	(100.0)
1987-88	288044	82411	23947	8318	402720
	(71.5)	(20.5)	(5.9)	(2.1)	(100.0)

Note: The figures in the parenthesis indicate percentage.

Taking 1975-76 as the base, the growth rate of enrolment for the 12-year period from 1975-76 to 1987-88 has been calculated and it works out to be 16.53 per cent per annum. This may be described as High Growth Scenario.

Scenario II

Three-yearly averages for 1975-76 to 1977-78, 1980-81 to 1982-83 and 1985-86 to 1987-88 have been worked out. This has been done to even out some normal fluctuations during a particular year. Using this, the growth rate between triennia 1975-78 and 1980-83 to 1985-88 works out to be 14.87 per cent. Taking the entire period, 1975-78 to 1985-88, the growth rate works out to be 15.54 per cent per annum. This may be described as Medium Growth Scenario.

Scenario III

Since 1975-76 is a low base year, we have used 1980-81 as the base year and worked out the growth rate between 1980-81 and 1987-88. This works out to be 13.46 per cent per annum. This may be described as Low Growth Scenario.

High Growth Scenario I, reveals an annual growth rate of 16.53 for distance education and 3.80 for universities and colleges.

It may be noted that in the three Scenarios, the Growth rate for universities and colleges show marginal variation but the growth rate in the three scenarios for distance education show relatively large variation—from 13.46 per cent in Scenario III to 16.53 per cent in Scenario I. It may also be observed that whereas the growth rates in distance education decline in our assumptions from Scenario I to Scenario II and to Scenario III, the situation with reference to universities and colleges is in the opposite direction with the annual growth rate of 3.80 per cent in Scenario I, 3.90 per cent in Scenario II and 4.25 per cent in Scenario III.

The results of the projections are tabulated in Table 5.

The Scenarios indicate that the total enrolment in higher education will be around 65 lakhs by 1995-96, although the share of distance education according to the three scenarios would be different. Scenario I and Scenario II indicate an enrolment of 13.69 lakhs and 13.65 lakhs respectively. However, the Low Growth Scenario III shows an enrolment of 11.06 lakhs by 1995- 96. Given the same trends, Scenario I and Scenario II indicate an enrolment of 29.42 lakhs and 28.09 lakhs in Distance Education by 2000-01. However, Scenario III gives an enrolment projection of 20.79 lakhs for 2000-01.

Differences in the three scenarios for Colleges and Universities are much narrower. Scenario I and II give a projection of 51.5 lakhs for 1995-96 and 62.0 lakhs for 2000-01. Scenario III shows a enrolment of 53.5 lakhs for 1995-96 and 65.9 lakhs for 2000-01.

The Fourth and the Fifth Five Year Plans have provided data regarding University enrolment and also indicated enrolment as a proportion of the relevant age group (17-23).

Two observations may be made here. First the data given in the Five Year Plans are at variance with the data provided by the UGC in its annual reports. Secondly, this does not include enrolment in correspondence education. Even if we assume that the data provided by the Planning Commission are correct, we find that in 1973-74, university enrolment accounted for 3.8 per cent of the population in the relevant age-group (17-23). The target indicated by the Fifth Plan of achieving an enrolment of 46.5 lakhs by 1978-79 was abandoned in view of the restrictive policy adopted for higher education. This is evidenced by the slow growth of actual enrolment to 26.18 lakhs as indicated by UGC data for 1978-79.

After the introduction of 10 + 2 system in the country, pre-university classes were largely transferred to the higher secondary schools. The UGC also decided to exclude the students enrolled in PUC from its figures of enrolment in higher education. We have, therefore, taken 18-23 age-group as the relevant age-group for University education since most of the state in India have switched over to the 10 + 2 system which requires an age of 17 years for its completion in the normal course.

Reveals that in 1985-86, enrolment in higher education accounted for 4.65 per cent of the population in the age-group 18-23—4.23 per cent being accounted for by the enrolment in Universities and colleges, and 0.42 per cent by the enrolment in higher education. By 1995-96, taking the Moderate Growth Scenario II, enrolment in higher education would be 6.59 per cent of the total population in the age-group 18-23, out of which 5.20 per cent would be accounted for by enrolment in Universities and colleges, and 1.39 per cent by enrolment in distance education. By 2000-01, the figure for higher education will rise to 7.83 per cent—5.95 per cent for the enrolment in Universities and colleges, and 1.88 per cent by the enrolment in distance education.

It may be noted that India is far behind the developed countries in the race for providing higher education. Even with reference to the developing countries, the position of India is not comparable. (For comparison see the data given in Table 8 regarding enrolment in relevant age group). The present restrictive policy of higher education may operate on the supply side, but with the rapid growth of distance education in the next decade, the supply constraint will become relatively less operative and the urge for higher education will be satisfied by this relatively cheap technology of higher education.

Figures of total population in the age-group 18-23 have been worked out from the Report of the Expert Committee on the Population Projections, Census of India, 1981, Occasional Paper No. 4 of 1988.

REFERENCES

Abraham, V. (1985), *A Brief Note on School of Correspondence Courses,* Waltair, July 1988 (Mimeo).

Datt, Ruddar, *Distance Education in India: Its Development and Significance,* Workshop on Education, Open School, New Delhi.

Distance education in Asia and Pacific, Vol. II, Proceedings of the Regional Seminar on Distance Education, 26th November—3rd December 1986, Asian Development Bank (1987), Article by S.P. Mullick, Distance Education in India.

Report of the Expert Committee on the Population Projections (1988), Census of India, 1981, Occasional Paper No.4 of 1981.

University Grants Commission, Annual Reports from 1975-76 to 1986-87.

11

Social Education in India

> "Natural abilities are like natural plants; they need pruning by study."
>
> —*Francis Bacon*

> "The world expects results. Don't tell others about the labour pains. Show them baby."
>
> —*Arnold Glasow*

It is a well-known fact that in India only about 35% of people are literate; rest 65% are foundering in a swamp of illiteracy. Under the changing political, economic and social circumstances, illiteracy of Indian people is a mighty obstacle in the way of their progress. With the advent of independence, India is making significant experience in democracy. But the success of the experiment admits of doubt and uncertainty owing to the incapability of the illiterate masses to understand and appreciate the higher principles of democracy, social justice and civic responsibilities. Our democracy is nothing but a humbug, so long as the voter or the tax-payer does not realise the value and significance either of vote or tax. There is the danger of its being abused by incapable and illiterate persons. Hence the preparation of suitable field through eradicating illiteracy for introducing any political, social or economic reform in the country is a pre-requisite. Social education is mighty instrument in this respect.

Fundamentals of Adult Education

The significance of the term 'Adult education' has undergone a change in the recent times. Sometime ago, adult education meant simply literacy. But literacy should not be confused with education, though it is key to the acquisition of knowledge and education. Literacy opens the gateway of education leading ultimately to the sacred shrine of knowledge. So long as ignorance prevails in society, exploitation cannot be eradicated root and branch. The exploitation leads to poverty which in turn gives birth to ignorance and misery. Thus the vicious circle goes on; and under such circumstances, the noble sentiments of social justice and democracy become extinct. The success of democracy finally rests on such citizens as are wise and understand fully the aims add implications of democracy.

Paul Bergevin, an American expert in adult education has stated, "democracy depends upon an intelligent, everwatchful citizenship intelligent enough to recognise the political charlatan, intelligent enough to weigh and evaluate ideas in terms of their worth to themselves and their fellow-citizens, intelligent enough to know that there are forces constantly at work which would sell a package in a pretty wrapping that does not contain what the purchaser bargained for, and intelligent enough to recognise the right of those with whom they disagree to express their opinion."

It is evident that giving of mere bookish learning to the adults would not be sufficient in order to achieve the objective of adult education. In fact, education is a constantly flowing stream. Man acquires knowledge consciously or unconsciously throughout his life. Therefore, there is the urgent need of well-organised and permanent provision of adult education for the sake of making any plan successful. Mere pious and good intentions and high-sounding words, as unfortunately has been the case in India so far in the sphere of adult education, are not enough. Proper opportunities should be provided to the adults to acquire general, special and vocational education. For this purpose, first of all, such subjects should be prescribed for their studies as might be related to their practical life. The attractive and interesting way in which a particular subject is presented to them can possibly induce them to understand the fundamental benefits of education. Thus when their mental horizons are widened, they will naturally try to understand their own environment and their education will, in this way, also develop.

Another important thing that is worth bearing in mind is that we cannot achieve desired success in our objective, if we wish to organise adult education merely to meet some temporary and emergent problems. Unfortunately, Indian society is in the grip of many an evil. Under such circumstances, temporary prescriptions of adult education are nothing but mere wastage of time and energy for the objective of eliminating all those vices. In fact, adult education should develop in the form of a permanent system of Social education which might bring about an all-round and stable development of the masses. In India, the efforts of certain so called enthusiastic social reformers and educationists generally end in teaching the illiterates the art of putting signatures in a few hours without understanding the alphabet at all. No doubt, this aim of adult education is quite insufficient, narrow and ridiculous. It has been experience during the past four decades that all the movements in the sphere of adult education have proved quite futile and temporary and the so-called literates have not been benefited in any sense. They have soon lapsed into illiteracy.

The primary need in this respect is that any plan of adult education whatsoever it might be, should take into its purview the mental development, qualities of ideal citizenship, cultural growth and vocational training of the adult concerned. The exploit the plan of adult education for political ends is a gross social crime: but as ill luck would have it, the evil practice is still rampant in our country. The Adult education campaign has not been launched successfully in India on the governmental level or in the form of well-planned and organised programmes of the social reformers. Adult education will remain merely a pious hope and we shall have to wait for long before the vast masses may be educated, so long as a movement is not launched on a larger scale and the State does not take active steps in this direction. Happily, a National Programme of Adult Education has recently been launched at last which we shall discuss later in this Chapter.

In the end, before giving a historical retrospect of gradual development of adult education in India, it is, however, essential to emphasise that the supreme aim of adult education in relation to democracy should be the widening of horizons of social, cultural, vocational and physical knowledge of the citizens so that the country might produce happy and prosperous citizens, wise electors, ingenious artisans and artists.

Preliminary Efforts for Adult Education in British India

During the first two decades of the twentieth century, no appreciable attempts were made in the field of adult education. A few night schools were organised here and there but children, too, would join them. They were not established exclusively for the purpose of adult education. They were but mere efforts to provide temporary education to those children who were compelled to seek menial employments by adverse circumstances. Adults, too, were admitted to those schools along with other boys. The movement of night schools for adults was started only in Madras, Bombay and Bengal Provinces. In 1909, there were 775 night schools in Madras, 1802 in Bengal and 107 in Bombay. Later on, the number of these schools dwindled. But the importance of adult education was realised when in 1921, the Provincial Governments were granted more powers and the members of Provincial Legislative Assemblies were mainly sent by the people through education. When the public was sanctioned franchise, the need of utilising it profitably was felt by Indians. The politicians, social reformers and the Government now began to devote their attention to the important problem of adult education owing to the prevalence of universal mass illiteracy. Some libraries were accordingly brought into being afterwards.

"In some provinces the question received serious consideration and.... a few organised experiments were made. In the United Provinces, the local Government in 1921 offered a subsidy to six municipalities for the development of a system of night schools for adults.... In the Punjab, on the other hand, over a hundred night schools have been opened mostly in the rural areas and mostly under the auspices of the Co-operative Credit Societies... Bombay reports a similar development.... The schools are controlled by the Education Department and have special inspectors to look after them. These Bombay night schools are circulating schools stationed at each centre for two years." Similar efforts were made in Central Province, Bengal and Madras. But no such country-wide movement was launched as might eradicate the evil root and branch.

Scenario from 1921 to 1947

The control of education was transferred to representative Indian Ministers according to the Constitution of India framed in 1919. Consequently, appreciable efforts were made to promote the cause of adult education. The Punjab, Madras, Bombay and United Provinces were chief provinces worth naming in this respect. In the year 1927, there were 3,784 adult education schools in the Punjab, 5,604 in Madras, 193 in Bombay and 1519 in Bengal Province.

Progress made by adult education during the quinquennium of 1922-27 can be calculated from the table of figures given below:

Year	*Number of Schools*	*Number of Students*
1922-23	630	17,776
1923-24	1,528	40,883
1924-25	2,372	61,961
1925-26	3,206	85,371
1926-27	2,784	98,414

Adult education marked an upward trend upto 1928, but several adult education centres were closed down in 1929 owing to economic slump. Political and communal disturbances too affected education adversely. Some Christian missionaries carried on their work. Dr. Lucas did appreciable work in spreading adult education at Allahabad and wrote certain Hindustani books in Roman Script. Similarly, Dr. Lawrence organised Hindi classes in Manipur as Dr. Daniel organised Tamil classes in Madras and published some elementary books.

The Punjab while was hitherto on an ascending scale of progress in adult education, became stagnant during this period and many a school were closed down. Here the pupil-teachers of Normal classes did some creditable work in the field of adult education and some library facilities were provided in rural areas as well. Similarly, libraries were established in 1928 in Central Provinces and Bihar.

Mumbai along showed a uniform progress in comparison to other provinces during this period. During 1932-33, the number of adult education schools was attended by 5,660 students rising respectively to 180 and 6,299 in 1937. The progress is ascribable mainly to growing interest in adult education on the part of Bombay Government. Besides, other institutions like Rural Reorientation League at Poona and Sewa Sadan, Social League and Bombay City Literacy Association at Bombay also spread adult education. Libraries were established in Baroda State. Travancore also followed suit. The progress, however, was quite slow upto 1937.

After 1937, the problem of adult education invited the attention of the country. Provincial autonomy had been established in all the provinces according to the provisions of Indian Constitution of 1935. Adult education was much encouraged owing to the formation of Congress Ministries in seven provinces. It was very essential for the successful working of the newly formed Ministries that citizens should be educated so that they might realise their own privileges and responsibilities and understand the various projects of the government.

The Provincial Governments, therefore, put forth some organised efforts in the sphere of adult education. The general public appreciated these efforts and zealously took active part in the literacy movement. It was thus that Government, for the first time in Indian history acknowledge the spread of adult education as her essential obligatory duty and started the work accordingly. The new curriculum of adult education did not remain circumscribed only to the spread of literacy but included social education as well. As regards the means of spreading education, recourse was had to pamphlets, magic lanterns and cinema besides the use of books.

During 1939-40, literacy movement reached its culminating point. The slogan 'Each one Teach one' was very loud during these years. In the Punjab the slogan 'Learn and Teach' was used on a large scale. During 1939-40, the literacy campaign was zealously launched in the Punjab and the Provincial Government earmarked a sum of Rs. 28,800 for the promotion of adult education under a five-year scheme. The old adult education institutions were sanctioned grant-in aid and many fresh ones were established. The number of these schools shot to 201 at that time. Moreover, the volunteers spread adult education in villages, sub-divisions and districts through Laubboche system. In the province of Assam, a separate Department of Adult Education was established under the supervision of a literacy officer. In 1941, a post-literacy curriculum was set up for the adults having finished the literacy course and as many as 1,200 study centres were established in the Assam Valley. A proper provision was made for the distribution and teaching of Readers, books and newspapers for the adults.

In Orrisa during 1940-41, 425 adult education centres were started where 8,147 adults were made literate. The movement of adult education here could not achieve more success than that.

In Mumbai Province, the first Congress Ministry did appreciable work in the field of adult education. The Government has established the Provincial Board of Adult Education there in the year 1937. The system of grant-in-aid for the purpose of adult education was initiated and liberal grants were sanctioned. During 1942-43 an extra sum of 50,000 rupees was spent for villages. In 1945, provision was made for opening adult education centres at selected places and it was decided that at least one thousand adults would be made literate at each centre at a cost of Rs. 9,400.00 per annum. In addition to that, Bombay city itself made appreciable progress in this direction. An Adult Education Committee was appointed there. During 1940-41, this Committee had opened some 1,140 adult classes in Marathi, Gujarati, Hindi, Canarese, Telugu and Tamil attended by sixteen thousand men and five thousand women. Moreover in certain industrial areas also the work of disseminating adult education was done. In the Province of Bihar, the adult education campaign made good progress under the guidance of Dr. Syed Mahmud. The Provincial People's Education Committee was established there. The volunteers launched the movement of "Make Your Home Literate" and they made 24,289 adults literate during 1941-42. Further, during 1942-43 one lakh and eleven thousand adults passed the literacy course. The special feature of adult education movement in Bihar was that it remained in operation even during the disturbed period of the World War II and every two lakhs of adults continued to be literate. In 1946, with the re-establishment of Congress Ministry, the work was taken up with much zeal and enthusiasm.

In Bengal, adult education was placed under the Department of Rural Reconstruction. Appreciable progress was shown by this province in this field. The work of spreading adult education among the peasantry was crowned with success in Bengal. The curriculum included agriculture, animal husbandry, sanitation, promotion of heath and principles of co-operation etc., and separate officials were appointed for different subjects.

In U.P. much creditable work was done in the sphere of adult education. In 1937, the new Ministry undertook this work with great enthusiasm and zeal. New education centres, libraries and reading centres were established at different places. Innumerable night schools were opened and every year a literacy week began to be observed. As early as 1930 Department of Adult Education had been established which did much creditable work in the ensuing years. The Provincial Government established 768 libraries and 3,600 reading rooms in rural areas on the first literacy day. The number of libraries shot to 1040 during 1941-42. In addition to that, 40 separate liberaries were established for women in 1940. The same year a grant of Rs. 500/-was sanctioned to each of the centres in Faizabad for the welfare of women. Further, the Government undertook to publish books on Hindi, Urdu, Mathematics, History and Geography for the use of adults.

Besides these provinces, the work of adult education was undertaken by Sindh and other native states. In Mysore, the State Literacy Council has done appreciable work in this direction. The Mysore University too has contributed its own quota to the sacred cause of social education. Four thousand and fifty adult education centres were operated in Jammu and Kashmir State during 1942-43 and thus made twenty-eight thousand persons literate. The same year 480 libraries were established there out of which 300 libraries were established in rural areas. Besides these states, Baroda and Travancore were other ones where the percentage of literacy was higher than other sister states in British India. Efforts were made to disseminate seeds of adult education even in hilly regions, among the Harijans and aborigines.

Besides these efforts, a number of other philanthropic organisations such as Young Men's Christian Association, Servants of India Society, Bombay Literacy Sangh, Literacy Expansion League and Jamia Millia. Delhi etc., gave impetus to the movement of adult education. The Sargent Education Scheme placed a very effective plan for adult education under the post-war educational development plan, but it could not be implemented. The account of any literacy movement in India will not be complete without the mention of the name of Dr. Frank Laubboche. He was an American Philanthropist. He did much appreciable work in the Philippine Islands in the field of adult education. He visited India in 1935 and made a second tour of it in 1937. He prepared suitable charts in Marathi, Hindi, Tamil, Telugu Bengali and Gujarati languages. Dr. Laubboche first of all reduced these languages to four or five vowels and thirteen consonants. Thereafter he discovered five such fundamental letters as might form the basis of the formation of other letters. It was thus that he found out the method of making adults literate within a short span of time. He also published some papers and wrote some useful books for the education of adults. His method was followed in many provinces.

Thus ends the second period in the history of Indian adult education. Post-independence India witnessed still greater progress in this field. The experiences in the fields of adult education gleaned between 1921 and 1947 have presented many an important problem connected therewith in clear and vivid form. It was fully well realised during this period of what an immense magnitude adult education was and what literature and means were required or what methods were beneficial and practicable to implement the adult education plan. It was also felt strongly that mere literacy was not enough without the means to preserve it so that the literate person might be enabled to increase his knowledge afterwards.

Social education after Independence

Whereas progress was made in the entire sphere of education after the independence of the country, some progress was achieved in the field of adult education as well. Adult education was given the shape of Social Education which sought to produce ideal citizens and make their life prefect in all respects. Taking into consideration the importance of franchise in the context of our democratic setup, the problem of adult education in India has assumed greater importance and it is hoped that the present progress and future building of the nation will be determined to a considerable measure, by it. Illiteracy of well-nigh four hundred millions of Indian populace is a strong challenge and it should be tackled as soon as possible, else Indian democracy would be put a broad farce and lose its significance essentially.

The Government of India have accepted adult education in its following aspects.

(i) to spread literacy among the adult illiterates;

(ii) to educate the minds of the masses in view of the absence of literacy education; and

(iii) to create a conscious knowledge in the adult about rights and duties of citizenship in the capacity of an individual citizen and as a unit of mighty nation.

Abdul education has been given the form of Social Education but more emphasis is to be laid on the items 'b' and 'c' referred to above. The adoption of the following educational method has been recommended in order to inculcate the virtues of ideal citizenship in the adults and educate their mind:

1. Making them acquainted with the meaning of citizenship and the method of conducting democracy; tó give them education in history and geography of the country and making them well acquainted with the prevalent social conditions.

2. Telling them importance of Health and Hygiene and giving them the knowledge of personal cleanliness and principles of public sanitation.
3. To impart education and information with a view to raising the economic standard of the adult so that his education might be correlated to his economic life.
4. Refining and developing the aesthetic and cultural tastes and sensibilities of adults through such creative activities as art, literature, music and dancing.
5. Creating a knowledge of human fraternity and universal ethics among them and emphasizing the need of understanding and tolerating differing views of others pertaining to democracy.

A brief account of the progress achieved during the period of Five-Year Plans may be discussed below:

In 1951, the Social Education campaign was launched in the villages of Delhi State with great zeal and enthusiasm. In the first year, 60 centres were established in villages and 62 teachers were trained for them. Similarly, adult education centres started in the city and its suburban area. Moreover, educational fairs are being organised in rural areas where through propagation educational and industrial development is carried on.

The Government of India started Work Camps in the country on the lines of Work Camps conducted by UNESCO, during the First Plan period. The same *mutatis mutandis* is being applied to Indian villages. It is showing good progress in those areas where the refugees have settled. The chief aims of the scheme are: (i) the spread of literacy, (ii) citizenship, and (iii) sublimation of ideas.

For literacy of the adults the following methods were adopted:

1. Reading of ordinary printed matter and in the final stage, reading of weeklies and magazines.
2. Writing of their own names and those of their own relatives as well as the names of their native villages, tehsils and districts and writing of ordinary social letters.
3. Writing of figures upto hundred, doing of simple sums of adding, subtraction, multiplication and division; getting a knowledge of coins, weights and measurement, etc.

Adult Education Programmes: Strategy

Adult education is one of the most neglected fields of Indian education system. The whole field of adult literacy programme has virtually been left to the uncoordinated and unplanned activities of a few voluntary organisations and private agencies. The governmental efforts being done in the name of social education under the Community Development Programme are more known for their failure than for any measure of success. Under this programme, an ill-equipped Assistant Development Officer, mostly overbusy with file-work or duties other than social education, with practically no funds and no enthusiasm either, was asked to impart social education to more than 85 per cent of illiterates in about 100 villages. It is no wonder that such a programme must fail to touch even the fringe of the problem after wasting whatever meagre resources allocated for the purpose.

(i) Adult Education as a Factor in Economic Development

Adult education deals with that section of the population which is actually engaged in productive occupations in farms, factories and elsewhere. The mental, moral and technical competence of this vital group of our society, therefore is bound to reflect on the productive efficiency of the group engaged in production.

Mass illiteracy and mass poverty go hand in hand. While it can be conceded that a rise in national income depends on the well-directed investment in physical inputs, it can easily be realised that such an investment does not explain the whole of the process of economic growth. What has come to be recognised as a Residual factor which can be regarded largely the human factor, also contributes to the process of growth and along with other components education forms the most important part of the human factor. The other components may be scientific and technological progress, inventions, research and organisational and managerial skills. But all these are the various manifestations of education itself. It can, therefore, be argued that education of those who are engaged in production is a very important and productive investment. In India unfortunately it is this very class which is largely illiterate and hence handicapped to make its fullest contribution to the process of growth. The low industrial productivity of the factory workers, the resistance and inability of Indian farmers to innovations and scientific methods of cultivation, the tardy performance of the co-operative movement, the Panchayati Raj and the community development, the lack of mass appreciation of family planning measures and indeed the stagnation of the entire social structure, which has simultaneously contributed towards the economic and cultural stagnation, can largely be attributed to mass illiteracy in this country. The continued neglect of adult education programmes in our educational system has further aggravated the situation. The former Five-Year Plans had given a very low priority to this vital aspect of the investment in human resources. Happily the Planning Commission has now realised that 'widespread illiteracy is a real handicap in the way of both economic and social development'. They have also confessed that adult education has not been adequately attended to in the past and this has led to various problems.

(ii) Illiteracy

It is indeed a pity that India which aspires to establish the biggest democracy of the world and also desires to achieve a rapid economic development of its stagnant economy and a quicker change of its stagnant society through the democratic cooperation of her people, has paid scant attention to make those very people worthy and capable of comprehending the real significance and content of either democracy or planned economic development.

In the year 1951,166 per cent Indians could read and write. The percentage went up to 24.0 in 1961 and to 29.45 in 1971. There are however regional variations. For instance, Kerala had the highest literacy rate of about 70 per cent according to the census of 1971. Similarly Tamil Nadu and Maharashtra had 45.8 and 45.4 per cent respectively. Amongst the Union Territories Chandigarh topped with 70.5 per cent literacy. At the bottom there are States like U.P., Bihar, Jammu and Kashmir, M.P., Rajasthan, Sikkim and Arunachal Pradesh, where more than 70% of the population is illiterate. What is more alarming is the fact that in spite of rise in the percentage of literacy, the total number of illiterates is rising constantly owing to the rapid growth of population and failure of the Government to provide compulsory primary education to the children in the 6-11 year group. The number of illiterates grew from 33.4 crores in 1961 to 39.6 crores in 1971. Rural folk and women form the bulk of illiterates. In the rural India only 27.9% people were found literate in 1971. It is feared that in 1971 the gross number of illiterates in the country would go still further up though the literacy rate might increase in terms of percentage. So far as the literacy rate amongst the female population is concerned it is merely 22%, which means that 78 percentage of female population is still unable to read and write.

(iii) The Fifth R

For long the concept of literacy remained confined only

to the teaching of traditional 3-R's. It has been found that even the most elementary knowledge acquired was soon forgotten in the absence of any continuous follow-up programme resulting in relapse into illiteracy. This concept of literacy, though essential, is found to be inadequate and wasterful. Therefore, the concept of 'social education' which aims at a fuller and all- sided development of an adult as a more useful member of society became popular with the educationists, Social education consists of, besides the 3-R's, elementary, technical and vocational skills, domestic skills, cultural and recreational arts, understanding of the environment, working of government, civic education and knowledge of other societies. But in the context of developing countries like India, where the problem is stupendous but resources limited, it is necessary that we do not have an unnecessarily elaborate and complex programme of social education in the initial stages. What is pragmatic in this connection is a "Functional Literacy" approach, which means education and training the illiterate adults in their respective economic functions in order to improve the quality of their performance at work.

Prof. Radhakamal Mukerjee has added a fourth R to the traditional 3-R's, signifying 'Human Relations'. We could further venture to suggest a Fifth R, call it either 'Reconstruction' or 'Rate of Growth'. It is indeed in the fifty sense that literacy programme in India must be formulated, directed, implemented forthwith and made an integral part of the national educational system, and as such, he included in the development plans of the country. The vast possibilities of contribution adult functional literacy can make to the modernisation of agriculture and industries, in the increased mobility of labour and thus helping the nation to achieve a desired rate of growth, justified a renewed and vigorous effort on the part of the governmental, political as well as private agencies. This we would call a campaign to Reconstruct a New Man. We will have to consider adult literacy as an essential element in over-all development, and link it to the economic and social priorities as well as to the present and future man-power needs of the country. Adult literacy has to be regarded not an end in itself but a means to prepare man for social, civic and economic objectives. The simple process of reading and writing would provide them initial opportunity for acquiring knowledge that can immediately be used after functional training for greater production and higher productivity. This world ultimately provide wider opportunity for participation in a fuller civic life and finally paying the way of fundamental human civilisation. "Literacy instruction must enable illiterates, left behind by the course of events and producing too little, to become socially and economically integrated in a new world where scientific and technological progress calls for ever more knowledge and specialisation.

(iv) Planned Efforts

For a successful development of the adult education system it is necessary that a nationwide campaign be started after formulating effective and practical schemes. These schemes must be oriented towards development and be considered of fundamental importance for all the other aspects of national life. All this cannot be achieved by the government alone. It demands the active co-operation of non-governmental voluntary organisations, educational institutions, cultural and religious societies and above all, the political parties of the country. We have no doubt in our mind that unless political parties take up the responsibility of the eradication of mass illiteracy in a big and co-ordinated way, we cannot succeed soon in removing the scourge of ignorance and illiteracy. Those of the political parties which actually count in the life of the nation must now at long last develop a constructive attitude towards the various national problems, particularly adult education and after imparting required training—may be under State guidance or in Universities—

send their party cadres to implement a comprehensive and intensive programme of functional adult literacy. If this suggestion is accepted we can bring about an earlier social and economic revolution in the country—an objective which all the political parties claim to bring about.

(2) Sometimes suggestions are made to postpone all the efforts for adult education on the plea that universal elementary education would attain the objectives of universal literacy during the course of time. This is a wholly erroneous idea. In fact, there is no conflict between schooling and adult literacy programme. These can be regarded as two complementary aspects of one and the same activity. Moreover, by the time the country achieves the targets of universal elementary education, much loss of human resources would have taken place by keeping the adult workers and farmers illiterate and vocationally inefficient, backward and less productive. Besides, we have to consider the fact of relapse into illiteracy of millions of persons educated upto primary stage in the absence of a follow-up programme. Adult Education of functional type would obviate such shortcomings. It can, therefore, be further suggested that literacy work should not terminate when the universal literacy has been achieved and schools have been made available to provide elementary education. But on the other hand arrangements should be made to ensure that literacy work would eventually be formed into a continuing educational process for adults through the mass media of communication and through planned programmes of follow up efforts for neo-literates during the post-literacy period.

(3) Second most effective agency may be the millions of our young men and women studying or teaching in the Universities, colleges and schools. We can utilise with great benefits the services of the teachers and senior students of the primary and secondary schools situated in the rural areas, unfortunately, in the absence of any well planned national

programme of social service and constructive activities for our students, and also for the want of any firm will and sustained determination, unhealthy and destructive tendencies have been developing amongst our students, which do good neither to themselves nor to the society, which is educating them at a heavy cost. For this colossal wastage of talent and man-power, which could otherwise be directed to productive activities, the main responsibility is of those who have been managing or rather mismanaging the educational affairs of the country. The lack of leadership in general and educational leadership in particular to utilise the vast constructive potentialities of student community has deprived the nation of the voluntary services of the younger generation. We can certainly utilise their energy, enthusiasm, idealism and a high sense of patriotism for educating their more unfortunate brethren, who, for one reason or the other, could not get the benefit of schooling, but are themselves making important contribution in their own humble way by working in farms and factories. It is, therefore, suggested that a Department of Adult Education be established in each University and apart from research and training, the department should organise a 'Literacy Corps' consisting of students and teachers.

(4) The strategy for planning of adult education in India would remain incomplete if we fail to give a serious thought to the problem of illiteracy amongst women; because they play a supreme role in the education of the family and can be regarded the key- factor in the progress of the family and, therefore, of the entire nation. In view of their importance for nutrition and home-management, for maximising the benefits from the available food resources, increased productivity of workers and growth of children with healthy attitudes and sound personalities. It is absolutely necessary that special efforts be made to involve women into the programmes of functional literacy to suit their particular needs and aptitudes; and adequate financial, institutional and organisational provisions be made for the purpose.

(5) Besides the mobilisation of national resources, attempts should be made to seek the co-operation of developed countries in technical and financial matters. International agencies like UNESCO can contribute a great deal in the eradication of the scourge of adult illiteracy from Indian soil. Agencies like the Literacy House in U.P. can do a lot in preparing suitable literature, reading material and undertaking research on various problems pertaining to the adult education. Recent efforts done in Maharashtra under the Gram Shikshan Mohim Scheme for mass literacy programme can with success be emulated by other States. In the end, we could repeat that in any programme of adult education it is to be remembered that the same must be linked with economic development and social change and be of a continuous nature eventually leading towards a fuller and more purposeful living. It is a human problem but giant efforts are needed to solve it.

(6) Other aspects of the programme may include Farmers' education, recruitment and training of the teachers, psychological orientation of minds towards the objectives to be achieved, surveys of needs of human resources, calculation of the per capita cost of educating an adult, creation of suitable reading material, text-books and audio-visual aids and last but not the least, research and an evaluation system to determine scientifically the relationship between the cost of literacy and benefits derivable from it to the society. No national effort of adult education would be successful unless it is preceded and followed by research on the extent and dimensions of the problem and of the results achieved.

National Adult Education Programme

During the recent years efforts have been made in the field of adult education through the farmers' functional literacy projects for rural areas, the Shramik Vidyapeeths, National Service Schemes in Universities and colleges, the Nehru Yuvak Kendras and by providing assistance to voluntary organisations. But for the period of the 6th Five Year Plan the Central Government has come out with a proposal to mobilise all the efforts and organise a very large, intensive and nation-wide programme of adult education, with special emphasis on the age-group 15-35. This is being achieved through a well-planned National Adult Education Programme (NAEP).

It has been realised that adult education should emphasise imparting of literacy skills to persons belonging to the economically and socially deprived sections of the society. Therefore, under the NAEP the adult education, while emphasising acquisition of literacy, will also emphasise on the facts it should be:

1. *relevant* to the environment and learner's needs;
2. *flexible* regarding duration, time, location, instructional arrangements, etc.
3. *diversified* in regard to curriculum, teaching and learning materials and methods; and
4. *systematic* in all aspects of organisation.

After 1978, the scheme took one year in intensive preparatory efforts, which included stepping up of the programme from the existing 0.5 million to at least 1.5 million, creation of environment, preparation of case studies and detailed state plans, establishment of necessary administrative structures, identification of various agencies, official and non-official, development of training methodologies and actual training of the personnel required at various levels and creation of a system of evaluation and monitoring as well as the required applied research. The first phase of the NAEP is to end in 1983-84. After that it would be necessary to diversify the programmes and the aim would be to strive for a learning society in which life- long education is a cherished goal.

(i) The Target Group

The main target group of the NAEP is the illiterate and

unorganised people in the rural and urban areas who are the most exploited and weak and are forced to live below poverty time. Amongst these emphasis will be on those who are in the 15-35 age- group. Illiterate women, scheduled castes and tribes and landless labourers will receive special attention.

(ii) Methods

It can be asserted that the success of the Programme will depend upon stimulating the motivation of adults, proper selection and training of workers, preparation of suitable reading material, development and adoption of dynamic methods of learning by doing, organisation of mass movement and provision of adequate supervision and guidance.

(iii) Content of the Programme

Although literacy has a special place in this programme, its principal objective is to increase the awareness of the poor illiterates about their own plight and about the socio-economic realities around them. They will also be assisted to organise themselves to understand and strive to solve their day-to-day problems and to involve them in useful national work of development. This would, therefore, mean an appropriate "mix" suited to the needs of the individuals as well as the society. This may in content mean, besides literacy, themes like general education and family planning, upgrading of vocational skills, understanding of science and technology in day-to-day life and physical education and cultural activities.

(iv) Administration

It has been realised that such a programme can only be organised on a decentralised basis. A National Board of Adult Education has been set up at the Centre to guide the Programme. On the same pattern suitable agencies have been set up at the state and district levels. This setup may still go to the grass-roots upto the Block and local community levels. This may, however be stated that a programme of this magnitude cannot be implemented by a single Ministry of

Education. Therefore, every effort has to be made to involve other ministries and departments. It would be necessary for such ministries and departments to set apart within their sectoral budgets funds for the Programme. In any case the state Governments have to play the key-role, and the main responsibility for actual implementation would be with the States. The U.G.C. has also come forward for carrying on the work of the NAEP.

(v) Agencies of Implementation

The Policy Statement makes reference to various agencies to be deployed for organisation of instructional arrangements and to share responsibility with the Government. In the implementation of the NAEP full utilisation has to be made of the voluntary agencies, youths and students, teachers, social workers, ex- servicemen and other retired persons, workers' organisations and field level government and other functionaries. Besides, it is also proposed to seek cooperation from all the other agencies engaged in the task of development. The very fact of emphasis on diversity and flexibility would throw greater responsibility on voluntary agencies.

(vi) Financing the Programme

The total allocation proposed for the Programme is Rs. 200 crores or 10% of the total Plan outlay as against 18 crores of about 1% during the Fifth Plan. It may however be pointed out that this is only one source of funds in a Programme in which multiple agencies are expected to participate and which will, therefore be funded from multiple sources. For instance, the different employer groups and project authorities might finance their own adult education programmes. The requirement of funds for tribals or agricultural workers and farmers or industrial workers might be financed out of their respective budgets. International bodies like UNESCO can also come forward as and when approached as the frontiers of poverty and illiteracy go far beyond the national limitations.

It has been worked out that financial requirements of a Project with 10 adult education centres would be Rs. 14,000. This amount is to cover the emoluments to a part-time supervisor, out-pocket allowance to the instructor as well as the learners.

The NAEP: A Resume

A brief description of the National Adult Education Programme as given above throws light on the fact that adult education has been taken up on such a vast scale for the first time in the educational history of this country. A massive programme in this respect, if implemented sincerely, is going to make its own contribution in the social-economic and cultural life of the nation. It is a fact that many previous attempts at organising literacy programmes including the selective programmes of Farmer's Functional Literacy, have resulted in failure mainly due to lack of flexibility, appropriate training for instructors, supervisors and other functionaries. It is therefore crucial for the NAEP not to repeat the mistake of the past and make adequate arrangements for the same.

Then identification of the individuals and groups of individuals to benefited from such a programme has to be made. It is needless to emphasise that this could not be done in haste and to limit the entire programme within the four walls of a single five year plan may not be sufficient for its proper implement.

During a period of years to make literate a vast mass of illiterate, ignorant and poor humanity suffering from innumerable handicaps covering 100 million souls may indeed be highly exciting as well as challenging.

It may however be asserted that as formulated on paper with all the aspects of the scheme clearly defined and planned, it makes a very good model. But the crux of the problem lies in its actual implementation. It may further be stated that so far the progress made is extremely tardy. Some of the states have done practically nothing towards taking even the initial steps, while others have their own fears about the wisdom of the plan. Doubts have also been expressed mainly in political circles about the very motive of launching this programme. It has, for instance, been suspected that certain groups or organisations are being strengthened with public money in the name of adult education. Whether right or wrong, such impressions are highly disastrous for the success of the scheme.

Further, the scheme has also been criticised for the waste of money mainly by the genuine or fictitious so-called voluntary agencies. It has been a misfortune of this country that even in the past the huge amounts spent in the realm of adult or social education have rarely been utilised fruitfully.

Through diverting its meagre resources on educating the older generation the government it depriving the children and the younger generation of opportunity even for elementary education. It is indeed a fact that so far we have failed to achieve the targets of universal elementary education, and unless the fountains of future illiteracy by providing universal elementary education are not plugged, it is impossible to eradicate education illiteracy altogether. But this fact should not sound too much pessimistic and must not dampen national efforts for adult education.

Summing Up

It is needless to say that in view of the monstrous illiteracy prevalent in the country, the efforts directed so far its eradication are quite far from being adequate. In this country, the scope of the problem of adult education is not limited only to the spread of literacy but it should include higher objective of making the lives of male and female adults richer and fuller. Moreover, there is need for such colleges as might provide facilities of higher education to those educated adults who, owing to one reason or the other, had been compelled to discontinue academic career.

Moreover, there is no an urgent need of increased number of libraries and reading centres for the purpose of keeping the taste and knowledge of adults alive. In addition to that, there are certain other needs which require immediate fulfilment for the sake of providing greater impetus to the movement of adult education. In short, they are change in mental outlook of the educated class, creation of the noble sentiments of constructive social service in their minds and hearts, forsaking a life of ease and luxury by political leaders in order to enter the field of real social service, change in the bureaucratic outlook of Government servants and concentration of their energy and attention on the promotion of the general good of society, and lastly, provision of funds in large quantity etc. In the end, we can subscribe to the views of Lenin who observes that the liquidation of illiteracy is not a political problem; it is a condition without which it is impossible to speak of politics. An illiterate man is outside of politics, and before he can be brought in, he must first be taught the alphabet.

12

Higher Education and the UGC in India

The higher education system has many issues of concern at present, like financing and management including access, equity and relevance, reorientation of programmes by laying emphasis on health consciousness, values and ethics and quality of higher education together with the assessment of institutions and their accreditation. These issues are important for the country, as it is now engaged in the use of higher education as a powerful tool to build a 21st Century knowledge-based information society.

Accepting the above and the basic fact, that the Universities have to perform multiple roles, like creating new knowledge, acquiring new capabilities and producing an intelligent human resource pool, through challenging teaching, research and extension activities so as to balance both the need and the demand, the University Grants commission (UGC) had initiated nation wise discussion on the said issues during its *Golden Jubilee Year, 2003.* Eleven Universities located in different regions of the were assigned the task of conducting Seminars on identified topics in the above areas, during Aug-Nov., 2003 and come out with their Reports and Recommendations.

It is very appropriate here to reproduce some deliberations in this regard.

An Editorial Committee was constituted by UGC to consider the outcome of these Seminars and compile them suitably so that an appropriate publication can be brought out for the use of UGC, higher education planners and the University system itself. The following discussion will put ample light on higher education and role of UGC in India.

Executive Summary

The University Grants Commission, as a part of its Golden Jubilee Celebrations, entrusted Eleven Universities located in different regions of the country to organize Seminars on topical subjects, addressing different *issues and concerns of higher education* in India. The Organizers of the Seminars were specifically requested to bring out the important recommendations arising out of the deliberations in the Seminars leading to *new directions in higher education* in the country.

The Seminar topics have been suitably categorized and presented in three Sections:

1) Management of Higher Education;
2) Reorientation of Higher Education and
3) Quality Assurance in Higher Education.

Issues of Public/Private Partnership, Governance, Access and Equity as well as Policy Planning for Export under WTO and GATT regime and Economics of Higher Education have been addressed in Section I, whereas Health Consciousness, Physical Fitness, Professional Ethics, Value Education and Evaluation / Assessment Systems have been focussed in Section II. The most important issue of Sustaining Quality in Higher Education through periodic Assessment and Accreditation of institutions has been highlighted in Section III.

The new challenge before the country at the beginning of the twenty first century is to become a developed society by the year 2020, which requires that not only a vibrant economy driven by knowledge has to be ushered in soon, but also a new society where justice and human values prevail has to be created. Moreover, challenges in higher education are no longer only nation centric. They have already attained global dimensions, particularly after trade in services has been brought under the purview of the WTO regime. With the explosive growth of knowledge in the past century and with the development of handy tools of information and communication technologies as well as of other scientific innovations, competition has become a hallmark of growth all over the World. As a result, knowledge is not only going to be the driver of Indian economy, but also, it is going to permeate into all the strata of Indian society for a better quality of life and living conditions. Therefore, India has to rise to the occasion urgently and reorient its higher education system to be vibrant, competitive, meaningful and purposeful, Besides, there is absolutely no substitute to quality of higher education, although the country has been faced for a long time with the serious problem of meeting the quantity needs of our society. It is, therefore, essential that a careful balancing of the two is given priority to meet the twin requirements of the society in the foreseeable future.

This publication gives highlights of the deliberations of the UGC Golden Jubilee Seminars organized at Eleven Universities in the country during August-November 2003, focussing on their specific recommendations for charting new directions in higher education in India. It is hoped that the stakeholders of higher education all over the country, will receive this publication with all the seriousness it deserves and become partners in creating a Higher Education System for the country, comparable to the best in the World.

I. Management of Higher Education

The Indian higher education system is one of the largest such systems in the World. It is estimated that during the X Five Year Plan period (2002-07), there will be a tremendous pressure of numbers on this system and a large number of additional students will be knocking at the doors of higher education institutions in the country. There are also new challenges of management and regulation being faced by these institutions, which require serious attention, both at the institutions in the public sector and also those in the private sector now growing at a fast pace. As a result, the old structures of management established in pre-independent India and working during most of the twentieth century are now required to undergo drastic changes. Besides, the demands of the society for equity and accommodation cannot be neglected any more.

The new regime under WTO where competence is the cardinal principle of success in international operations has made it abundantly clear that the country should exploit its excellent potential in higher education and training facilities and prepare itself to export the Indian brand of education to foreign countries. Policy planning and evolving strategies for this task are somewhat new for the country. But, this is an opportunity which cannot be missed by India, as it offers interesting possibilities for strengthening of the nation's talent and resourcefulness.

The following five sub-sections, cover important aspects of the deliberations, recommendations and action plans of UGC Golden Jubilee Seminars organized at different Universities in the country:

- Public/Private Partnership in Higher Education, at University of Calicut, Kozhikode, Kerala;
- Governance of higher Education, at University of Jammu, Jammu, J&K;
- Access and Equity in Higher Education, at G.C.D. University, Bilaspur, Chattisgarh;
- Export of Higher Education, at J.N.V. University, Jodhpur, Rajasthan and
- Policy Planning for Higher Education under WTO

and GATT regimes at North Bengal University, Darjeeling, West-Bengal.

— Economics of Higher Education, at N. E. Hill University, Shillong, Meghalaya.

1.1. Public/Private Partnership

Indian higher education system has undergone massive expansion in post-independent India with a national resolve to establish several Universities, Technical Institutes, Research Institutions and Professional / Non-professional Colleges all over the country to generate and disseminate knowledge coupled with the noble intention of providing easy access to higher education to the common Indian. The Public initiatives played a dominant and controlling role in this phase. Most of the Universities were Public institutions with powers to regulate academic activities on their campuses as well as in their areas of jurisdiction through the affiliating system. Even the private institutions enjoyed large-scale financial support in the form of grants from the public exchequer. Private funds as well as individuals played key roles in the cause of higher education.

With the public funding being no more in a position to take-up the challenging task of expansion and diversification of the higher education system in the country to meet the continuously growing demands at present, there is little option other than bringing in private initiatives in a massive way to meet the various challenges. The deregulating mechanism of controls started with the granting of "Autonomous Status" to identified Colleges in the 1970s.. Some of these Colleges have graduated further to receive the "Deemed to be University" status in later years. Now, the country is on the threshold of the establishment of Private Universities in different States. These and related issues figured prominently in the discussions at this Seminar, whose recommendations are as follows:

1.1.1. *Recommendations*

1. It is the primary responsibility of the State to provide the eligible with good quality higher education at reasonable cost. There shall be no withdrawal of the State from this responsibility. In fact, the investment in this area by the State shall be stepped-up to 3% of the GDP. This is essential for the intellectual strength of the State to address equity concerns.
2. A huge dedicated fund say, *National Human Resource Development Fund,* to the tune of at least one- percent of the GDP, may be created to tackle the equity problems. It shall be the accepted principle that *'no talented person shall be denied access to higher education opportunities on the grounds of economic and social backwardness'*. This fund may be dedicated to offer direct financial support in the form of scholarships, partial financial assistance and educational loans to students directly, based on the criteria of talent and financial and social backwardness. A well-designed mechanism to spot talents in different disciplines of knowledge is needed for this purpose. Further, foolproof criteria to determine financial or any other social backwardness is required.
3. Taxing the individuals, who had the benefit of the State resources in the past for their education, and the industries, which are likely to derive advantage from good human resources, are the options for creating such a fund. While it is difficult to arrive at an ideal solution to the equity problems, the absence of a credible and efficient method of addressing these problems will lead to lowering of the quality of human ware and large-scale discontent. The society may be the ultimate looser.
4. Industries may be encouraged to be partners with educational institutions directly for the development

of human resources dedicated to their interests. This could happen in the areas of creating infrastructure, faculty sharing and direct support with funds. The UGC may set-up a *High Power Committee* to explore these possibilities and to workout the modalities for such a partnership.

5. The industries belonging to a specific discipline or related disciplines shall be encouraged to establish state of the art Research and Training centres to develop the necessary specialized man power. Automobile industry is a case point. Existing Public and Private Institutions and possible new Institutions may generate ample provisions for partnerships in this regard. A Committee shall work out the modalities and norms for this.
6. The areas not capable of attracting private funds shall be supported sufficiently well from public funds. This, as indicated earlier, is essential for the balanced intellectual growth of the society.
7. Industries and individuals may be encouraged to channel a percentage of their profits to the higher education sector, with no strings attached to such contributions. Viable incentives may be offered for attracting such investments from the private resources. A Committee may work out the modalities.
8. Strong quality control measures to assure performance above an acceptable benchmark is essential for the institutions. We are at the moment weak in this regard. The various rating agencies shall evolve scientific, transparent and consistent benchmarking techniques for this purpose. A regulatory system to ensure compliance to the set bench marking is needed with sufficient powers to close down non-complying institutions is a need of the hour. The Higher Education Policy needs to

incorporate such features in it in the interest of the nation.

9. A Total Quality Management for courses offered, monitoring the achievement of the students at all stages of the course, shall be introduced at all higher education institutions.
10. An accreditation system for individuals in various disciplines may be thought of. Indeed, GATE and NET examinations with limited objectives are forerunners of such a system. The performance of students in such examinations may be made an important parameter for the accreditation of the institution.
11. The idea of allowing students to do Diploma or Certificate courses side by side with their Degrees, recently put forward by the UGC, is a welcome step towards empowering the students to take-up work soon after their Degree courses. This is an area where private initiatives can come up to augment the activities of the Colleges. The Colleges can develop in-house faculty and other facilities for this purpose and make these facilities available at a reasonable cost. Such a measure will turn around many Colleges from the non-performing class to the performing class. There shall be a mechanism to accredit these courses and facilities to ensure quality. This is an area where public/private partnership has a creative role to play.
12. It is important to realize that we live in a fast changing world, dictated by the developments in technology. Quick access to information has made knowledge creation fast, and the multiplier effect has made it even explosive. It is increasingly difficult to anticipate changes and respond to them with creative purpose. Designing courses with relevance to the future and

developing the necessary manpower to deliver them is a challenging task. All this calls for a team of professionals in different areas to come together to develop proactive strategies for higher education to meet the future demands. A Strategy Planning Body and an Institution to design and develop futuristic courses for transferring them to the Universities and Colleges may be created.

13. Good Faculty is a must for any higher education institution aspiring for Quality. It is high time that an Indian Higher Educational Service, along the lines of the IAS, is formed. This has the advantage of quality control of the teaching faculty for higher education. A new Human Resource Development Policy shall be evolved to facilitate this. This could assure that there is continuous infusion of young blood in to the teaching cadre; which is not happening at the moment. With some restrictions on faculty appointments, the present evil of inbreeding can be eliminated. The inbreeding has destroyed many departments at Indian Universities.

14. Private Universities are a reality now and, as such, strong regulatory mechanisms are to be put in place immediately to monitor and control their activities with the objective of ensuring quality and social accountability. Higher education is a Public Good and cannot be left to the market forces to control. Those who venture investment in this area shall be properly scrutinized. Those with commercial interests dominating over the interests and ethics of higher education shall be eliminated.

15. The present archaic administrative practices need a thorough reform. A healthy Public/Private partnership can do much in this regard by way of exchanging good practices. A management system, lean but professional, making use of modern

communication and information technologies is required to facilitate quality higher education.

16. According autonomous status to all performing institutions will facilitate rapid development of efficient and state of the art higher education institutions.
17. There shall be a dominant role for genuine academics in the governing structure of higher education institutions. The proposed regulatory mechanism shall have instruments to ensure this.

1.2. Governance

It has been observed that policy framework is carefully planned at the level of the Planning Commission, Ministry of Human Resource Development and University Grants Commission. However, the policies are not fully implemented mostly because of faulty management of the institutions of higher education. The administrative structure of the Universities, which was devised in the pre-independence period seems to be still continuing. The new challenges facing the system of higher education in the country cannot be met without a total overhaul of the structure of management of higher education institutions. This has become all the more necessary because of globalization, which requires talent, competence, drive, initiative and innovation at several levels. This cannot be achieved without overhauling the administrative set up of Universities/Institutions. Therefore *Governance of Higher Education* was deliberated at length at this Seminar, the main recommendations of which are summarized below.

1.2.1. *Recommendations*

1. The Governmental control in the Universities must be reduced, so that the University autonomy and accountability are strengthened and academic decisions are taken on merit.

2. New methods and procedures of financial regulations should be devised and direct interference of the finance department in the financial management of Universities, which is counter productive should be stopped.
3. As the Colleges are the feeding sources of the Universities, a better coordination in their working and activities is very much required. The participation of the teaching faculty in through a democratic process should be ensured.
4. Complete transparency should be maintained in the working of Executive/ Academic Bodies and other Governing Councils of the Universities.

   There is an urgency to review the University Acts in different States and revise the same in the light of the new requirements and the challenges being faced by the Universities.. New technologies of information and communication should be utilized for obtaining administrative efficiency.
5. Higher Education should be developed as an infrastructure for social and economic growth of the Country.
6. Students involvement in the area of University/ College governance should be encouraged.
7. Political interference in the appointment of University teachers and administrators should be totally stopped..

1.3. Access and Equity

Today the world economy is experiencing an unprecedented change. New developments in science and technology, media revaluation and internationalization of education and the ever expanding competitive environment are revolutionizing the education scene. A paradigm shift has been noticed in higher education now a days, from 'national education' to 'global education', from 'one time education for a few' to 'life long education for all', from 'teacher- centric education' to 'learner centric education'. These changes make new demands and pose fresh challenges to the established education systems and practices in the country. Because of interdependence and integration of world economy in recent years, the Indian higher education system has a new rôle and a challenge to provide to the nation and the world at large, skilled human power at all levels, having breadth of knowledge and confidence to effectively confront the social and economic realities.

It is worth noting that while India has the second largest system of higher education, next only to USA, the total number of students hardly represent 6 percent of the relevant age group, i.e., 18-23, which is much below the average of developed countries, which is about 47%. Thus, access, equity, accountability and quality should form the four guiding principles, while planning for higher education development in India in the twenty-first century.

It is true that enhancing social access to higher education is still important in the country. But, the major challenge before the Indian higher education system is to bring equity in quality of education across the length and breadth of the country. This is more close to the heart of students in rural, semi urban and urban areas, because they also wish to be able to participate in the new economic revolution.

Several social, economic and political reasons seem to act as constraints to access and equity in higher education in India. Poverty leads to high drop- out rates even at primary, middle and secondary school levels. Lower status of women, lack of easy access, lack of implementation of existing programmes, inadequate utilization of resources, absence of political will and inadequacies in coordinated actions across all equity fronts within institutions seem to be the other reason. Financial constrains also often form a significant factor in advancing equity. These and related issues in *Equity and Access of Higher Education* formed the subject matter of this Seminar, whose major recommendations are as follows:

1.3.1. *Recommendations*

1. Strategies for higher education should be set within an educational chain extending from early childhood to post- graduate education to career advancement. Improving the interrelationship of all stages and levels of education should be a long - term policy goal.
2. Rural, urban and gender disparities must be kept in mind by policy makers in planning and implementing the higher education system.
3. While quantity is important, say achieving, double digit percentage for higher education, quality is paramount. Higher education should continue to be subsidized by the Government in an adequate manner. For improving the quality in education the role of public sector should be enhanced.
4. While the Western models of higher education should be suitably adopted, the education planners/ implementers and the institutions should devise and develop indigenous ones.
5. A liberal milieu in the Indian Universities must be reconstructed. Diversity of opinion and critique of society and its processes need to be encouraged.
6. The appointment of bureaucrats, police officers/ generals as Vice Chancellors and Registrars must be avoided as far as possible
7. Policies of higher education should be designed to strengthen indigenous research agenda.
8. One reform that is urgently needed is the right to information in the institutions of higher learning. Transparency in the functioning at all levels is required so that those committing wrong are deterred.

9. It is recommended that the method of selection of Vice Chancellors must be changed urgently, to make them accountable to the academic community and not to the political or bureaucratic bosses.
10. Policies of our country based on simplicity and sharing of facilities within and across institutions must be established and encouraged.
11. The WTO pushing the trade in services will have far reaching consequences in India, particularly for the remote areas and poorer sections of the Society. Therefore, the World Bank, WTO and GATT policies on higher education need serious consideration, National interests must be safe guarded. And, the opportunities for the deprived and under privileged people and regions must be ensured
12. There have been significant changes recently in the policies on financing of Universities in India affecting the pattern of financing and expenditure in the Universities. Given the increasing importance of higher education, it is important that the State continues to take major responsibility of financing the Universities. All other sources of income , including fees should be viewed only as peripheral. It is to be noted that reliance on students' fees has its own limitation.
13. Increasing reliance on the generation of internal revenues through consultancy and interaction with industry may produce imbalances in the Universities across various disciplines of study. So, efforts for the mobilization of resources have to be made extremely cautiously. Keeping in view our concerns of equity, efficiency and excellence in University education. Hence, the best method of financing of the Universities may still be by the State.
14. Universities have to attempt seriously to improve the pattern of allocation of resources between various

activities and items of expenditure. Core academic activities should obviously receive top priority.

15. At the Universities, students' welfare, particularly scholarships, stipends etc., should be given due importance. Expenditure on administration and other miscellaneous activities needs to be rationalized.
16. New models for higher education including the following aspects need to be created and adopted in the country: (a) extended traditional Universities, (b) technology based Universities, and (c) corporate Universities.

1.4. Policy Planning for Export

Increasing economic integration across the World over the past decade has cast tumultuous impact on all the areas supporting human life in the developing countries, which constitutes about 80% of the work force. The so-called structural adjustments in national policies and the new international economic order have brought about severe stresses never perceived before. There are exhortations to the policy planners of higher education emanating from GATT regulations made under WTO formulation e.g. withdrawal of subsidies, reduced control of the State, larger privatization and access to corporate players, designing of courses to meet the human resource needs of the markets in the changed scenario, and reliance on self-financing type management. There are also obligations to allow free import of higher education as a service commodity from developed nations in the form of cross-border supply, consumption abroad etc. The cumulative effect of all these factors and the prevailing competitive environment have hustled the morale, confidence and commitment of the University community in general, even inducing trepidation.

Improving the low level of enrolment 6% in the 18-23

age group) ratio, ensuring better equity, access, sound and realistic man-power planning, faster growth of skilled human resource for a self-reliant course of economic development and universalization of basic education are the other major challenges.

In such a skewed and gruelling perspective, the University academics and administrators, are confronted with so many challenges calling for knee-jerk response and pro-active approaches to management of institutions of higher education with a high level of professionalism, competence and quality assurance. They are duty bound to tide over the challenges facing the institutions and deliver quality goods and services to the customers and users without any opacity, obsession or prejudice. Outline of the strategies, the imperative scope of expansion, dimensions of diversification, potentials for both short- and long-term planning and modalities of placid administrative processes warranted in the contemporary ambience, but in the changed context, have been discussed by experts and researchers.

There was a consensus that without compromising the national ethos of equity and access to higher education to all the intending learners at reasonable cost and to the socially disadvantaged ones at subsidized levels, higher education institutions in India must boost their activities to provide diversified academic products and services of high quality and with a strong market orientation. These issues and concerns were the focus of attention at these two Seminars, whose main recommendations are outlined below.

1.4.1. *Recommendations*

1. Most of the areas identified for export of higher education are directly concerned with industries. Therefore, Central and State Governments should introduce a range of programmes and incentives designed specially to improve the links between Universities and Industry.

2. The Universities and National Institutes of higher Learning should design their courses in collaboration with industry and such courses be updated regularly, e.g., every year, according to need.
3. There should be uniformity, as far as possible, in the standards of the courses, academic calendar and the examination system of Universities.
4. To provide a broad choice of courses, credit system should be introduced in the Universities.
5. Libraries should be fully equipped with the latest books, journals and periodicals
6. Laboratories should be updated and obsolescence in equipment/facilities should be removed on a regular basis.
7. Working facilities and workload of teachers should be as per the international norms.
8. Teachers should be encouraged to attend various Conventions, Conferences, Seminars, Workshops in their disciplines to update their subject know how.
9. As per need, hostel facilities should be developed for foreign students in the Universities. And a Foreign Students' Advisor's Office should be created to look after the foreign students in a proper way.
10. There should be regular monitoring and evaluation of teaching and research in the Universities and other Institutions of higher learning . A Monitoring & Evaluation (M & E) Unit should be set-up at State level preferably attached to Chancellor's Office; and for its effective functioning, a Statistical Cell should be set-up in each University in the State, under the over all supervision of the M & E Unit.
11. Necessary steps should be taken to attract bright students after graduation/post graduation to the teaching profession.

12. Campuses of top Indian Universities and other premier institutions should be established in the target countries with the permission of the concerned Governments.
13. A tie-up with a foreign institution of higher education could also be a possible way by which the Indian institutions of higher education can make entry into the target markets.
14. Franchising was also suggested by the speakers as one of the modes of entry into foreign countries. The Indian institution could offer our educational system and the operational details to a foreign institution, allowing the use of its name in exchange of an agreed fee. But, this requires careful monitoring and follow up.
15. E-Learning appears to be a fast emerging mode of global entry at the present time. The Universities and other Institutions of higher education can design their web sites for offering online education worldwide.
16. Deputing teachers of Indian Institutions to different Universities abroad on contractual basis with the built-in condition of introducing and operating the Indian higher education system there, is also a likely mode of entry into the foreign market. This should be given due consideration.
17. Other desirable initiatives for export of higher education include:
    - Developing educational products of new models based on flexibility and learner's choice;
    - Preparing students for the knowledge society;
    - Providing methods and styles of working for life-long learning;
    - Arranging facilities for E-learning and distance learning;

- — Ensuring total quality management in the higher education system;
- — Catering to the changing market demands and churn out adaptable work force, instead of providing them scope for narrow specialization.

1.5. Economics of Higher Education

Access to higher education needs to be widened in the country, both within the formal system and through other effective innovative measures, such as a truly *open* system and networking of Universities. It is now imperative on the part of Indian Universities to generate their own resources to a large extent. This could be done through several methods, like raising tuition fee and collecting capitation fee, both of which having severe limitations; and others like, launching courses for foreign students, obtaining donations from philanthropists, etc., which have a good potential.

In the globalized World, the State-protected educational system cannot withstand the pressure without making itself competitive. There seem to be four reasons why new policy initiatives should be taken by the Government in this connection. They are : (i) that the economic returns of primary education far exceed the returns of higher education; (ii) that the private returns on higher education far exceed the social returns; (iii) that the State funding for higher education is insufficient in countries like India; and (iv) that since private sector benefits the most from higher education, it is only just that it should make a decisive contribution. Whether or not one accepts the Government's rationale, new strategies need to be developed for the survival and well being of the higher education system in the present scenario.

Taking the problem of resource crunch in higher education at face value, some alternative ways were considered at this Seminar to combat the present situation, such as: research grants from industries, donations for admissions etc. which were found to be inadequate. It was observed that an organized structure for higher-educational fund raising and creating a culture of giving are the only possible solutions. Major recommendations of this Seminar are summarized below.

1.5.1. Recommendations

1. Raising of student fees to some extent, in consultation with student bodies and parents' organizations.
2. Charging capitation fees and obtaining donations.
3. Launching lucrative and specific courses for foreign students.
4. Developing philanthropy and cultivating an organized culture of giving.
5. Promoting income tax inducement for obtaining donations..
6. Reorientation of educational programmes.
7. Linking education with employment.
8. Launching industry linked human resource development programmes.
9. Reorientation of the management system of Colleges and Universities.
10. Better allocation/utilization of the resources already available
11. Encouraging accountability at various levels of decision making.
12. Obtaining research grants from industries
13. Reorganization of the educational system in the country in line with the changes.
14. Providing professional and vocational education and preparation of students for this.
15. Making general education costlier and less widely available than vocational education as to induce more students to take up the latter.

16. Developing innovative educational programmes/ products, having high potential for raising resources, making use of the institutional autonomy.
17. Minimizing wastage and under utilization of facilities.
18. Harnessing competitive advantages.
19. Harnessing the institution's locational advantages.
20. Promotion of publication activities and printing College/University stationery.
21. Encouraging taking up national/international and Government funded R&D projects.
22. Using marketing strategies to attract funded projects from industry and other sources.
23. Setting up Alumni Associations, to benefit from alumni contacts/contributions.
24. Encouraging knowledge – based consultancy services at the institutions.
25. Interrelating with industry; some suggestions for which are:
    - Undergraduate industry-related courses should be organized with care, exposing the students to industry problems and requirements;
    - Undergraduate students should take up industry-related projects and come out with viable solutions;
    - Industry personnel should be invited for extension lectures;
    - Industry personnel should be associated in curriculum development;
    - Faculty should visit industries and get acquainted with current problems;
    - Better contact with alumni to evaluate teaching methodologies and new demands;

— Vocationalization of Degree programmes;

— Establishing Liaison Cell for getting feedback from industries;

— Introducing entrepreneurship development programmes for students;

26. Fixing of minimum intake for a course and closing it if the intake is low.
27. Reducing manpower costs based on a formula developed by each University.
28. Encouraging optimum utilization of infrastructure and equipment.
29. Introducing students' loan scheme.
30. Providing a rational student-teacher ratio.
31. Levying education cess from users of technical manpower.
32. Encouraging the application of ICT in all processes at the institutions..
33. Networking the systems for efficient management.
34. Setting up cost effective institutions, e.g., Open-Universities, Community Colleges;
35. Taking up productive assignments from the Government.
36. Encouraging a policy of rewarding merit in the institutions.
37. Implementing a differential fee structure for different courses.
38. Developing nursery for vegetables, fruit trees, herbs and ornamental plants.
39. Providing pay-and-use internet connection to campus residents.
40. Encouraging donations by large companies
41. Introducing 'earn while you learn' scheme for needy students.

42. Starting new initiatives in a discipline, like "English for Special Purposes Course".
43. Government to make initial investments to make institutions globally competitive.
44. Funding liberal education by the State and skill oriented education by private sector.
45. Locally relevant higher education to be imparted through vocational courses..
46. Distinction be made between teaching/research Universities to enhance their roles.
47. Sensitizing the students' community regarding raising of resources for Universities.
48. Biodiversity being vital in areas like NE, there could be a University for this..
49. Colleges to assess local needs and frame their own syllabi/courses flexibly.
50. Introducing a scheme for rewards/punishments to ensure accountability work.

II. Reorientation of Higher Education

Educational opportunities and traditions that Indian Universities have built up, since independence have been able to produce graduates, capable only of pursuing limited careers, but, in the new globally competitive environment that is emerging in the country, the Indian student is now required to develop a multifaceted personality to cope up with the rapid changes in the world at large. This calls for the development of body, mind and spirit, through the educational processes in the institutions of higher education. *Health consciousness and physical fitness* for a healthy body should be an essential part of the University culture. But, a healthy body alone cannot be attained and maintained without a healthy mind. Therefore *value education* becomes a desirable moral necessity for meeting the challenges of the contemporary World. Professional competence is of little value if professional ethics are forgotten. Similarly, brilliance is of no use if it is employed for anti social activities. In order to achieve all these ends effectively one has to see that the processes of education are properly regulated in terms of assessment and evaluation of learning. A close interaction between the teachers and the students in the evaluation of the progress of learning is desirable, so that teaching-learning process is not superficial.

The following three sub-sections included in this Section, cover important aspects of the discussions, recommendations and action plans of UGC Golden Jubilee Seminars held at different Universities in the country, as listed below:

— Physical Fitness/Health Consciousness/Yoga Studies, at Gulbarga University, Gulbarga, Karnataka;

— Promotion of Value Education and Ethics, at SSS Institute of Higher Learning, Prasanthinilayam, Andhra Pradesh.

— Examination Reforms at M. S. University of Baroda, Vadodara, Gujarat.

2.1. Health Consciousness and Physical Fitness

Physical fitness and sports are two sides of the same coin and are mutually dependent on each other. As the famous dictum goes, mind is the key to man and eyes cannot see what mind cannot perceive. The relationship between mind and body has been acknowledged scientifically. It is generally believed that a healthy body has a healthy mind; but it could be the other way around also i.e. a healthy mind has a healthy body. However, this requires appropriate training.

Present day education is largely academic. Realistically, this orientation needs to be changed for a balanced development through inculcating health conscious amongst students. This includes the development at physical, mental and social levels. With the increasing emphasis on academics in the World of employment and elsewhere and the rapid advances in science and technology all over the World, parental pressure has been driving academic training at the cost of health and physical fitness of the youth .It is in this context that there is now an urgency to lay a strong foundation and strengthen physical education and sports programmes in the higher education institutions. This calls for the integration of physical education, sports, yoga and recreation activities in the higher education system for the overall good of the younger generation. These and related issues were deliberated at this Seminar and its major recommendations are given below.

2.1.1. *Recommendations*

1. At present Physical Education is the only course taught at Schools and Colleges. It is important new subjects like, Health Management, Fitness Management and Sports Marketing are included in the curriculum, preferably as. core/specialization subjects at professional preparation courses.
2. Olympics Education may be included from the elementary/ secondary level to higher secondary level of education to develop sports awareness among the children.
3. Raising the standard of professional preparation courses in physical education and sports sciences is an urgent requirement in order to produce competent physical education teachers. This calls for institutions offering physical education courses to take effective measures in attracting students with sports background and achievements. There is need for counselling centres for providing guidance to the students aspiring to take up physical education as a career.

4. Standardised physical fitness testing procedures should be applied on a uniform basis at the professional Colleges at the entry level. Besides, there is a need for restructuring professional programmes to update the courses in the field of physical education and sports so as to provide opportunities for the physical educators to adopt the emerging trends.
5. Physical education programmes need to strengthen the supervisory set up at the School system level to make the existing programmes to be implemented in a more effective manner.
6. Parent-Teacher Associations at the Schools should find ways and means to strengthen/ popularise the physical education programmes at each School by involving the entire students' population in the sports activities.
7. Physical education programmes should also include yoga and meditation in order to create a positive attitude among the students so as to achieve success in life and make physical education more meaningful and relevant in terms of education for life. All the Universities may be encouraged to establish facilities for education/training in yoga and meditation.
8. All the agencies working in the field of sports should take immediate measures to check the menace of drug abuse in sports and create an awareness on its ill effects..
9. It would be desirable to offer orientation programmes covering sports medicine, sports nutrition, sports psychology and other allied subjects to all physical education teachers to update their professional knowledge and skills.
10. The development of fitness culture among University youth has to be given due priority. In this direction,

Physical Fitness Centres need be established at all the Universities to provide fitness programmes for University teachers, students, and employees. These Centres may also conduct special fitness programmes at various levels during holidays and vacations. Necessary financial allocation may be provided in the University budget and UGC may also consider suitable grants in this regard. *'Fitness for all'* may be accepted as a fundamental need in the University system in India.

2.2. *Professional Ethics and Value Education*

The rapid developments in science and technology and the challenges of globalization are posing additional challenges to the education system in the country. This is also the time when parental care to the children is on the wane. The adverse effects of the media on the mental development and moral values of the younger generation are being felt increasingly in all spheres of life. Gross consumerism has distorted the outlook of persons into one of equating possessions with richness. Exploitation of natural resources is proceeding without reference to sustainability. The hiatus between the rich and the poor is getting wider. While the education system needs to keep pace with the scientific and technological developments in terms of building the skills and knowledge, it also needs to address the more fundamental issues of the social and moral consequences of such unregulated activities. In this context, there is now a growing demand to lay greater emphasis on education to inculcate, nurture and develop values, particularly among the youth of the country. Major recommendations of this seminar are given below:

2.2.1. *Recommendations*

1. The need of the hour is to inculcate human values in the University students, like quest for peace, adherence to truth and right conduct, non-violence,

compassion, tolerance, love for all living beings, respect for the Motherland and the glory of its culture and traditions, in order to promote *societal* concern and responsible citizenship; so that such an effort is in the interest of the students, society and the nation. The UGC may take up the nodal responsibility for this, in pursuance of its X Plan Policy document.

2. It is entirely feasible to inculcate 'values' in the students at the tertiary level, and there are several institutions in the country where such value-based education is imparted with impressive results. Nowever, it requires sustained efforts to practice, absorb, and assimilate values. A Cell for Value Education may be established at the UGC to plan, implement and oversee this requirement. The UGC together with NAAC could play a crucial role in realizing this objective..
3. It is desirable that human values should permeate and form part of the teaching in all disciplines and subjects. Here again, the UGC can play an important role in spreading this message in the University system in the country.
4. The UGC may work towards evolving a syllabus for a compulsory paper of appropriate credits at the undergraduate level of all disciplines, to stress human values and the duties laid down in the constitution [Art. 51 – A], and the same may be suitably supported by the methodology and examination/evaluation criteria facilitating a learner-centric approach. A Committee of Value Education Experts may be constituted by the UGC for taking appropriate steps in this connection.
5. Alternately, the compulsory paper on "Environmental Science", recently introduced by UGC, may be suitably elaborated to bring forth environmental concerns in the backdrop of human

values. However, introducing an optional paper on this subject, with the possibility of giving some incentives for taking such papers may not be a wise step. .The UGC Committees of Experts on Value Education as well as on Environmental Science may consider this issue jointly and work out a suitable strategy in this regard.

6. The S.S.S. Institute of Higher Learning may be recognized by UGC as a "National Centre of Excellence for Value Education". At the same time, a few institutions having the potential for imparting value-based education may be identified by following the UGC scheme of 'Institutions of Excellence' and necessary support extended to them. The UGC may give due consideration to this recommendation.
7. .Recognizing the special role of teachers in this effort, it would be desirable to impart them the necessary skills and insights into value education by devising suitable orientation courses and extending support to institutions for imparting such training. This may be given due consideration by the UGC and effective steps taken to introduce these courses at identified Academic Staff Colleges. Also, NCTE could play a crucial role in preparing the school teachers to meet this requirement.
8. Human Values should be the guiding parameters for governance processes at higher education institutions. The University system may take note of this. Also, the UGC may consider taking suitable measures for disseminating this information in the higher education system.
9. .Due recognition should be given to the expanding socially relevant role of open education and to explore the methods of communicating and internalizing 'Human Values' among the students. Special attention should also be given to develop appropriate

study material for this on a priority basis through proper supportive measures .The UGC Expert committee on Value Education has a crucial role to play in this connection. Besides, the Distance Education Council and IGNOU could also play useful roles.

10. .It is also recommended that the evaluation criteria of institutions should be so spelt out as to give due weight to the inculcation of human values, and that the 'Healthy Practices' identified during the Assessment exercises be widely disseminated by NAAC for the benefit of other institutions. Both the UGC and the NAAC can play useful roles in this initiative.

2.3. Evaluation and Assessment Systems

During the last 50 years, higher education in India has made great strides leading to the Indian higher education system becoming one of the largest systems in the World. Unfortunately, it is the Indian experience that this expansion in quantity has overshadowed the quality of higher education. Lately, a chorus of criticism is heard from various well-meaning quarters about the deteriorating quality of higher education. It is well known that one of the important components of higher education is the manner in which students' academic performance is evaluated. A concerted debate has been going on to determine the best system of assessment to be followed by the Universities in the twenty first century . A great degree of diversity has been observed in terms of assessment and grading of the students in the University system at present.. It is desirable that a certain optimum degree of standardization in the examination system and in the assessment of students is put in place before grades are awarded to them. These and related issues were deliberated at length at this Seminar leading to a set of recommendations given below.

2.3.1. *Recommendations*

1. The Semester System should be preferred to the annual system in teaching and evaluation at the Indian Universities.
2. Continuous Internal Assessment should be given the attention it merits in the students' academic programmes at the Universities.
3. The Grading System with a linear 10-point scale and its equivalence in terms of percentage of marks should be followed uniformly across Universities and disciplines. However, the evaluation methodology may vary across disciplines / Institutions.
4. Pre-and Post-processes of examinations should be made transparent. i.e. the pattern of papers, evaluation methodology, disciplinary rules etc. should be properly documented and communicated to students well in advance.
5. Appropriate and effective feedback mechanism (e.g. returning corrected answer books to students, responding to students' queries on the evaluation procedure, etc.) should be established at all institutions.
6. Examination should be designed in such a way that at least some portion of it evaluations the students' insight into the subject.
7. In the continuous evaluation based on objective-type questions, measuring the higher mental ability of students should be adopted and ICT may be effectively used to set and evaluate such papers.
8. Serious efforts should be made in developing question banks by following rigorous scientific procedures across disciplines. If need be, regional level workshops may be organized for the purpose. Computerized database may be created in each discipline.

9. Proper orientation on assessment methods should be given to all the teachers, particularly to the newly appointed teachers. The Academic Staff Colleges set up by the UGC at different Universities may be assigned this task
10. A proper structure for Examination Reforms Units for the Universities should be evolved, supported by UGC to keep the nationwide evaluation processes at Universities under continuous scrutiny.
11. All the examination processes should be computerized and recent advances in ICT should be exploited to make the process automated and efficient.
12. As a part of the continuous evaluation process in the Visual Arts area, student's portfolio consisting of the work during the entire year should be assessed and given due weightage.
13. In the Performing Arts examinations, video/audio recordings should be made of the performances for being jointly evaluated by the Board of Examiners to bring in more objectivity in the evaluation.
14. A proper methodology should be evolved for product evaluation in professional courses.
15. Research on the desirability and relevance of existing examination patterns and improvements there on in any given institution should be encouraged and facilitated. Innovative practices related to examination reforms should be empirically tested and institutionalized.
16. The UGC may encourage Universities to organize Regional Level Experts' Workshops to look into various qualitative aspects of Examination Reforms, such as:
    - — Testing Creativity;
    - — Testing Application Aspects;

— Testing both Fundamental and In-depth knowledge;
— Continuous Evaluation Strategies.

III. Quality Assurance in Higher Education

In an environment of global competitiveness it is important that Indian products of the higher education institutions are as competent as graduates of any other country,. not only in their scholastic attainments, but also in terms of the value system and richness of their personality. Unless the quality and standard of Indian higher education institutions is enhanced zealously and sustained at a high level through innovation, creativity and regular monitoring, it seems to be difficult for the Indian academics/professionals to compete in the World scene.

This calls for suitable assessment and accreditation mechanisms to be available in the country to ensure the quality and standard of the academic/training programmes at higher educational institutions. The assessment has to be continuous and the process has to be transparent to gain the acceptance of the society at large.

The subsequent two sub-sections cover important aspects of the discussions, recommendations and action plans at the UGC Golden Jubilee Seminars organized at different Universities as given below:

- Sustaining Quality in Higher Education Institutions, at University of Allahabad , Allahabad, U.P.
- How to complete the first cycle of assessment and accreditation, at Punjab University, Chandigarh

3.1. Sustaining Quality

Quality has both absolute and relative connotations. The concept of absoluteness in quality props up the morale of the higher education system at the delivery end i.e.

institutional, and at the receiving end i.e. students. Quality dimensions seem to have two implications, i.e., functionality of the output and meeting the basic standards. Hence, the quality of a higher education system may be seen from the point of view of norms and standards, which may evolve depending on the need of the hour. In the 21st century, it is crucial to identify the relative norms for different components of a higher education system. The alternative dynamics for teacher preparation and the sustaining quality in teacher input, like: Curriculum design and development; Curricular practices vis-à-vis emerging principles of pedagogy; Evaluation of learners performance and progress vis-à-vis curriculum evaluation; and, Quality management practices become crucial. The quality of these components may also differ from institution to institution. Therefore, sharing of the experiences among institutions on quality issues may generate ideas for evolving norms and strategies for their quality assurance of management processes, curricular inputs and practices and the evaluation system as well.

Of late, various developments have been witnessed relating to quality assurance mainly through the intervention of information and communications technologies (ICT) in education, like networking of the open learning system with traditional Universities, interdisciplinary interactions at intra-institutional and inter-institutional levels, networking of institutions globally, data based management of higher education, changing the orientation of institutions by incorporating self financing in their financial management, assessment and accreditation of higher education institutions and creation of different statutory and regulatory bodies at the national level. These and related issues were discussed at length at this Seminar, whose main recommendations are given below.

3.1.1. *Recommendations*

1. Curriculum Planning and Management should be

studied in the perspective of knowledge management.

2. Integrated approach by involving experts from different fields with major focus on sharing of experiences in a holistic framework and having dialogues at different levels such as : at core committee level and at sub committee level. Multidisciplinary curriculum must be developed with a view to cater to the needs and fulfillment of expectations of learners, teachers parents, employers and society in general.
3. Decentralization must be encouraged with a broad frame work of University system.
4. Every University must have its own curriculum. There should not be any mechanism for central curriculum framework at higher education level. Context, specificity and inquiry oriented experience must be reflected in the curriculum. Learners' participation in the generation of knowledge must be the focus of constructiveist curriculum. Problem solving abilities must be developed through experimentation life-like situations.
5. Augmentation of Cognitive capital through the University curriculum will be the indicator of quality education.
6. Indegeneous knowledge system must be kept in mind while adopting scientific and technological developments as core components of University curriculum. Context specificity and global developments must be visualised with a holistic perspective.
7. Curriculum construction should transact in an authentic and real environment.
8. Curriculum transaction should involve social negotiation and mediation. Encourage group

activities and make optimum use of peer as resources of higher learning.

9. Knowledge and skills must be developed with a view to provide relevance and meaningfulness.
10. Learners involvement must be encouraged to link previous experience with present learning. The learner should have full opportunity to scrutinize the learning experiences.
11. The principles of self regulation, self mediation and self awareness on the part of learners must be reflected in curriculum transaction.
12. Teachers should plan a mentor's of guiding learners to learn instead of directing them or instructing them all the time.
13. Learners must have ample scope to formulate their own queries and have multiple interpretations of knowledge through self search and experiential learning.
14. During curriculum transaction learners should be assessed formatively on a continuous basis to create the basis for acquiring new experiences.

3.2. Assessment and Accreditation

The fact of the matter is that the Indian elite and middle classes have not cared for making education, what to say of higher education, accessible to the other sections of society. It is ironic that the beneficiaries of privileged access to institutions of higher learning are ever ready to persuade others to believe that the Indian education system has expanded beyond reasonable limits. The fact of the matter is that the system needs to be expanded to a much greater scale to serve the needs of the Indian youth..

Many institutions of higher education in the country are excellent in the sense that their infrastructure, resources, faculty, programmes of teaching and research are almost as good as the best in the advanced countries. But, the same cannot be said of the average institutions of higher education in the country. They do not come anywhere near the level of average institutions of higher education in the advanced countries. This vast gap in standards and facilities has been a cause of constant anxiety and concern to the policy planners of higher education in India..

The issue of accessibility to quality higher education needs to be addressed in the light of the vast economic and social disparities, cultural and linguistic diversities, and extremely uneven opportunities of learning at the school level together with the aspirations and capacities of the potential students. Therefore, the question of access to higher education needs to be addressed at the local, regional, national and international levels from trans-disciplinary, inter-disciplinary and discipline-specific perspectives. The issue of accessibility of quality higher education arises in the context of the transition in the country from elitist to mass education in the post-independence period. The issue has significant implications in the sense that it demands a redefinition of the aims of higher education. This and related issues were discussed at this Seminar, resulting in the following major recommendations.

3.2.1. *Recommendations*

1. Accessibility and quality upgradation are inseparable dimensions of higher education. Over-emphasis on one at the cost of the other would be counterproductive.
2. India being a country of the sub-continental size with a population above 1 billion, the quantitative expansion of education (i.e. accessibility dimension) is of paramount importance to mitigate disparities across regions, gender and social strata in the field of education. This should be given due consideration.
3. Along with the necessary and inevitable quantitative

expansion of higher education, it is equally important to improve the quality of higher education. Institutions of higher education would find it difficult to meet the challenges of globalization of higher education if one fails on this front. Emphasis on quality parameters becomes all the more necessary in the light of mushrooming of private institutions with the opening up of the Indian economy.

4. Setting up of NAAC has sent the right and positive signals for generating and promoting awareness of the urgent need of quality upgradation of Colleges and Universities. The need is to identify effective ways and strategies to expedite the completion of assessment and accreditation by NAAC within a stipulated time frame.
5. Quality upgradation is not a one time phenomenon. Quest for excellence is a continuous and perennial pursuit. In view of this, post- accreditation complacency must be arrested by evolving quality assurance mechanism for self-regulation. The setting up of an Internal Quality Assurance Cell (IQAC), is one such mechanism. The IQAC comprising the Chief Executive, senior academics and officers of the institution should work as a steering group. The Cell may constitute two quality groups, one for academic excellence and another for administrative efficiency. These groups may design strategies for quality enhancement for consideration and implementation by IQAC.
6. Effectiveness of Quality upgradation initiatives in higher education largely depend on the quality of primary and secondary education. Institutional mechanisms on the pattern of NAAC, may be set up for upgrading the quality of education at these levels to further enhance the outcome of NAAC efforts.

7. Periodic assessment exercises in the future should be undertaken by IQAC as part of post assessment and accreditation exercises. These could be conducted in collaboration with NAAC.
8. With a view to ensure maximum participation of College teachers in Workshops/ Seminars/ Conferences and Orientation/Refresher Courses, it is suggested that these events be organized during lean periods in institutional academic work (i.e. March- July). This would help the teachers to participate in these activities without upsetting the teaching schedule.
9. The seven parameters identified by NAAC for evaluating the quality of institutions, although useful, need re-examination as they seem to be inadequate to fully assess the quality of higher education. .
10. WTO has brought far reaching implications for institutions of higher education. Assessment and accreditation bodies like NAAC should take into account these implications while reviewing the quality parameters.. The NAAC could also inform the institutions as to where they stand in terms of the standards of excellence from a global perspective.
11. At present NAAC is assessing and accrediting Universities and Colleges. This may not truly reflect the programmes/activities at the Departmental level. With a view to encourage this, NAAC could move a step further by starting the practice of assessing and accrediting teaching and research Departments within Universities/Colleges.
12. Multiple bodies have been undertaking assessment and accreditation of Universities and colleges. It was recommended that an institutional effort should be made to co-ordinate the activities of these bodies so that in togetherness they can address the issues of higher education in a broader societal perspective.

13. Other important recommendations for improving the quality of higher education include:

 (i) A well-planned and structured interaction to be developed between Centres of Academic Excellence and other Universities/Institutions;

 (ii) While restructuring the syllabi and courses, efforts should be made to develop an optimal combination of acquisition of theoretical and practical skills. The courses should be so designed that critical reading and interpretation of classics, practical field work wherever relevant, and application of readings and other skills are given importance;.

 (iii) Quality of higher education can improve considerably through an extensive and optimal use of audio-visual technologies and Internet. The courses should be so designed to make good use of these modern developments;

 (iv) In restructuring of syllabi, all stakeholders such as students, teachers and users of services should be involved. However, teachers should be given flexibility within the norms and benchmarks decided by the stakeholders;

 (v) Examination reforms, gradually shifting from the terminal, annual and semester examinations to regular and continuous assessment of student's performance in learning should be implemented.

 (vi) Quality of higher education can also be improved by inducting quality-oriented objectivity in merit promotions of teaching faculty. Specification of weightages for teaching, research publications/ supervision would help in making this transparent and credible;.

 (vii) Re-organization and integration of various faculties, particularly in social sciences, around inter-disciplinary and multi-disciplinary courses can also help in quality improvement in teaching, research and consultancy. UGC, ICSSR and other research funding bodies should encourage inter-disciplinary/ multi-disciplinary Seminars/ Conferences/ Research projects. These bodies could allocate at least 50 percent of their research funds for inter-disciplinary activities. UGC could also take initiatives to open Centres/ Schools for promoting multi-disciplinary teaching and research.

(viii) Basic Parameters of Academic Merit need to be developed for bringing transparency and credibility in the process of granting promotions under the Career Advancement Scheme. There should be no disparity between Readers/ Professors appointed through open selections and those promoted on the basis of the Career Advancement Scheme.

(ix) A critical review of activities of higher educational institutions as well as their budgets needs to be conducted to phase out obsolete activities and create the necessary space for new activities. The shifting from traditional incremental budgeting to performance based one is now necessary to arrest the erosion in quality inspite of the resource crunch.

Higher Education System in India

Its potential has been realised in the context of socio-economic and political development in the society. Simultaneously, its development has been influenced by several intricate factors related to social, cultural, political and economic aspects of life. It can be said that "while education can be a pace setter for society, equally and even more, education including the university, is also a faithful mirror of society." (Adiseshiah, 1985). In the Indian context, with a view to bring about further development of the system, it becomes essential to study the future of higher education in coming decades taking into consideration both the trend of this system since independence and projection of a desirable future. Here is an attempt to examine the future of different dimensions of higher education on the basis of trend of growth and development of this system and the expected role and functioning of Selected Educational Statistics, 1986-87, Ministry of Human Resource Development (Department of Education, Government of India. Higher education in future. Moreover, this analysis has been done carefully taking into consideration the ideological and practical aspects of social, political, cultural, and economic life in the country.

Expansion of Higher Education in India

The post-independence period, the demand for higher education has increased 20 times in relation to its position during 1950-51. The post-independence era has exhibited higher education as a means for social mobility, especially for the downtrodden masses. Various facilities, in accordance with the constitutional provisions, provided for lower sections' entry into higher education have encouraged the growth trend. Establishment of new colleges and universities in different parts of the country, particularly the growth of higher educational institutions in rural areas, has facilitated to some extent the democratisation of enrolment policies in higher educational institutions. As a whole, the fifties and sixties showed the trend of rapid expansion, may be for another significant reason of accommodating large number of products of higher education in the employment market. The growth rate came down in seventies. Further, the eighties made an upward trend. However, the rates is quite small as compared to the percentage in the sixties. The total picture of expansion rate at all-India level deviates from the expansion rate witnessed in the case of few states like Andhra Pradesh, Assam, Bihar, Manipur, West Bengal, Tripura, Sikkim, and Himachal Pradesh. It can be noticed that the eastern zones of the country in addition to their neighbour states of Andhra Pradesh and Bihar have maintained the earlier trend of expansion of all India level till date. However, there are mismatches of rate of expansion of enrolment with the rate of expansion of institutions, especially in the context of Maharashtra, Karnataka, Orissa and Madhya Pradesh. In such cases, there is every possibility of problem of increase of non-viable institutions which may result in the disfunctioning of the institutions. As a whole, it can be visualised that, with a view to meet social and individual needs, the higher education system would follow the positive trend of growth in the coming decades, of course, accommodating necessary structural changes expected from time to time.

Structure of Higher Education

The special feature of higher education in India is that around 88 per cent of the total enrolment remains in undergraduate courses, whereas around 10 per cent students enroll in post-graduate courses, and around one per cent students go for research. The position of the percentage of total enrolment during 1984-85 does not show any marked deviation from the average position of enrolment at different stages during the last three and half decades.

Continuation of this trend of higher education, concentrating on undergraduation does not reflect an ideal feature of higher education. The crisis goes on increasing, as undergraduate education is treated as some kind of compensatory education. In general, at undergraduate stage, teaching has taken the form of imparting knowledge without generating scope for questioning about the validity of the information which is being transferred to the students. A degree holder 'is sometimes treated as having finished his schooling and sometimes as having done only a part of the degree course' (Singh, 1985). The static structure of higher education over a period of three and half decades has not been responsive to the ideological issues, and developmental needs of the society. Especially the persistence of the low share of post graduate and research involvement restricts the efficiency of higher education system in research and development activities. Further, it proves its inability to keep pace with structural changes that take place in the field of economy. It is apprehended that continuation of low share of post graduate and research would reflect the weakness of human resource system to adapt to the increasing complexities of the process of modernisation and change. With a view to strengthen the functioning of university education, every effort should be made to expand postgraduate and research activities in proper direction. In the post independence period it was realised that the qualified and technically skilled manpower would be of immense value in a developing economy. During this period, in spite of high rate of expansion of economic system, major share of enrolment in higher education remained with non-professional courses as compared to professional courses.

Social Accountability of Higher Education

With a view to attain egalitarian values of the society, it is expected that the phenomenal growth in educational facilities would lead to a balanced development of human resources. However, the lion's share of available educational facilities goes to the advantaged sections of the society. The dismal picture of educational development of weaker sections of the society viz. SC, ST and women can be noticed.

Firstly, we have to go a long way with regard to equal distribution of educational opportunities for SC and ST who remained oppressed for ages.

Secondly, even though, a positive trend is marked with regard to women's enrolment, attainment of their equal share with men population remains a far fetched goal. Especially, women's enrolment has reflected under achieving position with regard to Science, Engineering and Technology, Law, Agriculture, and Veterinary Sciences. Further the problem of enrolment of women among SC and ST groups can be treated as the problems of weakest among weaker ones. There is a hunch that in a stratified society the rapid rate of expansion in enrolment may corroborate the possibility of increment of entrance of students from weaker sections of the society. While the rate of growth of enrolment comes down to a very low level, there is every possibility that the ratio of enrolment position of such groups may not increase further. Keeping this in view, while efforts are made to stabilise the enrolment position in higher education, special efforts must be made for encouraging the upward mobility among weaker sections, by providing financial assistance, hostel facilities and extra coaching to them and establishing colleges/universities in rural and tribal zones of the country.

It is a fact that Indian higher education system has not matched to the manpower requirements of the country. While the problem of unemployment has been acute for the products of all the faculties,there have been instances of existence of shortages of manpower. The former category problem is in vogue with regard to the products of general education. On the other hand, higher level skill shortages are noted in technical and professional occupation, craftmanship, and production workers. There are instances, where vertical mismatches have taken place because of availability of over qualified persons on the labour market.

The problem lies outside the scope of higher education. The empirical studies quote the large gap in availability of higher educated manpower between India and developed countries. In the process of economic self-sufficiency, India is still in need of large number of trained manpower. The real problem as witnessed today "is not in the expansion of higher education or with the products of higher education but with its unplanned expansion, the type of expansion which has not matched with the type of manpower demand and the country's level of absorption of technology and management" (Agarwal, 1985). In this context; it can be presumed that in the absence of identification of appropriate approaches of manpower planning, educated unemployment phenomena will have its strong hold in the country. Vocationalisation of secondary education may solve the problem of faster expansion of higher education. Still, the problem of unemployment of products of vocational streams would persist, as it is witnessed in the cases of states like Maharashtra, Karnataka and Gujarat which have already vocationalised the +2 stage of education.

Future Perspectives and Quality Improvement

It has been emphasised time and again that appropriate measures must be taken to check the expansion rate and to improve the standard of higher education. However, with a view to maintain egalitarian norm in the functioning of the system, compromising steps are taken between academic performances and popular demand for expansion of education. As UGC (1985) statement reads, "although there is need to regulate expansion in view of the limitation of resources, it is not easy to deny expansion altogether as weaker sections of the society have looked for Higher Educations as a means of social and economic mobility; the demand for education should not be judged purely from the point of view of the labour market alone, but due consideration should also be given to the social, cultural and humanistic aspects of education". Thus, a conservative stand cannot be taken to attain quality at the cost of quantity. The expansion of higher education system will continue further with an imbalanced rate of growth in different zones of the country. Keeping in view the popular demands of higher education, efforts should be made to provide appropriate infrastructure to all the institutions for the maintenance of quality and standards. Moreover, the autonomy of the universities must be secured while granting affiliation to new colleges according to the guidelines provided by the UGC from time to time. Appropriate measures should be taken for teacher training programmes and upgrading research endeavours of teachers of higher education. Moreover, stable policies should be evolved for academic and professional incentives to devoted and effective teachers. Use of modern methods of teaching, validated learning materials, and electronic equipments must be encouraged to stabilise higher education teaching programmes. With a view to improve research activities, the university teaching departments and leading post graduate departments of affiliated colleges should be provided with appropriate physical and human resources.

The existing schemes of Centre of Advanced studies, special assistance and post graduate teaching and research grants must be upgraded and expanded to a larger number of institutions of the country. Along with the UGC, the State Governments should extend similar facilities for upgradation of research schemes of universities and post-graduate institutions.

Higher Education: Divergent Forms

With a liberal outlook, certain social scientists opine that within a long range perspective, equity and efficiency are complementary to each other "if educational resources are not being put to the best use, it is inefficient; if those who can profit and who have to profit are not able to do so, it is inefficient". (Raza et al., 1985). A country following democratic ideals will have to democratise the higher education system. All care must be taken for providing educational opportunities for those eligible students who desire to study further. In this context, the Education Commission (1964-66) had recommended for a dual practice, viz. (i) selective admissions can be done for full time institutions only for ensuring the quality of higher education and (ii) part-time courses like Correspondence Courses and own-time education can be encouraged for meeting the popular demand of education. However, looking at the socio-political influences, the National Policy of Education of 1968 was silent over the issue of selective admission. But, it is well understood that education can be both efficient and equitable if the majority of the people, the disadvantaged having proportionately more opportunities, are able to benefit from it. Further, looking at the total university enrolment in relation to population in the age cohort of 17-23 years, it can be expected that the situation is not that much alarming from the point of view of rate of expansion in a highly populous country. This position has been perceived by the UGC as hardly adequate in spite of expansion of numbers.

Due to several influential factors like change of structure of secondary education, introduction of vocational education, rapid progress of science and technology, fast changes taking place in knowledge etc. the level of demand for higher education would take a different turn in future. *First,* while the glamour of higher education will continue among the products of academic streams of +2 stage, the products of vocational stream would seek 'further education' while being in job. Also, in a technology biased society the semi-skilled workers would be in need of tertiary level education. *Second,* the products of higher education system working in different sectors of employment i.e. management, teaching, technology and engineering, public administration etc. would be the aspirants for updating the knowledge and skills of respective fields.

Especially, the need for continuing higher education would increase in future among the technicians, semi skilled labourers, professionals, scientists, engineers and others. Accommodation of clients of diversified groups into higher education would be possible through identification of different suitable means of non-formal education in addition to the age old structure of formal system. Hence the need for popularising continuing education programmes; Distance Education System functioning inside the frame work of formal system and outside the traditional universities.

Distance Education System in the form of Correspondence Courses has been in existence in Indian Universities since 1962. Of late, two open universities, viz., Andhra Pradesh Open University and Indira Gandhi National Open University have added a new dimension to the existing structure of higher education in the country. The success of correspondence system of instruction can be recognised in the Indian universities, as around 40 universities are offearing as many as 50 courses in general and professional fields and at undergraduate, post graduate, Research, Diploma and certificate courses. These institutions have been gaining ground by annually enrolling around 1.5 lakh students constituting 5 per cent of total enrolment in all the universities of the country. The enrolment position at different stages reveals that unlike formal streams, the correspondence system has accommodated a very high percentage (33%) of post graduate students. Among all post graduate course several Arts courses, in total have been enrolling highest number of courses. However, the courses like M.Com and M.Ed, have attracted very high number of students. The trend shows that popularisation of non-formal/Distance Education streams would bring a change in the existing structure of enrolment in different stages.

In all, courses offered by correspondence institutions have been mostly traditional degree-oriented ones and have been limited in number. The innovative courses which have been restricted to a few institutions have attracted around 2 per cent of the total enrolment. Till date, it seems the distance education system has remained a sub-component of traditional university structure. It is high time to realise the significance of this system to meet the specific requirements of target group learners. These institutions are supposed to follow flexible approaches in offering much multi-disciplinary courses, which may be very much different from traditional courses. In the meanwhile, it would be essential to maintain parity between distance system and regular system of education. Further, establishment of open universities in different zones of the country would enable strengthening the scope of higher education among the needy group of learners. Use of advanced educational technology in both software and hardware forms would enrich the efficiency of self learning system with appropriate guidance from the distance education institutions.

Higher Education: Multiple Roles

It is often criticised that the higher education system must come out of its conservative functions of teaching and research activities which may be indifferent to social development. The social responsiveness of higher education can be directly realised through appropriate use of its own resources for integrated rural development activities, removal of illiteracy and awareness development programmes, application of research findings in developmental activities and policy formation, training of planners and teachers, preparation of learning materials and use of innovative communication strategies for extension programmes. In this context, while encouraging these activities there will be a shift from dominance of individual disciplines to inter-disciplinary and multi- disciplinary approach in the pursuit of meeting diversified developmental needs of the society. A handful of teaching departments and independent institutions have already made a breakthrough in this line. It can be hoped that the traditional institutions of higher learning will adapt their roles in carrying out interacting activities with the developmental programmes. Further, there is every possibility that new forms of higher educational institutions would come up to concentrate on developmental programmes through inter-disciplinary research activities; on-the-job training activities for labour forces, and management personnel; policy oriented evaluation activities; community service camps; and performing via-media roles between the traditional university resources and outside community. The nature of functioning of such institutions would be non-formal, innovative and participatory.

The present day activities of universities are directed towards two major dimensions (i) producing, conserving and diffusing knowledge and (ii) grading and certification. The latter has dominated the scene to such an extent that the entire management of the university is mostly occupied with it at the cost of the former basic functions. The implication of national policy (1986) of delinking degrees from jobs may bring "are-fashioning of job specific courses and afford greater justice to those candidates who, despite being equipped for a given job, are unable to get it because of an unnecessary preference for graduate candidates". In addition to these implications, if implemented properly, this would promote learning and competitive atmosphere in the educational institutions. Major concentration of the universities would remain on the basic functions of teaching, research and extension activities, with due emphasis on continuous evaluation of learners' performance in curricular programmes. Of course, the success of implementation of this scheme would solely depend upon the co-operation of public.

Therefore, in the process of socio-economic changes of the country, Higher Education system will undergo changes both at structural and functional levels. Controversial situations created in the context of social mobility among different sections of the society will continue to be reflected in the higher education system for a considerable period of time. Of course, efforts should continue to expand and consolidate the system keeping in view sociological ideals of the country. Mostly changes in the structure of secondary education; faster expansion of technology and exposition of knowledge; and requirement of updated skills in developmental programmes would demand expansion of non-formal streams like open university system, correspondence courses, extension education-programmes and continuing education programmes. The future of higher education will demand special attention of policy makers and educationists for improvement in instructional systems of both formal and non-formal streams through appropriate use of modern educational technology.

13

Privatisation of Higher Education

"He who buys what he needs not, sells what he needs."

—*A Japanese Proverb*

With the advent of British regime in India, Indian education system was also devised as per suitability of Rulers. MaCauley the father of English Educational Policy in India, was interested in creating Indians with "English in taste, in opinions in morals and in intellect". But MaCauley never wanted unpatriotic Indians for which he was stalled in the British Parliament for introducing a system of education that was responsible for American War of Independence. The East India Company was also not interested in making everybody literate and therefore encouraged private initiative in education through grant-in-aid. The aim of grant-in-aid of the company was that, "any system of education provided by the Government may be discontinued with gradual advance of the system of grant-in-aid and many of the existing institutions specially those of the higher order may be safely closed". This was the aim of a colonial power to enslave Indians by denying an opportunity to improve the native abilities, skills and technology for its sustenance through education was the basic motive of the British. But the present World Trade Organisation (WTO) regime is much more wider, powerful and vicious than the lone East India company that ruled India for about two centuries.

Yet, many scholars and policy makers are inviting Privatisation and globalisation without realizing the implications of it at the present juncture. The paper is addressed to the issues involved in the Privatisation of education in a pluralistic society with wide inequities.

The root idea of Privatisation is widely used in literature to show that more number of self-financing institutions are to be established to reduce the burden on the State. Privatisation is applicable where the provision of education is entirely done by public and its conversion to private sector thereafter. The educational history shows that education was never under the total control of the State. The provision of education in India was never universally democratic. Several groups of people were denied the right and forcefully kept outside the learning system. The community, the private philanthropists and the missionaries have started providing education particularly higher education in the country to fill the gap with a democratic spirit. Realising the danger of multiplicity of educational agencies and the spread of parochial education, the British dragged their feet into it in the name of grant-in-aid. Different types of managements started emerging in the management of collegiate or higher education in different parts of the country during the British regime. Therefore, Privatisation is not simply allowing private individuals to start commercial enterprises in education business or industry.

Nobody can deny that for many years private institutions of education were in existence in different forms in the country. Some institutions were established by private philanthropic organizations, but aid was granted to them by the State. Practically, there were no institutions in the higher education sector that were not receiving any grant from the state till 1980s. It was only during the late 1980s, the emergence of purely self-financing institutions with the given syllabus of the universities were started. The proliferation of the self-financing institutions became a reality after induction of so-called liberalization in 1991. All these institutions were following the given syllabus and mandate of the respective governments in India. No private institution was given a mandate to develop and market their own courses in the private sector till the GATTs regime helped promote commercial enterprises to enter Indian market.

Currently, in India there are three types of private institutions; (1) institutions that receive grant from the government, but the management is vested with private people, (2) institutes that are purely private commercial entities with their own products (own course structure, fees and content) with foreign collaboration or with franchise to market products in Indian market, and (3) institutions that charge fees and offer approved syllabus of the government through university structures.

"Private returns are higher than social returns". It is assumed that it is possible to take care of the problems of monetisation of rural markets, identification and valuation of all kinds of tangible benefits, etc., of education. These studies have done some good to the education sector and a lot of damage to groups and countries, which are disadvantaged. It is on the basis of the results of these studies, economists and policymakers have started generalizing the policies relating to investment in education. It is said that as long as the investment benefits are related to individual, why should the state fund such investments despite market imperfections, social rigidities, etc. But we should remember that barring some spurious arguments education, particularly higher education is not a public good.

It is said that, "the expansion of higher education has not yet extended to the talented and best from all backgrounds. In Britain today too many of those born into less advantaged families still see a university place as being beyond their reach, whatever their ability... Having a university education brings big benefits and while the government will continue to pay most of the cost involved in studying for a degree, it is also reasonable to ask students to contribute to this. But we need to make sure that no student is put off from going into higher education because they cannot afford the cost of studying while they are at university" (DES, UK 2003, p. 2). Thus privatization of education is different from private management of education. The government of U.K. has committed substantial investment to education. "Between 1997 and 2006, the proportion of GDP spent on education will rise from 4.5 per cent to 5.6 per cent. Spending on higher education will rise from a total of around $7.5 billion in 2002-2003 to almost $10 billion in 2005-06 a real terms increase of over 6 per cent each year". This the UK scenario.

Now coming to India, pravatisation efforts in education will harm the average Indian lot. The Dalits, women and other weaker sections of the society in particular will remain deprived of higher education under privatisaion. The Ambani and Birla Committee spoke about 'weightless goods' that are created by knowledge workers. Perhaps, they are interested to export these goods and get a comparative advantage in the international market. The present euphoria of Information Technology professionals going abroad and the value of their remittances need to be kept in proper perspective and context. The British sent indentured labourers as plantation workers to Africa, Latin America, Europe and elsewhere. There was no 'body shopping' at that time. Is there any difference between the status of the indentured labourer of 18th and 19th century and the educated labour force today.

A number of questions are there that need to be posed and answered before we go in for privatization under WTO regime. The relative advantage of a country in the global market comes out of its investment in R & D, technology and higher education. The knowledge content of goods that are traded in the international market will continue to increase and the countries that have an advantage in these areas will triumph in the market. The West including the US have sufficiently invested in higher education and R & D through state support for about a century till they reach a threshold level. No country can pursue an independent development policy as long as it depends on others for its technological needs. Further, the technology developed in the West might flow into the country through the MNCs but may not suit the conditions. Even if the technology is adopted like that of the Japanese, the country will be made to follow the dictates of the donor or sponsorer. Therefore, a country like India with its present base in knowledge and technology need to develop and possess its own technology. The private sector will never come forward to invest where risk is involved.

The impact of GATTs is clearly perceptible in the higher education market in India. Several educational service providers including As per recent AIU published data relating to number of foreign students studying in India indicate how the GATTs provisions are helping the free trade in education, particularly higher education. As of now, it is not favourable to India as the number of foreign students educating in India has come down substantially from around 8000 to 4000 during 1995-2000. It is reported that international student mobility in OECD countries during the last 20 years is doubled. They receive around 85 per cent of the world foreign students.

Realising the dangers of GATTs provisions for higher education, the international organizations representing 5500 assocaitions signed a declaration in 2002 at Porto Alegre. The Porto Alegre Declaration on education opposed the move to introduce free trade in education through GATTs. Interestingly, the signatories include university presidents from Latin American, American and third world educational organizations. It is an important and major activity in the life span of an individual that will help to mould the destiny of a nation. The white paper presented by the Tony Blair government in the UK in January 2003 clearly demonstrates that if a country needs its identity and keep pace with the progress of others, the state has no alternative except to invest in education.

To conclude, everyone should know that 'education' is not a 'consumer item' of sort. It shapes the destiny of a nation. Donot measure everything on the scales of economics. Remember experience may be a good teacher, but some people never graduate from kindergarten.

REFERENCES

Chalam, K.S. (1994), "Union Budget and Decline in Educational Effort", *Economic and Political Weekly,* April (special).

George, P. Sacharopoulos and Harry Anthony Patrinos (2002), *Returns to Investment in Education: A Further Update,* World Bank Policy Research Working paper, 2881, September.

Department of Education and Skills, U.K. (2003), *The Future of Higher Education,* January.

Sharma, G.D. (2002), "Trade in Education Service under WTO Regime – An Indian Response" in *Studies in Higher Education,* Andhra University.

14

Towards Future Education

> "To stand for the freedom of others is one of the marks of those who are face, just as to fail to do so is one of the marks of those who are ready to be enslaved."
>
> —*Alam Paton*

> "Give the best you've got today.
> That's a recipe for a better tommorrow."

The basic restructuring of the earthly home of the *homo sapiens* on the micro-dot of a planet along desirable directions calls for a deep understanding of the current processed of social change, of this being as becoming; for freedom is the cognition of necessity; and knowledge is power "not only to interpret reality but to change it." Education is the ability to generate such an understanding by abstracting universals of varying orders from the specifics of social experience, to systematise them into a hierarchy of intellectual constructs and to impart them to the newer generation so as to enable it to build upon its heritage and continue the task of further generation and systematisation. It is this unique ability of mankind which enables it to actively interact with other elements of nature is widening realms of increasing complexity and not only to passively adjust itself to them in an inflexible system of rigorous interdependencies. It is through this process that the species moves into the ambience of freedom; for necessity is blind only till it is cognised. Viewed thus, education is humanisation. Having transformed *homonidae* into the *homo sapiens,* it continues to guide mankind along the tortuous and unending road to humanity.

The ethos of the contemporary phase is characterised by the opening up of new vistas through the unfolding of the scientific-technological revolution, on the one hand, and, on the other, by the unique incapacity of the contemporary social systems to actualise and come to terms with these immense possibilities. It is in this contradiction that both the hope and the despair of our times are deeply rooted; and education is intrinsically involved with both. It is a necessary input in this revolution which has enabled man to interact with non-human nature at a qualitatively higher level and to hope for the ecstasies of fulfillment. It is, at the same time, the receptacle of a moribund value system and of and obsolete *Weltanschauung*. The essential inadequacies of this sub-system are not indigenous to it but are products of the system as whole. They, however, in their turn, buttress the infirmities of the system and thus become the harbingers of the despair of impending disasters. The future of education is thus the future of mankind, and the education of the future is synonymous with the humanisation of the *homo sapiens* through the mutual inter penetration of form and function, means and ends, work and knowledge in that distant and yet hazy layer of time wherein the good, the beautiful and the true become one in the spirit of man.

Technological development essentially increased labour productivity by an increasingly efficient utilisation of natural laws. Each innovation, therefore, calls for a *smaller quantity* and a *highest quality* of labour input for producing the some output. It calls for less hours of work and more hours of education; for the former is the measure of quantity of labour and the latter of its quality. A historical trend is clearly discernible in this contest and may be projected in the future.

The life span of generation may be divided into two parts—each spent in either learning to live or in living to learn. With every phase of technological development in history, the share of time in a life span devoted to learning and leisure has been increasing and the share of working has been decreasing. This process may be disaggregated as follows.

(1) The requirements of education and training before the induction of the young citizen in the work force have been increasing and becoming more rigorous and the number of years needed for it has been increasing with time. From near zero in the case of the Greek slave (who, incidentally, worked for no less a person than the great educationist Plato) to about seventeen years of compulsory schooling in most countries of the modern world—the change is reflective of the increasing humanisation of man.

(2) The share of the highly skilled in the workforce has been increasing constantly, so much so that the emergence of the quarternary sector has already presented its sterile apron in the company of the blue and the white collar.

(3) The number of working days in a week as well as the number of working hours in a day has been decreasing and the number of paid holidays in a year has been increasing from the seven day week of Spartacus to a five day week in modern Europe, from 18 hours a day in Zola's Germinal to the May day slaughter for an eight hour day in mid-nineteenth century and to a six hour day in many industries of today—this has been a long road from the near animal to the near human. Technological advances and increased labour productivity could have led to a situation wherein either less number of people work for more hours or more number of people work for less hours. Labour and capital have been waging and continue to wage battles around this question but, by and large, the trend has been towards less hours of work and more hours of leisure and rest.

(4) With increasing longevity and improvements in the health of the aged, a new phase of creative and productive life is opening out for those who have retired from work but have not retired from life. The past which is fast disappearing,

equated youth with adventure and age with resignation, youth with innovation and age with conservation, youth with restlessness and age with serenity. The scenario for the future is bound to be different. The old would be mature not senile; they would week adventure through experience unlike the youth who seek experience through adventure. Instead of playing make-believe games for hollow and stuffed men in the gilded cages of old peoples' homes, they would be seeking newer and greener pastures with serene restlessness or restless serenity in an ethos of timeless grace which transcends beauty.

Education is increasingly becoming a continuing process stretched over the entire life span of man—in terms of the Quranix imagery "from the lap to the grave." It is available to the new generation as the quintessence of the accumulated social experience of mankind before its initiation into the world of work; it would continue to complement and supplement work through leisure time activities through the formal as well as non-formal channels during the working age, and it would steer the life of the aged in meaningful directions after retirement. Education of the future is bound to be united intimately with the life of mankind through every fiber of its being. From being only a preparation for work, education is becoming the nagrance of life itself and of the whole of it.

The educational sector will play such an all-pervasive role in the world of tomorrow only to the extent that it is able to respond adequately and properly first, to the pressures being exogenously exerted on it by the deepening contradictions between man and non-human as well as between the unity of the globe and the fragmentation of the world; and second, to the stresses and strains being generated indigeneously within itself by the sharpening contradictions between tradition and modernity, between integration and specialisation, as well as between work and knowledge.

Naturalisation of Man vis-a-vis Humanisation of Nature

The education of the future must restore the primeval unity of man and nature; but restore it, of course, at a qualitatively higher level of the eco-system and get rooted again in the monist view of reality which had been lost in the mad rush to conquer nature generated within the profit syndromes of class societies. Such a monist view of objective reality is contingent upon the recognition of this unity, operationalised through the mechanism of interactions between social man and non-human nature. The essentiality of man and nature is based on "man as a natural being and nature as a human reality." Since the naturalisation of man and the humanisation of nature proceed simultaneously through man's interaction with nature, human history may be viewed as the continuation of, and a qualitatively new stage in natural history—the two constituting a differentiated unity. It is no doubt true that primeval nature is prior to man and continues to exist without him every where except on our tiny planet earth in the vastness of the universe. This is non-humanised nature which has not neutralised man and is of only marginal significance in the social development process. Nature comes within the orbit of development primarily as a constituent element of the system of man-nature interaction, wherein man himself gets transformed in the process of transforming nature.

The development process unfolds itself through integrating the anthropogenetic and the non-human components into a system of interdependencies—the eco-system. This intellectual construct has emerged as a timely corrective to the academic tradition of the post-industrial society based on the disgeregation of the totality into facets, aspects, parts or fragments for deeper study and analysis, thereby engendering the knowing of more and more about less and less till, as a wag remarked, one finally ends up knowing everything about nothing. The gap between the essentially holistic character of the objectively existing system and its fragmented cognition through disaggregregated analysis has already become a serious constraint on and hasled to a crisis in knowledge. It is the experience of history that at such moments, unifying principles emerge critical moments to provide the basis for a new *weltanschauung*, an integrated view of totality. It is being suggested that the concept of the eco-system is a unifying principle of this order, which, though rooted in all the sciences still transcends them. It provides the closest conceptual approximation to the integrated complexity of objective reality and may, therefore, serve as the basis for the most relevant twenty- first century ideology.

Like all the significant ideas of science, the scientific conceptualisation of the eco-system, which is a recent product of the intellectual crisis of the post-industrial society, is rooted in a pre-scientific tradition of great chronological depth and is, in fact, embedded in the basal psyche of the *homo- sapiens.* The system of animistic and totemistic beliefs, characterising the proto-iodeology of the Palaeolithi age, was based on a unity of all that exists and transcended the duality of the biota and the abiota, of the animal and the human, of the material and the spiritual. The worship of the Mother Goddess, which has provided the sub-stratum for the spiritual ideas of the agricultural people all over the world was similarly rooted in a holistic view of the Universe, which subsumed the man-nature dichotomy into a broader unity though in an inverted form. The mysticism of the orient, which continues to wield considerable influence over the mind, resolved the subject-object, man-nature contradiction through a monist view of reality. The modern concept of the eco-system has such a distinguished parentage. Just as science has arisen out of magic so has this scientific conceptualisation emerged from pre-scientific intellection by assimilating with it the kernel of truth in the latter and rejecting its pseudo-spiritual clap-trap, by moving from the realm of false consciousness to that of consciousness.

While the social sciences have moved towards a certain degree of internal cohesion, the world of non- human nature is still alien to it, at best producing unnecessary noise in their sophisticated computer programmes. The agricultural economist would rather not dirty his hands with the soil, this nauseating residual in his regression model, which cannot be wished away. The incapacity of the natural sciences to go beyond the rigid limits of their sub-system is no less alarming. The internal integration of the natural sciences has at best produced the science of ecology. In their just concern with the autotrophs and the hetrotrophs, the ecologists tend to forget that the *homo-sapoens* constitutes a category qualitatively different from the other hetrotrophs; that their explanatory system is incapable of accounting for the behaviour of social man; that they are asking only limited questions and can, therefore, get only inadequate and partial answers. At best, they recognise man as an element in the man nature syndromes and have shown a unique incapacity to recognise the reality of man *in* nature. They fail to see that the rationality of man is as much *natural* as the irrationality of the monsoon wind, the cheronozem or the xerophyte. The unifying concept of the eco- system has arisen to break the constraints imposed by the complementary inadequacies of the social and the natural sciences.

Let it be stated clearly that development is operationalised through a triangle of forces, wherein nature lays down the limits of freedom and indicates the direction of optimal advance, wherein technology extends the area of freedom within the general orbit of necessity; and wherein institutions are either conducive for or restrictive of man's interaction with nature through technology. The ecocrisis of the contemporary times is a consequence not of a technology gone berserk but of an institutional frame, which is no longer capable of coping with it. The crisis, therefore, calls not for a stoppage of technological advance but for a new world order—a just, equitable and humane world order which can regulate man's relation with nature as well as man's relation with man.

Integration, Differentiation and Fragmentation

The education of the future has to come to terms with the globalisation of society and has to bridge the gap between parochial perceptions of narrow minds and the concerns of a one-world reality. The spread of modern industrialisation has already—towards the beginning of the nineteenth century—replaced the aggregate of closed or semi-closed systems of the pre-capitalist for formations by a loosely integrated world market. The peasants of Asia and Africa, living for millennia in the isolated small world of petty production, were used to natural calamities like floods and droughts, cyclones and earthquakes but were for the first time exposed to blind forces of the market which they did not know. The suction mechanism of international exploitation extended its tentacles to the remotest hamlet and united the developed and the underdeveloped in world economy. Advances in transport and communication during recent years have further strengthened such trends, have brought the entire world to our doors and have made everybody everybody's neighbour. Walls have crumbled; and ideas ride the winds. A poem, created on the Left Bank today, provides spiritual sustenance to young scientists in the Silicon Valley or Novoibirisk the next day.

The findings of a research project in the Kolar mines reach Triestein minutes and become inputs in the work of a Nobel laureate, whose words are heard with batted breath in Tokyo, Princeton and Oxford over the week-end. The agro-biological researches in Mexico provide the basis for the green revolution across the oceans in India and Pakistan. The heartbeat of the young in Europe become faster on the rhythm of African drums, or the *swara* of the Indian sitar. The world has become one indeed! The integration of the globe should not be confused with its homogenisation. The jean clad, hamburger eating, coca cola drinking, hashish smoking young men and women with vacant eyes roaming around the bylanes of large cities the world over constitute the thin layer of froth over the multi-splendoured sub-stratum of profound meaning in all traditions over the globe. Unity lies in plurality; not in the negation of it. Development is a process in which integration and differentiation are dialectically united, being contingent upon each other. The uni-cellular amoeba is neither integrated nor differentiated. The complex human organism is both. While homogenisation is the function of the breaking up identities and their assimilation in synthesised melting pot products, integration is articulated through a multi-level and hierarchical system of interdependencies. Homogenisation, in fact, is the anti-thesis of integration. One has not to be less of an Indian to be more of a man; one has not to be less of a Pathan to be more of a Pakistani. Universals exist through specifics; and specifics acquire deeper and wider meaning through universals. They make each other possible and sustain each other. Brothers Karamazav are so deeply Russian that they transcend their Russian-ness and become universal. Semetna's "My Motherland" sings of the pride in his mother or his country or in the mother earth or the Milky Way or the expanding universe or all of them at the same time; for the lilt of the Valtava in the opening bars of the symphony is so like a lullaby as well as the music of the stars! The Blue Danube of Strauss, the Ol'Man River of the Negro spiritual, the Ganga Maiya of India folk lore—are'nt they the specific forms of the same universal. The mystic search for the river in a drop was based on a dialectical relationship between the whole and the part-of unity in diversity and of diversity in unity articulated by the simultaneous integration of the differentiated and the differentiation of the integrated.

Education of the future has to come to terms with the specific without becoming parochial, philistine and mundane; and with the universal without becoming other—worldly, ethereal and divine. It should become human and humane, the conscience of mankind, smelling of the earth and yet gazing into the stars.

Now, differentiation articulates and reflects diversity, fragmentation generates and sharpens disparity. While differentiation of an integrated world is a function of development, fragmentation of the world has been a function of the development of a few have nations proceeding along and causatively linked with the underdevelopment of the mass of mankind. This is the most agonizing tragedy of our times; for development like freedom is indivisible. The industrial revolution marks the watershed in history. The surpluses generated by the sweat and toil of people all over the world, since then, were swallowed up by the ruling classes of a few nations through colonial suction mechanisms 'to build industrial empires and to transform the rest of the world into their raw material appendage.

North is becoming increasingly non-rural with most of its population living in urban settlements, South is being transformed into a large aggregate of villages inhabited by most of the rural population of the world. The percentage of the population of the more developed countries who inhabit their urban settlements goes on increasing at an alarming rate and getting concentrated in fever and fewer megalopolises. The North is threatening to become one large urban connurbation—the cruel and sick city with the anomie and loneliness of an alienated humanity, the windowless silos full to the brim with discarded hopes and nameless fears, the concrete jungles inhabited not by neighbours—neither love nor hate, neither friends nor foes, but by faceless non-persons: data units of an animated demography.

There are three altars in this big city—one each for the revered gods of an industrial capitalism run amuck—economies of scale, economy of agglomeration and economies of urbanisation. The industrial revolution ushered in the era of factory city- smoke belching chimneys rising over working class slums, the refuge for expropriated peasantry in an alien world. Viewed in the contest of history, the emergence of the industrial city was a positive step in the right direction. It converted the vertical shift in the work force from the primary to the secondary sector into horizontal mobility from the rural to the urban settlement. The city was thus an instrument of history and the three-fold economies provided the *raison d'etr* for this historical process.

However, the modern science-technological revolution has transformed the situation qualitatively. The microchip has taken quite a bit of the wind out of the sail of the economies of scale. A highly skilled white aproned workforce of two figures working in a villa within a park may produce higher value added than a blue collared.workforce of four figures breathing polluted air in the jungle of chimneys of a four acre factory. It is not being suggested that the small is always and necessarily beautiful. The argument is based on the realisation that the scientific technological revolution has made it possible for economies to be available along the whole spectrum of scales. It is, therefor, not surprising that the North is increasingly shifting the resource-based, large scale polluting industries to the South and is concentrating instead on the innovative highly skilled, R and D based wherein the laboratory imperceptibly merges into the production line. The 'clean' scientific- technological revolution, unfolding in the North is pushing the polluting industrial revolution into the South. By the time the North is in the twenty-first century, the South would be struggling into the nineteenth.

The autonomy of the shopping plaza from the residential neighbourhood and of the latter from the industrial area has already been made possible by qualitative improvements in short-range transport. The home computer has brought about an information revolution, and interconnected terminals of large systems make it possible for some economies to become available in small and medium sized settlements as well. The perspective for the twenty-first century is, therefore, not necessarily of cannibal megalopolises swallowing up smaller specimens of their own species but of a balanced and humane system of settlements where the large, the medium and the small flourish in symbiosis. There is too much of urbanisation in the North and too little of it in the South. The polluted city of the North and the filthy village of the South are two sides of the same coin. The former is sick with affluence, the latter is diseased with poverty. The former has the paunch of the over-fed, the latter has the bloated belly of the scurvy stricken: the former needs slimming, the latter needs nutrition. Glorification of the former is inhuman and romanticisation of the latter is cruel. There is no escape from one to the other.

Education of the future must contribute to the resolution of the contradiction between the integration of the globe and its fragmentation. The fracture in the human condition brought about by the hammer strokes of industrial capitalism must be healed in the interest of not only those who have been at the receiving end but for mankind as a whole. Educational policies must be intrinsically intertwined with the basic structural changes without which the new international order would remain just an idle dream. It must clean deterministic cobwebs which posit that poverty is nature's gift and the deprived must learn to live with it as with natural catastrophes. It must correct the perspectives of those who search solace in the spurious spirituality of poverty as well as those who seek meaning and purpose at the consumerist counters of affluence. Education of the future must combine the sophistication of the city with the earthiness of the village and thus restore the urban rural continuum in the living style of mankind.

It is really surprising that the models of the Club of Rome, the Japanese Club of Rome and of Leontiev have no place for education. Unless this serious limitation of our futurological models is removed, the world mayget broken up in three fragments instead of two, as has been pointed out by a UNESCO study: "this means that without basic structural change (the New International Economic Order), we shall end up with the world divided into three types of countries; at the bottom, countries with primary (basic) education doing extraction work and subsistence labour; in the middle, countries up to the level of secondary (including vocational) education doing some simple processing; and at the third and top level, countries where everybody is a university graduate and working highly in research-intensive industries with large science and technology components?" The tragedy of the modern era is that the Third World is already getting fragmented into the Third and the Fourth; and the developing countries into the less and the least developed. Education is unfortunately playing a key role in this process of inequalisation.

The above discussion on the context of the educational process may generate the misconception that education is largely a derived parameter, that it is essentially determined by exogenous forces or that it does not have an indigenous mechanism within its own autonomy which contributes to its transformation. This would be a serious, error with far reaching implications for the future. It is, therefore, desirable to focus attention on some of the internal forces of self-articulation within the educational sphere itself.

The most potent of the contradictory pulls regulating the trend line of educational development are those exerted by tradition and modernity. The contradiction is resolved by the modernisation of tradition itself through a simultaneous process of rejection of the moribund, the dead and the obsolete in tradition and of the assimilation of its live, and relevant elements into the modern. This is how astrology transformed itself into astronomy by, for example, rejecting the geocentricity of the solar system but assimilating some of its mathematical formulations. The modern does not generate in a vacuum; it grows in the womb of tradition. It does not replace it; it transforms it. The modern is modernised tradition, a new wave in the ocean of time. If the modern rejects the whole of tradition it ceases to be modern; it becomes rootless and anemic; a spurious product—glossy but ephemeral—destined for the dustbin of history. If tradition does not eschew the obsolete by modernizing itself, it ceases to be tradition; it becomes sterile a stagnant pool of decay and degeneration.

This rejuvenating process of the modernisation of tradition proceeded, albeit at a slow pace and having many ups and downs, within all the major civilisations of the earth till the industrial revolution and the emergence of industrial and financial capital on the scene. This was a turning point in history. While the Greeco-Roman tradition, which had survived the suffocating atmosphere of the inquisition, modernised itself and flourished in the metropolitan countries of Western Europe on the basis of the flowering of rationalism and humanism. The traditions of the colonial empires faced crises of an unprecedented magnitude. The overseas territories within temperate latitudes provided *lebensraum* for European immigrants, who,with a rifle in one hand and the Bible in the other. Liquidated whole peoples and, out of sheer benevolence permitted civilisations to breath their last peacefully in the soul killing ambience of encapsulated reservations. This brutal genocide was called colonisation and a new genre of literature, painting and films arose to glorify the civilising mission of the wild West. Imported modernity flourished in the graveyard of native traditions both in America and Australia. The situation was different in the tropics. They provided an arena not for colonisation but for colonialism. Traditions in these lands which were deeply rooted in the native soil and were, as in the case of India, the quintessence of millennia of social experience were, so to say, frozen into immobility, became sterile, atrophied and fossilised. The obsolete, the backward looking and the decaying elements of tradition were not allowed to die a natural death, fertilising the soil for the sprouting of newer shoots. The colonial powers preserved the festering sores of casteism and communalism, parochialism and obscurantism so as to pollute the atmosphere of national resurgence and to induce ideological debility in the system. Over this oozing sub-stratum of decaying tradition was superimposed a thin veneer of rootless modernity imported from across the seas. These structural inadequacies were expressing themselves most sharply in the sensitive sphere of educational under-development. While the *pathshalas, gurukuls* and the *madrasahs* continued to teach the outdated doctrine of geocentricity as late as in the first half of the twentieth century, Macaulay's educational system could produce only graduated flunkeys. While tradition was dying, modernity was powerless to be born. Modern renaissance in India, as in most colonial countries was, therefore, neither really modern nor substantively a renaissance. It is no doubt, true that the anti-imperialist struggle for national independence inspired the search for alternative models of education; but perhaps, with the possible exception of the intellectual contributions of Rabindranath Tagore and Jawaharlal Nehru, the tradition-modernity gulf could not be satisfactorily bridged.

Contemporary education not only in India but in the entire South is still grappling with the complexities of this problem; and its growing concern with academic colonialism or neocolonialism may be appreciated in this context. Education of the future in a hopefully more equal world would, therefore, be required to face the challenge of import substitution in the field of education endeavour on the basis of the flowering of self-reliant national traditions into modernity.

The second internal force of self-articulation within the autonomy of the educational realm relates to the knowledge explosion. Since the humanising task of education essentially lies in passing on the accumulated social experience of mankind to the newer generation and since knowledge is the abstraction of this experience, the accelerating expansion of the knowledge realm has serious implications for education. The invention of writing, the movable type and the computer mark three quantum jumps in the expansion of and practice. Just as the production processes were fragmented knowledge. As many titles are produced in a day now as were in a whole year during the fifteenth century; and perhaps in the whole of the first millennia.

The increase in the load of the learner as well as in the rigour of learning calls for a fresh look on pedagogic theory in the wake of the industrial revolution into smaller and smaller units on grounds of 'efficiency', knowledge was also broken up into fragments for analytical purposes. The vital search for the multi-splendoured knowledge of the multi-faceted reality quite often tended to degenerate into the soulless technical exercise by the alienated. The scientific technological revolution of our times is generating a qualitatively different model of the learning process which emphasises the nomothetic rather than the ideographic, the holistic rather than the fragmented. The encyclopedic holism of ancient and medieval learning was transformed by the industrial revolution into its opposite, that is, into fragmented units of knowledge. The latter is once again being transformed into its opposite by the scientific- technological revolution and its primeval unity is being restored, albeit at a higher level. The education of the future will be required to build the intellectual milieu for such a restoration. There are indications that this would be done in the following ways.

First, there would be greater emphasis on the generic rather than the specific. It would become possible to encompass the expanding universe of knowledge by basing pedagogy not on the minute of detailed information units but on unifying intellectual constructs of a higher order. Mendaleyev's periodic tables make the "load" of chemistry on the learner substantially lighter.

Second, there would be greater emphasis on knowing rather than on the known, on how to know than on what to know. Logic—both quantitative and qualitative—would acquire a pre-eminent position in the educational endeavour as it embodies the finest abstraction from the concrete and the *terra incognita* is explored with its help. It may be noted that the ratio of the area that is known to that which is known to be unknown remains constant. In other words, every knowing is at the same time a not-knowing. The answer to one question generates ten questions that clamour for answers. Such a model of the expanding realm of knowledge calls for an educational system which essentially sharpens the tools of knowing.

Third, there would be greater emphasis on multi and inter- disciplinary approaches. Like the seven blind men, the aspectual disciplines focus their attention on limited segments and tend to get a distorted view not only of the whole but of that segment as well. This realisation has influenced the educational endeavours of our times quite profoundly. It has led, firstly, to the strengthening of the common base of general education in the schools; secondly, to the combining of the principle of disciplinary specialisation with that of inter-disciplinary concerns; thirdly, to the emergence of binomial disciplines along disciplinary borders e.g., Chemical Physics or Historical Demography; fourthly, to the diffusion of concepts from the source discipline to others, e.g. of gravity from physics to migration studies in Demography and commodity flows analysis in Economics and Geography; and lastly, to the sharpening of the philosophical concerns in all disciplines particularly in the hard sciences.

Fourth, there would be greater emphasis on holistic principles of organisation of knowledge—the *chronological* and the chronological principles. The realm of matter in motion which man cognises through social practice exists in a time-space continuum. Time and space constitute the principal forms of the existence of material phenomena; and are, therefore, as objective as matter itself. If that, which is, exists in a space-time continuum, its proper understanding not only requires the disagration of the totality into aspects for deeper study but also its synthesisation in terms of the two elements of the continuum. Thus alone would the products of cognition—from primary perceptions to the most complex intellectual constructs—get systematised properly and adequately. Academic 'disciplines', the resultants of first of the two processes, concern themselves with segments or facets of the multi-dimensional reality. The second of these processes has led to the emergence in the world of knowledge not only of two 'disciplines' in the narrow sense of an organised body of knowledge but also as the embodiment of two complimentary principles of the organisation of knowledge of that which exists and can only exist in a time-space continuum—the disciplines of History and Geography. That which studies variation and interconnections essentially along the time scale is History; that which studies variations and interconnections essentially along the space scale is Geography.

Educational theories of the ancient and medieval times were based on the assumption that those who work should not think and those who think should not work. Thinking emasculates work and working pollutes thinking. *A brahmin* should not touch the plough and a *Shudra* should not touch the vedas. Contemplation was the only source of knowledge and this could be best achieved in the solitude of a Himalayan peak or under the shade of a banyan tree in the seclusion of a jungle. That was the road to *Nirvana,* to the acquisition of true knowledge. But if someone tilled the soil with a plough or fashioned iron or with a hammer his or her capacity to think would wither away. These theories were propagated by the propertied classes to ensure their monopolistic ownership of and control over the means of production and the knowledge of production. As long as they monopolised these two crucial sectors, they could continue to get work done by others, and to appropriate the surpluses generated by such work. As long as they owned and controlled these sources and levers of power, they could go on enjoying the fruits without working for it. Such has been the social basis of educational theory as it evolved in ancient and medieval times not only in India but all over the world. The Platonic view of education, for example, heralded the debut of the intellectual Prince on the stage of state power.

The separation of work from knowledge was operationlised by the separation of training from education. The former was intended to transfer the skills of labour and the secrets of craftsmanship to the younger generation of the toiling poor so as to enable them to produce value from the sweat of their labour. The latter was intended to pass on the abstracted generalisations of social practice as gems of knowledge to the younger generations of the propertied classes so as to enable them to wield power through a monopoly of such knowledge and appropriate surpluses generated by the labour of the former. The essentially integrated task of transferring the accumulated social experience of mankind to the younger generation was thus fractured. The continuum of the primitive stage was transformed into the dichotomy of class societies. The world of the master craftsmen and his disciples was a world apart from the protected cloisters wherein the wise debated on the number of angels that could comfortably sit on the point of a needle. This tradition of separating work from knowledge and work from power has been the basis for the exclusion of the toilers from the domain of acknowledge by denying education to them; and from the domain of power by closing its door to the uneducated. Viewed thus, education may be considered to be the most potent instrument of inequalisation in history.

This distortion was partially corrected in the developed

countries of the West under the impact of the Industrial Revolution. With qualitative transformation of technology, it was no longer possible for the skilled craftsman to participate in production without transcending the boundaries of training and moving into the world of education. The blacksmith was to be rooted in the science of metallurgy and the tanner in chemical technology. The hitherto unsurmountable wall between training and education had to be breached in the new situation. It became possible to do so in the traditionally virgin ethos of the lands across the Atlantic wherein the tanner and the historian, the blacksmith and the physicist, the tiller and the poet were put together in the wilderness of the wild West to fashion their common destiny. Separation of work from knowledge in the ambience of the new world would have meant death. The carpet beggar carried the agronomy textbook, the works of Join Paine and the Bible along with his chisel, his hammer, his axe and his ploughshare. The sophisticated anaemia of theory divorced from practice and the rustic vitality of practice divorced from theory were melted together in the crucible of the pioneer green settlements of the emerging continent to produce sophisticated vitality.

The continental universities, the citadels of unpolluted traditional learning, sneered at the frowned upon the new hybrid campus wherein the supposedly illegitimate union of work and knowledge was providing new dimensions to both. The prized isolation of a Cambridge or a Padua, a Sorbonne or a Karlova had been broken in the new world and the din and bustle of the workshop had finally managed to enter the sacred elisyum. The universities of Europe had to come to terms with the new requirements of the new times. The initial response was in the form of the emergence of the 'Scheduled Caste' red brick universities, a world apart from the clostered affluence of the Oxbridge tradition. But the movement spread at a rapid rate. The avalanche could not be stopped by outdated prejudices. Vocationalisation of secondary and professionalisation of higher education became a common feature of the educational system in the developed world.

The tragedy of the Third World lies in the fact that the Industrial Revolution was not allowed to take place therein and the gulf between work and knowledge in the societal set up of these countries continues to be still quite wide. The requirements of colonial rule thwarted their economic development, acted as an impediment in the path of technological advances in agriculture, did not permit the emergence of a self- reliant industrial sector; and consequently acted as a serious constraint on the inter-sectoral transfer within the work force from the primary to the secondary sector—at best, permitting the development of underdevelopment. While the collapse of the handicraft based secondary sector led to the over burdening of the technologically stagnant primary activities, the needs of colonial administration were met by a bloated tertiary sector, which was divorced from and contemptuous of work. The socioeconomic conditions, which had led to the narrowing of the gap between work and education in the developed countries of today is the wake of the Industrial Revolution, were thus not allowed to emerge in the countries of the Third world. The educational systems of the colonial countries, in fact, tended to considerably strengthen the separation of work from education. Even though many decades have passed since the attainment of political independence in these countries and a number of educational reforms aimed at narrowing this gap have been experimented with, the situation still continues to be highly unsatisfactory in most countries of the South. The future of education in these countries largely depends on the capacity of these societies to reforge these basic links which were broken by the emergence of social stratification along with private property. Education has to get rooted in work in order to become the education of the future.

The scientific-technological revolution of our times which has paved the way for many positive changes in the North is, however, creating dangers of a new king in the brave new world of developed capitalism. The work force is tending to get divided between a tiny minority of the highly skilled and the vast majority of human robots. The educational system is likely to become the instrumentality of screening the human minority from the machine like multitude. The danger becomes all the more serious because information and its communication is being increasingly monopolised by fewer and fewer people. The advantages of the individuation of the learning process which has become possible due to technological developments is being thus brought to naught. While it is true that every household in the North has a television set, it is also true that only a few trans-national companies have a monopoly over the software that is televised.

Education of the future will face this challenge of strengthening the links between work and knowledge as well as of ensuring that the great majority of the work force is not reduced to the status of robots.

It is very apt to conclude the discussion with the following quote of Henry Ford II:

> "No can really guarantee the future. The best we can do is size up the chances, calculate the risks involved, estimate your ability to deal with them, and then make our plans with confidence."

APPENDIX I

Programme-wise and School-wise Enrolment of Students at IGNOU (1996-2001)

PROGRAMME	1996	1997	1998	1999	2000	2001
Certificates	11274	23587	26235	30029	32598	59363
Diploma	5276	11146	10964	8338	3346	4824
P.G. Diploma	4044	3358	3726	5992	5337	8713
Advance Diploma	-	-	32	9	676	2
Bachelors	35584	50655	61228	69594	83456	120993
Masters	66429	61216	50817	47793	60917	90298
Miscellaneous	7621	12683	10392	10793	10320	20206
TOTAL	130228	162645	163394	172548	196650	304681
SCHOOLS	1996	1997	1998	1999	2000	2001
Computers	14614	44162	57697	70888	94082	151859
Continuing Education	6791	5508	4816	6422	5752	8637
Education	1685	1199	1119	1631	3704	5029
Engg. & Technology	763	2220	1202	559	963	1513
Health Sciences	830	1086	1662	1764	1810	2659
Humanities	475	1067	1273	2221	1949	7815
Management	69504	65194	52274	43006	38623	46512
Social Sciences	31266	38259	38346	41105	44022	67990
Sciences	4140	3924	5005	4753	4764	6135
Miscellaneous	160	26	-	199	981	6532
TOTAL	130228	162245	163394	172548	196650	304681

Source: Convocation Reports of IGNOU and SR&E Division from 1996-2001.

Bibliography

A.C. Harberger, 'Investment in men versus investment in machines: The case of India' in *Education and Economic Development.*

Adiseshiah, M.S. (1985), "Role of Universities as Agents of change" in J.V. Raghavan (Ed.), *Higher Education in Eighties.* New Delhi: Lancer International.

Adiseshiah, Malcolm S. (1970), *Lifelong Education,* Document No. 7, International Educational Year Special Unit, Pans: UNESCO.

Agarwal, B.L. (1985), "Nexus Between Jobs and Degrees" in J.V. Raghavan (Ed.), *Higher Education in Eighties.* New Delhi: Lancer International.

Agarwal, B.L. (1985), "Nexus Between Jobs and Degrees" in J.V. Raghavan (Ed.), *Higher Education in Eighties.* New Delhi: Lancer International.

Aggarwal, J.C. (1982), *Development and Planning of Modern Education,* Vikas Publishing House, New Delhi.

Ahuja, Y.L., Kulkarni S. & Sharma H. (1988), *Active Education Policy for Skill Development,* Theme Paper of the Seminar, IAMR, New Delhi, Unpublished.

AIEPA, *Lifelong Education,* Report of the Meeting of Experts held in August 1970. New Delhi: Asian Institute of Educational Planning and Administration, 1970.

A.M Nalla Gounden (1967), 'Investment in Education in India', *Journal of Human Resources,* Summer, pp. 347-358.

Anderson, H.H. and Anderson, G.L. (ed.) (1951): *An Introduction to Projective Techniques,* Prentice Hall, NY. 1951.

Association of Indian Universities (1980), *Handbook of Distance Education*, New Delhi.

Association of Indian Universities (1985), *Higher Education and Development*. New Delhi.

Association of Indian Universities (1985), *Three Aspects of University Education*. New Delhi.

Ausubel, D. 'In Defence of advance organisers : A reply to the Critics', Review of Educational Research, 1978,48, pp. 251-257.

Azad, J.L. (1975), *Financing of Higher Education in India*, New Delhi: Sterling Publishers Pvt. Ltd.

Barker, R.G., "Success and Failure in the Classroom," *Progressive Education*, 19: 221-24, 1942.

Barnes, B.R. and Clawson, E.V. (1975), 'Do advance Organisers facilitate learning? Recommendations for further research based on an analysis of thirty-two studies'. Review of Educational Research, 45,637-659.

Bell, J.E. (1948), *Projective Technique*, Longmans, Green and Co., NY.

Bell, R.E. and Youngron A.J. (Ed.) (1973), *Present and Future in Higher Education*. London: Tavistock Publications Ltd.

Bell, R.E. and Youngron A.J. (Ed.) (1973), *Present and Future in Higher Education*. London: Tavistock Publications Ltd.

Bloom, Benjaim S. (1964), *Stability and Change in Human Characteristics*, New York: Wiley.

Buros, D.K. (ed) (1959), *The Fifth Mental Measurements Year Book*, Highland Park, NY.

Burton, W.H. (1952), *The Guidance of Learning Activities, 2nd ed., New York:* Appleton-Century Crofts.

C.V. Good (ed.) (1959), *Dictionery of Education*, New York, MacGraw Hill Book Co.

Cantor, L.M. and J.F. Roberts (1983), *Further Education Today. (2nd* Ed.) London: Routledge and Kegan Paul.

Cantor, N., *The Teaching-Learning Process.* New York: The Dryden Press, Inc., 1953. Chapter 3.

Cantor, N., *The Teaching-Learning Process.* New York: The Dryden Press, Inc., 1953. Chapter 3.

Centre of Advanced Study in Education (1985), *Vocationalisation of Education at +2 Stage.* A Planning Commission Sponsored Project, Baroda.

Chauhank, K.S., (1994), "Union Budget and Decline in Educational Efforts," *Economic and Political Weekly,* April (Special).

Chauhan, S.S. (1978), *Advance Educational Psychology,* Vikas, New Delhi).

Coombs, Philip H. (1968), *The World Educational Crisis,* New York: Oxford University Press.

Council of Europe (1970), *Permanent Education, A Compendium of Studies,* Strasbourg: Council of Europe.

Cronback, Lee. J. (1960), *Essential of Psychological Testing,* Harper and Brothers, NY.

Datt, Ruddar ((1985), *Distance Education in India: Its Development and Significance,* Workshop on Education, Open School, New Delhi.

Dave, R.H. (1986), *Towards a Theory of Educational Extension, Teacher Education* 10, No. 4 , New Delhi: National Council of Educational Research and Training.

Dept. of Education and Skills, UK (2003), *The Future of Higher Education.*

Douglas, H.R., and H. H. Mills (1948), *Teaching in High School* New York: The Ronald Press Co.

E.F. Denison, (1964), 'Measuring the Contribution of Education (and the Residual) to Economic Growth in O.E.C.D.' *The Residual Factor and Economic Growth,* Paris.

F. Harbisen (1967), *Educational Planning and Human Resource Development,* UNESCO.

Freeman, F.S. (1962), *Theory and Practice of Psychological Testing*, Holt Richart, NY.

Garrison, N.L. (1955), *Improvement of Teaching*. New York: The Dryden Press, Inc.

George S. Counts (1932), *Dare the School Build a Social Order?* New York, John Day.

Government of India (1948-49), *Report of the University Education Commission*. New Delhi.

Government of India (1964-66), *The Report of the Education Commission*. New Delhi.

Govt. of India, Min. of HRD, Dept. of Education (1988), *Nonformal Education*, New Delhi.

Grambs, J.D., and W. Iverson (1952), *Modern Methods in Secondary Education*. New York: William Sloane Associates.

Greenough, Richard (1972), *Adult Education and National Development*. *UNESCO Chronicle* 18, No. 4, pp. 131-134.

Guthrie, E.R. (1952), *The Psychology of Learning*, rev. ed. New York: Harper and Brothers, Publishers.

Hansen, K.H. (1957), *High School Teaching*. New Jersey: Prentice Hall, Inc.

Harris, M.L. and Harris, C.W. (1973) 'A Structure of Concept Attainment Abilities', Madison: Wisconsin Research and Development Center for Cognitive Learning, Quoted by *Encyclopaedia of Educational Research*, Vol. 2, 1982.

Hartely, J. and Davies, I.K., (1976) "Preinstructional Strategies: The role of pre-tests-behavioural objectives, overviews, and advance organisers". *Review of Educational Research*, 46, pp. 239-265.

Hartung, H. (1966), *Pour une education permanente*. Paris: Fayard.

Hershfield, A.F. (1990), *Minorities,' United States of America* in *Distance Education: A Spectrum of Case Studies*, (Eds. Koul, B.N. and Jenkins, J.), Kogan Page. London.

Hilgard, E.R. (1948), *Theories of Learning*. New York: Appleton-Century Crofts, Inc.

Houle, C.O. (1969), "Continued Professional Education in the USA, *Lifelong Learning—A Symposium on Continuing Education* edited by F.W. Jessup. Oxford., Pergamon.

Hughes and Hughes (1960), *Education: Some Fundamental Problems*, Longmans.

Husen, Torsten (1968), "Talent, Opportunity and Career: A Twenty-six-year Follow-up. *The School Review*, June, pp. 109-209.

Illich, Ivan (1970), *Deschooling Society, World Perspectives*. New York: Harper and Row.

J.K. Folger and C.B. Nam (1964), 'Trends in Education in Relation to Occupational Structure', *Sociology of Education*, Fall, pp. 19-34.

Jessup, F.W., ed. (1969), *Lifelong Learning—A Symposium on Continuing Education*. Oxford: Pergamon.

John Dewey (1916), *Democracy and Education*, New York, The Macmillan Co.

Johnson, E., and R.E. Michael (1958), *Principles of Teaching*. Boston: Allyn and Bacon, Inc.

Joyce, B.R. and Weil, M. (1980), *'Models of Teaching'* (2nd Ed.), Printice Hall.

Kaul, J.N. (1975), *Higher Education, Social Change and National Development*. Simla: Indian Institute of Advanced Study.

Kingsiey, H.L. (1946), *The Nature and Conditions of Learning*. New York: Prentice-Hall, Inc.

Klausmeier, H.J. (1982), 'Educational Experience and Cognitive Development', *Educational Psychologist*, 1977, 12, pp. 179-196, Quoted by *Encyclopaedia of Educational Research*. Fifth Edition, Vol. 2, pp. 891-916.

Klausmeier, H.J., and Feldman, K.V. (1975), 'Effect of a definition and a Varying number of examples and nonexamples on concept attainment'. Journal of *Educational Psychology*, 67, pp. 174-178.

Klausmeier, H.T., and Harris C.W. (1966), Analysis of Concept Learning, Academic Press, New York, London.

Koul, B.N. (1984), *Need for Professional Training in Distance Education*, (Ed. Parmaji. S.), Sterling Publishers Pvt. Ltd., New Delhi.

Krishna Kripalani (1960), *All Men are Brothers*, Ahmedabad, Navajivan Publishing House.

Lawton, J.T. and Wanska, S.K. (1977), 'Advance Organiser as a teaching strategy. A reply to Barnes and Clawson.' Review of Educational Research.

Le Veugle, Jean (1970), *Initigtion a l'education permanente.* Paris: UNESCO.

Lengrand, Paul (1970), L'Education des adultes et le concept del' education permanente." Convergence 3, No. 2.

Leona, E. Tyler (1973), *Tests and Measurements*, Prentice Hall, NY.

Lister, I. (1971), "The Concept of Deschooling and the Future of Secondary Education, Mimeographed. Amsterdam: European Cultural Foundation.

M. Blaug (1967), 'Approaches of Educational Planning', *The Economic Journal, June.*

M.P. Follet (1920) , *The New State*, New York, Longmans Green.

Maneu, Rene (1968), "Pour une education permanente," *Convergence* 1, No. 1.

Mayer, R.E. (1978), 'Advance Organisers that compensate for the organisation of text,' *Journal of Educational Psychology*, 70, pp. 880-886.

Mayer, R.E. (1979), 'Can advance organisers influence meaningful learning?' Review of Educational Research, 49, pp. 371-383.

Mead, Margaret (1970), *Culture and Commitment: A Study of the Generation Gap*. Garden City, N.J.: Natural History Press.

Melvin, A.G. (1952), *General Methods of Teaching*. New York: McGraw-Hill Book Company, Inc.

Ministry of Human Resource Development, Government of India (1986), *National Policy on Education, 1986, Programme of Action*. MHRD: New Delhi.

Ministry of Human Resource Development (1986), Government of India, *National Policy of Education*, MHRD: New Delhi.

Mischel, W. (1968), *Personality and Assessment*.

Morrison, H.C., *The Practice of Teaching in the Secondary School*. Chicago: University of Chicago Press, 1931 (revised).

Mortensen, Dpmaid G. (1972), *Guidance in Today's Schools*, John Wiley and Sons, New York.

Myers, George E. (1976), *Principles and Techniques of Guidance*, McGraw Hill Book Co., New York.

Ojeman, R.H. (1952), "Identifying Effective Classroom Teachers, in Bases of Effective Learning," *1952 Yearbook* (Dept. of Elementary School Principal). Washington. D.C.: The N.E.A., pp. 130-138.

P.O. Shrimali (1967), *Pattern of Employment and Earnings Among Graduates in Lucknow*, Labour Research Centre. Deptt. of Economics, Lucknow University.

Purkait, B.R. (1987), *New Education in India*, The Associated Publishers, Ambala.

Raghavan J.V. (Ed.) (1985), *Higher Education in the Eighties: Opportunities and Objectives*. New Delhi: Lancer International.

Report of the Education Commission (1964-66), *Education & National Development*, Ministry of Education, Govt. of India.

Robert R. Rusk (1955), *The Doctrines of the Great Educators*, London, Macmillan & Co. Ltd., p. 176.

Sahoo P.K. (1983), "Higher Education in India — Certain Issues", *New Frontiers in Education,* Vol. XIII No. 4.

Schramm, W. et. al. (1967), *The New Media Memo to Educational Planners.* Paris: UNESCO International Institute for Educational Planning.

Seth, S.C. (1985), *India in the Next 7000 Days, New Delhi:* Wiley Eastern Ltd.

Shertzsr Stone (1976), *Fundamentals of Guidance,* Houghton Miftlin Co., Boston.

Singh, A. (1985), *Redeeming Higher Education.* New Delhi: Ajanta.

Singh, A. (1985), *Redeeming Higher Education.* New Delhi: Ajanta.

Singh, M.B. and Seth S.C. (1985), "Report on Teaching and Research in Futurology: A Special Report", *Indian Review of Management of future.*

Skinner, C.E. and others (1955), *Educational Psychology.* New Jersey: Prentice-Hall, Inc.

Smith, H.P. (1954), "Individual Differences in Ability to Learn," in *Psychology in Teaching.* New Jersey: Prentice-Hall, Inc.

Status Report of Non-formal Education from Some States in India, Dept. of School Education, NCERT, 1978.

Stephens, J.M. (1951), *Educational Psychology.* New York: Henry Holt and Company, Chapter 3.

University Grants Commission (1963), *Reports on Standards of University Education.* New Delhi, U.G.C.

University Grants Commission, (1985), *Annual Reports for Years: 1960-61 to 1984-85,* New Delhi.

Vernor, P.E. (1964), *Personality Assessment,* London, Metheun.

Voeks, V.W. (1950), "Formalisation and Clarification of a Theory of Learning," *Journal of Psychology.*

W.A. Lewis (1960), *Development Planning,* Allen and Unwin.

Wilhelmsen, Lief J. (1968), "Cultural Activities in Lifelong Education." Convergence 1, No. 4.

Wroczynski, Ryszard (1972), "Lifelong Education as a Result of the Scientific and Technological Revolution." *Society and Leisure,* No. 1, Prague : European Centre for Leisure and Education.

Yadav, M.S., Lakshmi, T.K.S., and Sahoo, P.K. (1985), "Higher Education in India: Survival and Revival". Paper presented in the 5th International Conference of Higher Education, University of Lancaster, U.K. *Indian Educational Review,* 20(3).

Index

□□□